CHANGE
ACROSS
CULTURES

BRUCE BRADSHAW was the director of transformation development research and training for World Vision International for more than twelve years and worked as a regional liaison officer in Somalia for the U.S. Agency for International Development. The author of *Bridging the Gap: Evangelism, Development, and Shalom,* he is currently assistant professor of economics and business at Bethel College, North Newton, Kansas.

CHANGE ACROSS CULTURES

A Narrative Approach to Social Transformation

Bruce Bradshaw

Baker Academic
A Division of Baker Book House Co
Grand Rapids, Michigan 49516

Published by Baker Academic
a division of Baker Book House Company
P.O. Box 6287, Grand Rapids, MI 49516-6287

Printed in the United States of America

Library of Congress Cataloging-in-Publication Data

Bradshaw, Bruce.
    Change across cultures : a narrative approach to social transformation / Bruce Bradshaw.
       p.   cm.
    Includes bibliographical references and index.
    ISBN 0-8010-2289-4 (pbk.)
     1. Social change. 2. Discourse analysis, Narrative. 3. Christianity and culture.
I. Title.
HM831 .B72 2001
303.4—dc21   2001052624

For information about Baker Academic, visit our web site:
www.bakeracademic.com

Contents

Foreword

The great mission outreach of the nineteenth and twentieth centuries planted churches around the world. It was less successful, however, in transforming the societies in which people lived. Poverty, injustice, corruption, violence, and oppression continue unchecked in much of the world, despite the growth of the church. How should we as Christians respond to this apparent contradiction?

In this thought-provoking book, Bruce Bradshaw challenges us to reexamine our Christian mission to the world. He points out that too often we interpret Scripture through the lenses of our own cultures and worldviews. In the past, we have been deeply shaped by modernity. Its stress on individualism has led to a personalized gospel that largely ignores the importance of social and cultural systems. Its Greek dualism, which divides the world into supernatural and natural realms—opposing spiritual to material, faith to fact, and miracle to natural order—has given rise to a spiritualized gospel that is concerned with saving the lost but overlooks the fact that God is concerned with redeeming his whole creation, including the world. The modern use of a mechanistic metaphor in understanding and organizing the world and society has led to a managerial approach to mission that is based on control, hierarchy, and techniques and formulas, which belies the fact that salvation and mission have ultimately to do with relationships between God, humans, and creation.

Bradshaw challenges us to reenvision our understanding of the Christian mission for the twenty-first century. He calls us to bear witness to the whole gospel, which includes salvation from sin, the transformation of societies and cultures, and ecological stewardship. This calls for new kinds of leadership, different understandings of gender relationships, alternative uses of power, and new economic responsibilities. Bradshaw invites us to make the building of relationships central to our mission task and to be open to the work of God in human situations. This calls for moral as well as cognitive transformations. We need to develop methods for dealing with the issues arising out of cross-cultural ethics, just as we have done for dealing with cross-cultural understandings.

To develop his model, the author draws on narratives to help us understand the mission task. He begins with biblical narratives and links these to present-day cases drawn from his wide field-experience in Christian development and transformation around the world. These cases raise the cognitive and moral dilemmas that we face and present the gospel as a transformative power in the world.

Bradshaw reexamines many biblical texts to support his view of mission. Not everyone will agree with his exegetical conclusions, even though he finds the support of Bible scholars for many of them, but we cannot avoid the critical questions he raises and his challenge to look for a new biblical paradigm that sees mission not only as the salvation of individuals but also as the transformation of Christian communities and whole societies.

Paul G. Hiebert
Professor of Mission and Anthropology
Trinity Evangelical Divinity School

Acknowledgments

While admitting to be the sole author of this book, I am keenly aware that writing is not a solitary effort. The book has had many sources. It was conceived in 1993 when John Steward and I happened to meet in Manila. I shared my idea for this book, and he affirmed it by stating that "values are transmitted through stories; the values won't change unless the stories change." I am indebted to him for his wisdom and encouragement.

There are others who made valuable contributions. The World Vision staff who participated in my workshops provided the case studies from which the stories are garnered. My students at Fuller Theological Seminary helped shape many of my ideas. Tone Lindheim, an emerging theologian from Norway, was particularly helpful, and Laura Pinho read the entire manuscript. I am grateful to them.

The book also provided much of the substance for my Sunday evening reflections at Peace Fellowship, a house church of Anabaptists in Claremont, California. The folks at Peace listened well, giving me the impression that the material was worth publishing. Peter Riddell of London Bible College, Lance Shaina, Rebecca Russell, and Edna Valdez all gave me encouragement. Steve Hoke, Patrice White, Carl Raser, Sherwood Lingenfelter, Eric Ram, Ted Yamamori, Bruce Brander, and Don Brandt were among the people who read sections of the early manuscript, influencing me to believe that this book was worthwhile.

I must also thank my family for their support and tolerance. This book had a two-year gestation period, and Mary, my wife, tolerated the piles of books, journals, and papers that littered our house during that time. Our children, Ellen, Amy, and Phillip, also endured its birth.

Introduction

*. . . fracture for fracture, eye for eye, tooth for tooth. As he has injured the
other, so he is to be injured.*

Leviticus 24:20

While Kosovo was being bombed during the spring of 1999, the
Rrushis confined themselves to their family home in northern Albania.
The bombing, however, was not their major concern; they were at war
with their neighbors, the Bardhoshises. Both families live according to
the moral code of the *Kanun of Lek Dukagjini*. Named after a fifteenth-cen-
tury Albanian hero, it comprises the plot of the cultural narratives of
northern Albania. The *Kanun* regulates justice, marriage, vengeance, and
family feuds. It dictates retaliatory justice, or that blood be paid with
blood, giving both the Rrushis and Bardhoshises moral justification to
avenge a death they believe the other caused; thus they live in constant
fear for their lives. The *Kanun* is responsible for the continuation of feuds
in Albania over long periods of time, some being revived after lying dor-
mant over a half century. There are, according to an independent blood-
feud reconciliation agency, over 2,700 ongoing feuds in Albania.[1] The
communist government that ruled Albania from 1944 to 1991 tried several times to curb the influence of the *Kanun* by legislative proposition.
The feuds, however, were embedded in the cultural narratives, rendering governmental legislation powerless to end the blood feuds and allowing the *Kanun* to survive.

1. Marjorie Miller, "Ancient Legal Code Fuels Surge in Vendetta Killings," *The Sydney
Morning Herald*, 7 August 1999.

Introduction

Sustainable cultural change requires the transformation of the values that permeate the cultural narratives, which are the stories of the social structures that comprise the communities in which people live. They also embody the values that govern their lives and inspire them to change their behavior. Christian missions and development agencies have engaged in numerous efforts to manage cultural change throughout the world. To a large extent, however, the projects have failed because the theology and ethics that influenced them were propositional, not narrative, in nature. They were, therefore, powerless to produce sustainable change.

Two primary concerns of this book are, first, the pervasive influence cultural narratives have on managing cultural change through development projects and, second, the way in which worldviews and moral assumptions inherent in cultural narratives govern biblical interpretations. Too often, biblical interpretations are culturally bound, influencing Christians who manage cultural change to believe they are implementing biblical solutions to cultural transformation. However, some of their solutions are less than redemptive.

Interpreting Scripture according to a specific worldview can produce interpretations opposed to each other. For example, the injunction "eye for eye, tooth for tooth" has frequently been interpreted as biblical justification for a personal ethic of revenge, influencing people to believe that they can rightly inflict on others the wounds that have been inflicted on them. Like the *Kanun of Lek Dukagjini*, the Levitical teaching can be interpreted as a prescription for everyone to be toothless and blind. The narrative context of the Levitical injunction, however, can also be interpreted to imply that communities can realize justice when their laws respect all people equally. Instead of suggesting that people are justified in destroying each other's limbs and lives, the ethical injunction can actually prevent such destruction by encouraging people to value their neighbors as much as they value themselves.

The two interpretations of the Levitical injunction emerge from moral assumptions embedded in different cultural narratives. The farmers in Albania, for example, can use this moral injunction to transform the values inherent in the *Kanun of Lek Dukagjini*, or they can use it to escalate the cycle of violence that perpetuates the ongoing feuds and wars. They need a story that shifts the human penchant for violence into an ethic that supports life; the gospel of Jesus Christ is such a story, with the power to break the cycle of violence and inspire people to love their enemies and to pray for those who persecute them (Matt. 5:44).

Christians engaged in managing change across cultures attempt to transform the values embedded in the narratives by using the story of God's redemptive relationship with creation through the life, death, and resurrection of Jesus Christ. Since narratives are the stories of the social structures that comprise one aspect of the biblical concept of the *kosmos*,[2] the ethics of managing cultural change is unavoidably wedded to transforming those structures. The biblical view of the *kosmos* is a central theme of this book. It is defined as the arena in which the drama of human life is lived, comprising the matrix of human cultures that people construct to provide order to their lives. People construct the cultures that comprise the *kosmos* according to the values their narratives contain.

A major implication of managing cultural change by transforming social structures is the union of evangelism and social ethics. The recent history of Christian missions has been plagued by a theology that separates personal salvation from social transformation, which has created a Gnostic theology that will be explored in chapter 4. Here it is sufficient to write that the presence of the God of Jesus Christ "must be perceptible not only in the individual conscience, but in social structures as well."[3] Jesus became human not merely to "inspire devotional exercises and metaphysical speculations and cultic communities; he came to inaugurate a kingdom."[4] The result of transformed social structures is a cultural narrative that bears the values Jesus cited when he inaugurated his ministry: preaching the gospel to the poor, proclaiming freedom for prisoners, recovering the sight of the blind, releasing the oppressed, and proclaiming the year of the Lord (Luke 4:18–19). The realization of these values challenges Christians to hold personal salvation and social ethics together and to read John 3:16–17 in the context of the biblical view of *kosmos:*

> For God so loved the world [*kosmos*] that he gave his one and only Son, that whoever believes in him shall not perish but have eternal life. For God did not send his Son into the world [*kosmos*] to condemn the world, but to save the world through him.

The concept of redeeming the *kosmos* introduces a new twist to a term that has had some negative connotations in Christian missions. The term

2. Throughout this book, *kosmos* is defined as the social structures that people create to provide order for their lives; *cosmos* defines the natural elements of creation.

3. Jacques Ellul, *The New Demons* (New York: Seabury, 1975), 4.

4. Paul Toews, *Mennonites in American Society, 1930–1970: Modernity and the Persistence of Religious Community* (Scottdale, Pa.: Herald, 1996), 335.

is *secularization* and is defined, throughout this book, as the practice of interpreting God's redemptive work in areas that we do not generally esteem as religious. While secularization is often associated with secularism, the difference between the two terms is significant. Secularism is an ideology that denies the presence of God. Secularization, in contrast, recognizes God's presence in all areas of life.

Secularization is a theological alternative to the liminal experience, a state of being that is "often seen as sacred, powerful, holy, and set apart time in which the old structures, rules of order, and identities are suspended."[5] Liminality, which is examined extensively in chapter 11, is the personal experience that people generally associate with spirituality. Conversion experiences often have a liminal nature, influencing people to interpret their spiritual experience as primarily personal. Liminal and secular, though, are two sides of the same coin, empowering Christians to hold salvation and ethics together in their effort to redeem the *kosmos*.

The redemption of the *kosmos*, including all of the cultures that comprise it, is a central aspect of Christian missions; this expression of redemption transforms the narratives containing the values that govern how people construct their cultures. The task is inherently moral; it determines how people are going to respond to the issues that impede the redemptive work of God in creation, issues such as famine, poverty, death, and economic and political decay. The gospel of Jesus Christ transforms these structures, releasing people from poverty, oppression, and other expressions of social bondage.

5. Paul G. Hiebert, R. Daniel Shaw, and Tite Tienou, *Understanding Folk Religion: A Christian Response to Popular Beliefs and Practices* (Grand Rapids: Baker, 1999), 297.

1

Narrative:
The Media of Ethical Inquiry

Stories have wings; they fly from peak to peak.

Romanian Proverb

To be human is to tell stories about ourselves and other human beings.

Tobin Silvers

That is why it was called Babel—because there the Lord confused the language of the whole world. From there the Lord scattered them over the face of the whole earth.

Genesis 11:9

People who read the Genesis account of the Tower of Babel from the perspective of Western culture invariably interpret the story as a curse. It tells how God defeated the human effort to become divine. At the beginning of the story, the "whole world had one language and a common speech" (Gen. 11:1), leading the people to believe that they could transcend human limitations, and they tried to build a tower to heaven as an expression of their power. God knew, however, that if they were successful, nothing they attempted would "be impossible for them" (Gen. 11:6). God, therefore, thwarted their aspirations by confusing their language, scattering the people over the face of all the earth (Gen. 11:9), and making the diversity of human language appear to be an expression of "divine punishment for the human act of arrogance."[1]

It is possible, however, to interpret the story as having redemptive qualities. Jose Miguez-Bonino, a Latin American theologian, sees the story as an expression of God's mercy. He writes from the perspective of a people subjugated by another culture, who, as conquered people, had lost their language and were compelled to "deny everything that gave meaning to their lives—stories, traditions, the 'naming of things,' the music of words, the sounds of love. To keep their own language, however, meant to be a stranger in their own land."[2]

Miguez-Bonino suggests that God's choice to confuse human language was "an act of deliverance"[3] for a subjugated people. The story of Babel, in his view, should not be interpreted as a curse but as a blessing. It reveals "that God's intention is a diverse humanity that can find its unity not in the domination of one city, one tower, or one language but in the 'blessings for all the families on the earth' (Genesis 12:3)."[4] The motive of the people who attempted to build the tower of Babel was to resist the "diversification which God had long before ordained and initiated. . . . Thus, the 'confusion of tongue' is not a punishment or a tragedy but the gift of new beginnings, liberation from a blind alley."[5] The contrasting interpretations of the story of Babel emerge from different cultural narratives, which influence people to perceive truth from various angles.

The What and Why of Ethical Inquiry

The influence that cultural narratives bear on our lives makes them the media of ethical inquiry, particularly as it pertains to managing cul-

1. Jose Miguez-Bonino, "Genesis 11:1–9: A Latin American Perspective," in *Return to Babel: Global Perspectives on the Bible*, ed. Priscilla Pope-Levison and John R. Levison (Louisville: Westminster John Knox, 1999), 14.

2. Ibid., 13.

3. Ibid., 15.

4. Ibid., 16.

5. John Howard Yoder, *For the Nations: Essays Public and Evangelical* (Grand Rapids: Eerdmans, 1997), 63.

tural change, which we do according to the values of some narrative. The central issue for Christians is discerning what that narrative is.

Take, for example, a successful immunization project in an East African village. Its purpose was to reduce infant mortality, and it achieved significant results. The village elders, however, perceived the success of the project in a manner different from that of the development practitioners. While the development practitioners celebrated the survival of infants, the village elders were relieved that they did not have to allow the elderly women in their village to die. The villagers attributed infant deaths to the witchcraft of the older women and required the life of one woman for the death of every child, thus defending the role of justice in the narrative of their community. The project evaluators realized that their efforts to increase the survival rate of children also increased the survival of the elderly, creating a geriatric problem and making more demands on the village's meager resources. An anthropologist who is committed to functionalism, as we shall later see, might question the benefit of this project, believing that the deaths of the children and the elderly are keeping the population in balance.

The project managers, however, drawing inspiration from the biblical narrative of God's concern for all human life, affirmed that the survival of both young and old was good. Because of their belief that they were participating in God's redemptive work in creation, they knew they were engaged in an ethical pursuit and were, thus, working to transform a major moral aspect of the community. As a result, they were challenged to support the villagers in their efforts to sustain the lives of the children as well as those of the elderly. In so doing, they were extending the narrative of God's redemptive relationship with creation into that village in a comprehensive manner.

All cultural change has a moral aspect and is intimately related to cultural narratives, which contain the values that shape human character and govern ethical action. Ethics, often defined as "*theories* of morality,"[6] seeks to maintain the integrity of the narratives through which people live. Ethics has to do with character as it is formed by a habitual way of life and demands that people take responsibility for shaping the nature of their cultural narratives. Jack Miles observed that character, not circumstance, governs our lives. He noted that if a wealthy young man chose to dispose of his wealth and live in poverty, his character would remain "that of a man raised in wealth, for he cannot give his

6. James W. McClendon Jr., *Systematic Theology: Ethics* (Nashville: Abingdon, 1986), 47.

history away."[7] He will have to make intentional efforts to change the narrative of his life if he wants to value poverty. Similarly, many of the people who lived through the economic depression of the 1930s continued to live within a narrative of poverty throughout the economic growth of the late twentieth century. The condition of poverty was embedded into their character, influencing them beyond the scope of their current life situations.

For Christians, ethics is expressing the integrity of God's redemptive relationship with creation in both words and deeds. Our narratives give us differing understandings of how we engage in this effort, influencing us to interpret Scripture differently and challenging us to discern which interpretations are redemptive: which ones illustrate God's commitment to reconciling the creation to himself through Christ. Likewise, Christians manage cultural change by supporting projects that nurture the dignity of human life, not because these programs are anthropologically functional or economically efficient, but because they participate in God's redemptive relationship with creation.

The Polarities of Ethical Inquiry

Narratives are the central media of ethical inquiry, but they do not preclude propositional truth. Instead, narratives and propositions are closely related, and we cannot fully appreciate the contributions narratives make to the ethical task of managing change across cultures until we understand that relationship. In this section, I want to explore the nature of the connection between propositions and narratives.

Toward Understanding Propositions

Propositions are statements about a perceived truth, based on the logic of a particular culture. They contain moral truths, such as "you shall not commit adultery" (Exod. 20:14), and they are generally invoked when people confront moral dilemmas. They usually offer ethicists two or more opposing moral alternatives that appear equally valid and often equally condemning. These alternatives can include refusing to baptize men who have two or more wives (thus requiring polygamists to violate the sanctity of marriage by divorcing second and subsequent wives) or condemning marriage after divorce as a form of adultery.

Norman L. Geisler, a leading proponent of engaging in ethical inquiry through propositions, sets forth six approaches for evaluating the moral

7. *God: A Biography* (New York: Random House, 1996), 3.

implications of human behavior and provides a definitive analysis of categories representative of propositional ethical inquiry. Geisler evaluates each of these approaches according to a variety of theological and ethical propositions. He chooses three that are acceptable for Christians and strongly supports one of the three alternatives as most conducive to facilitating Christian morality.

Geisler's six approaches to ethical reflection range from antinomianism to unqualified absolutism. Antinomianism denies the existence of any moral laws and allows morality to be evaluated on "subjective, personal and pragmatic grounds, but not on any objective moral grounds."[8] Unqualified absolutism, the opposite of antinomianism, affirms that "there are many nonconflicting moral laws, and none of them should ever be broken."[9] The other four options, situationism, generalism, conflicting absolutism, and graded absolutism, fall between the extremes of antinomianism and unqualified absolutism.

Situationism, popularized by Joseph Fletcher's *Situation Ethics: The New Morality,* claims that the law of love serves as the only basis of moral decisions. This position postulates that conflicting alternatives in any moral decision can be mediated by discerning which alternative results in the greatest expression of love. Generalism adds to situationism by postulating that there are two or more laws on which moral decisions are based. These laws can include love, but they might also include other values such as increasing happiness or pleasure or reducing pain. For decisions on the polygamy dilemma mentioned later (see p. 24), generalism might consider love in addition to the social and economic issues that are involved in having two or more spouses.

Geisler postulates that antinomianism, situationism, and generalism are insufficient models to support Christian ethical inquiry. He sees the remaining two alternatives, conflicting absolutism and graded absolutism, along with universal absolutism, as the only viable ethical models for Christians.

Conflicting absolutism contends that moral decisions can involve an obligation to fulfill two or more absolute norms that are mutually exclusive. If Christians choose one option, the option they rejected is still a moral obligation, and they have to repent for not choosing it. For example, polygamists who become Christians and decide to divorce their spouses have to repent for acting on this decision.

8. *Christian Ethics: Options and Issues* (Grand Rapids: Baker, 1989), 26.
9. Ibid., 27.

Graded absolutism is the position that Geisler supports. It claims that while ethical norms are absolute, they are ranked to prevent them from conflicting with each other. Graded absolutism acknowledges a pyramid of objective values determined by God in agreement with his "absolute, unchanging character"[10]: the only subjective aspect of values "is our understanding and acceptance of God's values."[11]

Geisler comes close to recognizing the cultural influences on graded absolutism. However, this recognition does not lead him to consider the cultural influences on perceiving the hierarchy of values in graded absolutism. Instead, he compares this subjective factor as "a limitation shared by other Christian views as well."[12] This limitation suggests that even the strongest approaches to propositional ethics have subjective natures, which questions the importance of propositions. Truth, however, can be communicated through narrative as well as propositions.[13]

Toward Understanding Narratives

Narratives, the "basic and essential genre for the characterization of human actions,"[14] are the stories that govern our lives. They empower people "to organize [their] institutions, to develop ideals, and to find authority for [their] actions."[15] William J. Bennett's recent work on the virtues of American culture illustrates that the narratives of American culture, at their best, are blends of Christian and Greek virtues and values.[16] He suggests that Americans become virtuous by living into the narratives of their culture. The apostle Paul expressed a similar thought when he urged the Christians in Rome, "Do not conform any longer to the pattern of this world, but be transformed by the renewing of your mind".

---

10. Ibid., 131.

11. Ibid., 124. Geisler's view of graded absolutism recognizes that the pyramid of ranked alternatives might cause Christians to sin by choosing a lesser evil. However, he believes Christians do not have to repent if they choose the alternative representing the greater good rather than the lesser good. John Jefferson Davis prefers *contextual absolutism*, which differs from graded absolutism by offering "a course of action that is morally right and free of sin" (*Evangelical Ethics: Issues Facing the Church Today*, 2d ed. [Phillipsburg, N.J.: Presbyterian and Reformed, 1993], 7).

12. Geisler, *Christian Ethics*, 124.

13. Douglas Groothuis echoes Geisler's commitment to propositions by stating that "revelation came through a variety of cultures and individuals, but it is no less propositional for that" (*Truth Decay: Defending Christianity against the Challenges of Postmodernism* [Downers Grove, Ill.: InterVarsity, 2000], 113).

14. Alasdair MacIntyre, *After Virtue: A Study in Moral Theory*, 2d ed. (South Bend, Ind.: University of Notre Dame Press, 1984), 208.

15. Ibid., 172.

16. See William J. Bennett, *The Book of Virtues* (New York: Simon & Schuster, 1993).

(Rom. 12:2). We renew our minds when we transform the narratives that govern our lives; only then can they empower us to live into a different story.

Narratives are both the templates through which we interpret reality and the means through which we seek continuity in our lives. They emerge from our history, and we could not tolerate life without them. They empower us to organize our perceptions of reality and to locate our place within it; they help us to see things not as they are, "but as *we* are."[17] They assist us in discerning the things that are important by communicating the truths about life's mysteries through metaphor and symbol.[18] Because they influence who we are and how we perceive God, they serve as the primary media of engaging in ethical inquiry.

Narratives influence the ethics of managing change, whether within or across cultures. They reveal how values and virtues are developed and shaped over time as well as the nature of the truth that governs them. For example, truth, for Christians, is not "a concept that 'works' but an incarnation that lives."[19] Jesus, in saying, "I am the way and the truth and the life" (John 14:6), issued an invitation to people to reconstruct the narratives of their lives around a relationship with him. The narrative of Christianity centers on Christ and his redemptive relationship with creation.

The Bible contains many stories of people who reconstructed their narratives by embracing the risen Christ. The story of Stephen (Acts 6:8–7:59), the first martyr of the church, is perhaps the best example. In order to persuade the Sanhedrin that Jesus was their long-expected Messiah, Stephen traced the history of the Hebrew nation from Abraham to the establishment of the monarchy and the building of the temple. The Sanhedrin seemed to agree with Stephen's account of their narrative until he concluded that they, like their ancestors who persecuted the prophets and "killed those who predicted the coming of the Righteous One" (Acts 7:52), were a "stiff-necked people, with uncircumcised hearts and ears," who always resisted the Holy Spirit (Acts 7:51). The Sanhedrin, who interpreted their history as the primary medium of revelation, were so offended by Stephen's judgment that they stoned him to death.

17. Neil Postman, "Science and the Story That We Need," *First Things* (January 1997): 30.
18. Charles Simpkin and Anne Simpkin, *Sacred Stories: A Celebration of the Power of Story to Transform and Heal* (San Francisco: Harper San Francisco 1993), 1.
19. Parker J. Palmer, *To Know As We Are Known: A Spirituality of Education* (San Francisco: Harper & Row, 1983), 14.

History, which is composed of narratives, reveals God's being and will[20] and is the arena of his activity; people confess their faith "by reciting the formative events of their history as the redemptive handiwork of God."[21] In so doing, they graft themselves and their communities into the narratives of their faith. Christianity has the power to transform history and thereby to transform cultures. God's redemptive work through Christ gives people another filter through which they can interpret their history.

Narratives lie at the heart of inspiration. According to Jacques Ellul, "all errors in Christian thought" began when Christianity shifted the center of theology from history to philosophy.[22]

People live in history as fish live in water, and "what we mean by the revelation of God can be indicated only as we point through the medium (history) in which we live."[23] Christian truth is revealed through the history of God's redemptive work in creation, giving God's relationship with creation a historic foundation. We know God, not through abstract philosophical propositions, but through our ability to interpret our history to reveal God's redemptive relationship with humankind, a relationship that is revealed through our personal and communal narratives. Historical evidence, however, is meaningless without interpretation. We study history through the context of some narrative, seeking ways to understand our present and future from the context of the past. "God's 'hand' in history is not found in the evidence and traces of the material past themselves, but in the interpretation and meaning of the past."[24]

Because history is the medium through which human beings realize the redemptive work of God, faith cannot get to God save through historic experience.[25] Without being integrated in narrative, history loses its meaning, its symbolic value, and its redemptive theme; it becomes nothing but "one damned thing after another."[26] In the thought of Lesslie Newbigin, Christian faith is itself an interpretation of history: "The acts

20. G. Ernest Wright, *God Who Acts: Biblical Theology as Recital* (Chicago: Regnery, 1952), 21.
21. Ibid., 38.
22. *The Subversion of Christianity*, trans. Geoffrey W. Bromiley (Grand Rapids: Eerdmans, 1986), 23.
23. Dale T. Irvin, *Christian Histories, Christian Traditioning: Rendering Accounts* (Maryknoll, N.Y.: Orbis, 1998), 18.
24. Ibid., 57.
25. H. Richard Niebuhr, "The Story of Our Life," in *Why Narrative? Readings in Narrative Theology*, ed. Stanley Hauerwas and L. Gregory Jones (Grand Rapids: Eerdmans, 1989), 42.
26. Richard John Neuhaus, *The Naked Public Square: Religion and Democracy in America* (Grand Rapids: Eerdmans, 1984), 11.

of God in history are the clue to its meaning and direction."[27] The Bible is the inspired narrative of God's relationship with creation, and history is the context in which the meaning of this narrative unfolds, revealing that God has a redemptive relationship with creation.

Propositions in the Context of Narrative

While propositions and narratives represent two polar modes of ethical inquiry, they also work in conjunction with each other, because narratives produce and absorb propositions. God's word is not culturally abstract but is embedded in the narratives of the cultures of the people to which it was directed, giving ethics a narrative nature.

Ethicists who focus on narrative are sympathetic to Geisler's conviction that ethical choices have to be based on God's absolute moral character, giving ethical inquiry an "objective, propositional and substantive nature."[28] However, this statement suggests that ethical propositions can be distilled from the narratives in which they are embedded. To some degree this is true; propositions can be extracted from the narratives of Scripture and transferred from one culture to another. However, this is an effort to engage in narrative ethics. Our cultural narratives influence our interpretation of Scripture as well as our selection of data from which we construct ethical propositions.

The notion that ethical inquiry is culturally influenced causes many Christians to feel insecure about the moral basis of their faith. It sounds theologically or philosophically less convincing than the conviction that our ethical decisions are objective, propositional, and substantive. This notion, however, actually affirms the wisdom of God's choice to relate to people through the context of multiple human cultures. People are culture-constructing beings, and God redeems human cultures to embody his narrative of redemption.

Efforts to create a culturally abstract ethical framework, in contrast to recognizing the value of multiple cultures, hint at the problem Jose Miguez-Bonino addressed in his interpretation of the story of the Tower of Babel. An abstract ethical framework makes truth instrumental, allowing people with power to produce what the powerless must accept as truth. However, ethical inquiry based on the narrative of God's redemptive relationship with creation seeks to empower peo-

27. George R. Hunsberger, *Bearing the Witness of the Spirit: Lesslie Newbigin's Theology of Cultural Plurality* (Grand Rapids: Eerdmans, 1998), 113.
28. Geisler, *Christian Ethics*, 131.

ple to perceive the redemptive work of God through Christ within the context of culture, preventing truth from being usurped by the powerful. A narrative approach to ethical inquiry acknowledges that ethical propositions cannot be culturally abstract and seeks to transform existing cultural narratives by integrating propositions into them.

This effort to integrate the transcultural propositions of the Christian faith into prevailing cultural narratives is common, and it is the source of the vitality of cross-cultural ethical inquiry from a Christian perspective. The celebration of the Sabbath, for example, is a proposition that emerged from the narrative of the Hebrew community, and it was subsumed into the narrative of the Christian church, albeit in a different form. The Decalogue clearly depicts the Sabbath as the seventh day. However, the Christian church, in its early effort to counter-identify with its Jewish roots, transformed the observation of the Sabbath from the seventh to the first day of the week.

A major concern of narrative ethics is the danger of implying that the redemptive truth of Christianity is culturally relative. However, a narrative approach to ethics removes this danger by applying revealed truth to cultural particularities. Before we address that issue, we must first examine the major functions of narrative in a culture and discern the implications of these functions for ethical engagement.

The Major Functions of Narrative

Narratives serve several functions that make them critical factors in cross-cultural ethical engagement. L. Gregory Jones extracted seven functions of narratives from the writings of Alasdair MacIntyre.[29] I want to add an eighth function to these seven and examine their roles in the context of several issues on managing change across cultures.

Explain and Legitimize Human Behavior

Cultural narratives explain why people behave as they do, and they can provide social justification for any behavior. This social justification is the starting point to discern how behavior can be redeemed. For example, a group of community elders in an African village claimed they had no regard for Christianity because they could not accept its monogamous teachings. They claimed that monogamists are selfish and that, in

29. "Alasdair MacIntyre on Narrative, Community and the Moral Life," *Modern Theology* 4.1 (1987): 53–69.

contrast, the respected men in their community practiced polygamy[30] to express generosity, a major virtue in their culture.

The ethical question was whether any particular form of marriage is central to expressing the redemptive work of God through Christ in that culture. The question, conversely, is whether Christians can accept polygamy as a valid expression of Christian marriage, if not as a Christian virtue. In a workshop seeking to answer this question, the participants cited 1 Timothy 3:12, "A deacon must be the husband of but one wife and must manage his children and his household well," and Titus 1:6, "An elder must be blameless, the husband of but one wife, a man whose children believe and are not open to the charge of being wild and disobedient," as unequivocal biblical support for their conviction that monogamy was normative for all Christians.

One of the participants, however, suggested that 1 Timothy 3:12 and Titus 1:6 prohibit digamy rather than polygamy, hinting that the Bible is silent about polygamy, or perhaps supportive of it.[31] Digamy is the practice of people remarrying after the termination of a previous marriage, generally because of death, but not excluding divorce. Digamy was prohibited in ancient Greece, and Greek tradition continues to discourage widows from remarrying.

If the Bible is equivocal on its position toward polygamy, we cannot consider whether polygamy has any redemptive value until we examine the narrative of the culture. Such an examination might inform us why polygamy is an expression of generosity, why the people place a value on marriage, and why that culture might have a surplus of women. Alternatively, it could tell us that men employ their power to exploit women and justify their exploitation as beneficial for women. Human behavior makes sense only in the narrative of a particular culture. Narratives help us understand why a particular behavior in a culture survives and might support a redemptive value in that culture.

Conversely, narratives also help us discern whether the biblical texts that are central to this issue, 1 Timothy 3:12 and Titus 1:6, as well as others, are concerned with digamy instead of polygamy. The exegetical evi-

30. Polygamy defines two expressions of plural marriage: polygyny is one man married to two or more women; polyandry is one woman married to two or more men. Since polyandry is rare, the popular use of polygamy has made it a synonym for polygyny. This book defines polygamy in its popular usage.

31. For a provocative discussion on polygamy and Christian ethics see Pamela S. Mann, "Toward a Biblical Understanding of Polygamy," *Missiology: An International Review* 17.1 (January 1989): 10–26.

dence indicates the passages are concerned with digamy. They were written to Christians in Greek cultures, and since the Greeks were not polygamous, there was no reason to mention polygamy to them. Digamy, however, unlike polygamy, was a major issue in the narratives of Greek cultures. The Greeks were frequently at war, and many of the men died or were missing for several years. Women displayed their virtue by expressing their loyalty to their deceased or missing husbands by not remarrying. The Greek classic *The Odyssey* portrays the virtue of Penelope as honoring the value her culture placed on the prohibition of digamy; she displayed her loyalty to Odysseus, who spent ten years returning from the Trojan war, by not remarrying.[32]

Christians in the twentieth century must decide what kind of behavior 1 Timothy 3:12 legitimizes. One side of the argument postulates that it forbids plural marriages whether polygamous or digamous. The other side of the argument says that the central issues in the passage are qualities of Christian leadership and that plural marriages are incidental to the passage. The point is not whether Christian leaders should be digamous or polygamous but whether they respect the indigenous qualities of leadership. Since the prohibition of polygamy is firmly embedded in the narrative of the Christian church, the tension will be resolved when the global church affirms the legitimacy of this tradition or seeks to transform it. If they seek to transform it, it will become one among several ethical issues that have been transformed throughout the history of the church.

Cultivate an Individual Self-Concept

Facilitating the development of self-concepts of both individuals and groups within a culture is the second function of narrative. People perceive themselves according to how they view their places in the narrative of their culture and how their cultural narrative relates to the narratives of other cultures. We know who we are, to some extent, in our relationships to others; likewise, we see redemption in narrative by affirming our values as complementary or contrasting to others.

An amusing illustration of this point occurred in the polygamous community of the Pokot of Kenya when a senior wife, noticing the dil-

32. Digamy was a problem for the Greeks but not for the Hebrews. The Sadducees, for example, remarried after the death of a spouse (Matt. 22:23–30). Paul's teaching concerning digamy suggests that he advised church leaders to honor a virtue that was deeply ingrained in the narrative of the host culture, whether or not it was part of the biblical tradition.

igence of the Roman Catholic nuns, thought that one of them would make a good co-wife for her husband. She recommended that the village elders arrange a marriage, which could be done without the husband's consent. The elders invited the husband and the Roman Catholic priest—who they assumed was the father of the nuns—to a meal to negotiate a bride price. The priest had to tactfully explain the Roman Catholic call to celibacy that he and the nuns shared. The Pokot people were completely unimpressed with a cultural narrative that de-emphasized progeny. They left the meal feeling bad for the nuns and affirming the superiority of their own culture. The Pokot women, like the elders in the community who associated polygamy with generosity, did not see any redemptive value in the narrative of a religious tradition that valued celibacy.

Foster a Collective Identity

Narratives serve a third function by empowering people to bear a particular social identity. They offer answers to some central questions, such as "Who am I? What is the nature, task, and purpose of human beings?"[33] They define "'What's wrong'? and 'What's the remedy?'"[34] The creation account (Gen. 1–2) in the Judeo-Christian faith, for example, declares that all people are created in the image of God and share an equal dignity. It also describes the fall of creation through the sinfulness of human beings and alludes to a redeemer who will overcome evil. It offers sin as the answer to the question of "what's wrong" and offers redemption as the remedy, defining people as sinful creatures who are being redeemed. To define humanity as sinful without offering hope for redemption is to ignore the main purpose of the salvation God offers to people.

The creation account also defines monogamy as the accepted form of marriage within the Judeo-Christian tradition, stating that a man should leave his father and mother "and be united to his wife, and they will become one flesh" (Gen. 2:24). If people in a polygamous culture become Christians, this passage will challenge them either to justify polygamy as a valid expression of marriage or to change the marriage laws of their society to be consistent with the creation narratives that they have grafted themselves into.

33. Brian J. Walsh and J. Richard Middleton, *The Transforming Vision: Shaping a Christian World View* (Downers Grove, Ill.: InterVarsity, 1984), 35.
34. Ibid., 44.

Empower People to Shape Their Histories

Empowering people to shape their histories, the fourth function of narrative, contains both the strongest and the weakest characteristic of narrative concerning its value in ethical inquiry. Its strongest feature is that it empowers people to participate in constructing the narratives that govern their lives, recognizing that people create the reality in which they live and that their decisions have moral consequences. Their decisions can bring them closer to experiencing the redemptive work of Christ or move them away from it.

The weakest point of narrative in ethical inquiry is that it is vulnerable to becoming self-congratulatory. In creating their narrative, people can look at it and declare that it is good. However, the values inherent in the narrative might not be good. A prescription for this weakness will be addressed later in the chapter. The immediate concern of empowering people to shape their narratives is the way in which that power is managed. The men of a community might shape a narrative that makes a positive relationship between polygamy and generosity. But the women of the community might shape it differently if they did not value polygamy in the same way. Both women and men will have to determine exactly what value polygamy, or any other virtue, has in their community. If they become Christians, they will need to participate equally in the transformation of their culture, determining what social practices are consistent with Christian values.

Foster the Creation of Traditions

The fifth function of narrative is creating and maintaining traditions. A tradition is any practice, argument, or belief extended over time, a "set of memories which are delivered from one generation to the other"[35] and which give people a particular identity. Traditions are historical and narrative in nature and exist, not because their value is rationally adduced, but because they are affirmed independently from reason. Tradition, for example, perpetuates female genital mutilation (FGM) in many cultures of the world, despite its widespread condemnation as cruel and irrational. The traditions of the cultures where it is practiced give it meaning and purpose. For instance, John S. Mbiti, an African theologian, explains that the shedding of blood from the reproductive organs symbolizes the flow of life. He says that FGM is "a pro-

---

35. Irvin, *Christian Histories*, 28.

found religious act by means of which the young people accept that they have to become bearers of children."[36]

Benezet Bujo, another African theologian, moves from explaining FGM to justifying it by suggesting that because of the woman's central position as the giver of life, she had to learn from youth "to dedicate her vital organ to God and the ancestors through the endurance of severe pain. She could only give life in the all-embracing sense, after having defeated death through suffering."[37] While many international organizations seek to abolish this practice, the traditions that perpetuate it will have to be transformed for the practice to terminate.

Define and Communicate Virtues and Values

Narratives fulfill a sixth function in ethical inquiry by communicating the virtues and values of a culture. They depict what the virtuous people in a culture do and the values they hold, whether or not they are moral. The Mauritanian government, for example, has banned slavery three times during the twentieth century; recent reports claim that between eighty and ninety thousand people in Mauritania are enslaved.[38] The legislative efforts to ban slavery affirm the immorality of the practice, but while legislation can embody moral values, it cannot produce them. The virtues of a culture emerge from their narratives and have their origins in what the culture perceives as ontological truth. Legislation, in contrast, produces instrumental truth; it is concerned with but cannot produce ontological truth.

Provide a Basis for Evaluating Morality

The seventh function of narratives is to provide a basis for evaluating the morality of particular behaviors. Cultural narratives create an epistemological framework by defining the basic assumptions people use to create and validate their knowledge of what is moral. For example, because the narratives of Western cultures define polygamy as a form of adultery, the people condemn polygamy as an immoral expression of marriage. In contrast, many African cultures, such as the Pokot in Kenya, esteem adultery as a serious offense, but they would not positively connect polygamy to adultery. If ethicists want to influence the people in a culture to shift their marital ethic from polygamy to monog-

36. John S. Mbiti, *Introduction to African Religion,* 2d ed. (Nairobi: East African Educational Publishers, 1991), 104.
37. Benezet Bujo, *The Ethical Dimension of Community: The African Model and the Dialogue between North and South* (Nairobi: Paulines Publications Africa, 1998), 127.
38. Joseph R. Gregory, "African Slavery 1996," *First Things* 63 (May 1996): 37–39.

amy, they have to shift the narrative through which people view marriage. Through narratives, "our epistemology is quietly transformed into our ethic."[39]

Provide a Vision for the Future

The final function of narrative is to provide people with a vision for their future that embodies the ultimate hope they esteem for themselves. The narratives of the various philosophies of modern cultures convey hopes for economic growth, scientific advancement, and an increase in pleasure, among other things. The narratives of traditional cultures focus on such things as social harmony as well as peace with God. The ultimate hope for Christians is the consummation of history at the second coming of Christ. The story of God's redemptive relationship with creation begins with humankind's alienation from God in the Garden of Eden and ends in the New Jerusalem, an image that "portrays a world purified from the Fall and its effects,"[40] where God's will dwells, once again, among his people.

Narrative and the Resolution of Ethical Dilemmas

Ethical inquiry based on propositions invariably creates dilemmas. The Old Testament Law, for example, says "You shall not murder" (Exod. 20:13), but the history of the Jewish and Christian communities is replete with stories of holy war and capital punishment, challenging theologians to discern the normative application of this ethic. Is it an unqualified absolute, a conflicting absolute, a graded absolute, or something else? Does it apply to personal, communal, or national behavior? Does it include both intentional and unintentional homicide? These are some of the issues through which we navigate when we seek to resolve ethical dilemmas through propositions. Narrative ethicists are not immune to the same difficulties, but they contextualize the dilemma in a manner that resolves some of the ambiguity of a proposition.

Consider how different narratives influence the ethical interpretations of the following story, which embodies the virtues and values of following Jesus, at least in one Christian tradition. In 1569, Dirk Willems, a faithful follower of Jesus Christ who lived in Asperen, Holland, was pursued by civil authorities for holding theological convictions contrary to the official orthodoxy. They hired a person, called a

39. Palmer, *To Know As We Are Known*, 21.
40. Walsh and Middleton, *Transforming Vision*, 58.

thiefcatcher, to apprehend Willems. When the thiefcatcher attempted to capture Willems, he fled by crossing a frozen lake. While pursuing Willems, the thiefcatcher fell through the ice, and Willems returned and rescued him from certain death. The thiefcatcher, however, took Willems to the civil authorities, and even though he advocated Willems's release, the magistrate condemned Willems to death.

Did Dirk Willems have a moral obligation to rescue the thief-catcher? Was the break in the ice a divine intervention that Willems did not take advantage of? Or was it a natural phenomenon that called Willems to rescue the thiefcatcher at the expense of his own self-interest? Our answer to these questions depends on the narratives we use to interpret the ethical value of Willems's decision. Jesus' teaching to his disciples to "love your enemies and pray for those who persecute you" (Matt. 5:44) evidently motivated Willems to make the decision that prevented his safety and freedom. This teaching seems to be normative for Christian behavior, and Willems appears to be justified because he followed it.

However, Jesus' teachings do not fully resolve the issue. Some Christians can argue, from the basis of self-preservation, if not from other biblical teachings, that Willems would have been morally justified to let the thiefcatcher drown. The view postulates that Jesus' teaching to love your enemies is not an instruction to be applied, but a vision to be esteemed, even for another age.

The biblical story of the Israelites' crossing the Red Sea is one biblical account that can be used to offer moral justification of allowing the thiefcatcher to drown. The Israelites, after safely crossing the Red Sea, rejoiced for "the great power the Lord displayed against the Egyptians" (Exod. 14:31) when the walls of water collapsed on them.

The moral struggle of reconciling the teachings of Jesus with the behavior of the Israelites raises several questions characteristic of the narrative approach to ethical inquiry. Did Jesus, for example, expect his teaching to transform the exodus story in the narrative of the Judeo-Christian tradition? Did he imply that the Israelites misinterpreted the role of God in causing the Egyptians to drown? Did he, like many contemporary Christians, believe there is a tension, but not a contradiction, between his teaching about love of enemies and the morality of celebrating their deaths?

Christians can garner an exhaustive number of biblical verses, interpretations, and arguments to support many views for or against Willems's decision and other ethical decisions. They can engage in "swapping text and counter-text for a while, with little likelihood of convincing themselves or anyone else"[41] about the moral validity of any ethical position. They often fail to develop moral principles to navigate through the ethical dilemmas that face us in life and confront us as we attempt to manage change across cultures.

Narratives, by telling "a story whose meaning unfolds through the interplay of characters and actions over time,"[42] cast some light on resolving moral tensions that emerge from ethical engagement. The essence of narrative is that it is not an abstract statement about truth. The Bible is the narrative about the living relationship between God and his people. Narratives offer interpretive contexts for biblical propositions and empower Christians to navigate through the moral impasses of life. They assume that biblical texts cannot be interpreted in cultural or historical vacuums, and Christians must "stop looking at doctrines and maxims in the abstract . . . [and] get the full story of what is happening in the situation."[43]

The place of reconciliation in the Jewish and Christian narratives gives us a clue to the interpretation of the exodus story and supports the virtue of Jews who celebrated their rescue at the expense of their enemies' deaths as well as the virtue of Christians who die at the hands of their foes. The unfolding of the Jewish and Christian narratives empowers Jews to look forward to reconciliation and liberates Christians to look back to it. The exodus story, celebrating the death of the Egyptians, is the prelude to the crucifixion story, empowering Christians to love enemies, including the Egyptians, as Michael Goldberg states:

> The story of the Jews is the story of the world in need of and waiting for reconciliation . . . in the Exodus story, the prelude to redemption and a new life is the death of sinners, the Egyptians—the enemies—at the hand of God. In the Christian story, the basis for salvation and new life is the death of Jesus—the self sacrifice of God, done for the sins of all.[44]

Christ's death, having transformed the Israelite narrative into a Christian narrative, commends the virtue of Dirk Willems's decision without devaluing that of the Israelites. Both behaviors were consistent within their respective narratives.

41. Christopher J. H. Wright, *An Eye for an Eye: The Place of Old Testament Ethics Today* (Downers Grove, Ill.: InterVarsity, 1983), 13.
42. Michael Goldberg, *Theology and Narrative: A Critical Introduction* (Nashville: Abingdon, 1982), 35.
43. Ibid., 25.
44. Ibid., 133.

Narrative Ethics and Cultural Relativism

In this section, I will explore the relationship between narrative ethics and cultural relativism, which are often confused, in order to substantiate the belief that God's redemptive relationship with creation subjects all cultures to truth.

Problems of Cultural Relativism

Cultural relativism proposes that "that which is right or wrong or good or bad depends on one's culture . . . no universal norms exist that apply to all people and all cultures."[45] It began as an opposition to the tendency to use European cultures as the standard for all cultures, creating the perception that people from non-European cultures were primitive, pre-logical, and nonrational, without the human consciousness to participate in a civilized community. Hegel, who was characteristic of these writers, saw Africa as a lawless and unethical wasteland, waiting for Europeans to conquer it and to impose morality.[46] E. B. Tylor's early anthropological writings on religion advanced the same belief that Western culture was the anthropological norm. Writing in the 1860s, he made continuous references to non-European people as the "lower races."[47] Similarly, the influential German theologian Ernst Troeltsch "believed that outside European civilization, true historical consciousness did not exist. The domains outside Europe lacked historical self-consciousness and the critical knowledge of the past for which only the European *Geist* has experienced a need."[48]

Narrative ethicists fully accept that Western culture is certainly not superior to other cultures and that all cultures have both morally positive as well as morally negative values. As we have seen for instance, the story of the Tower of Babel can be interpreted as God's decree that no culture is supreme. The rejection by cultural relativists, however, of any universal standards for ethics is problematic for managing cultural change. This idea gave birth to functionalism,[49] which proposes that all cultural beliefs, values, practices, and customs are beneficial, whether in-

45. Willie E. Hopkins, *Ethical Dimensions of Diversity* (Thousand Oaks, Calif.: Sage, 1997), 29.

46. Emmanuel Chukwudi Eze, ed., introduction in *Postcolonial African Philosophy: A Critical Reader* (Oxford: Blackwell, 1997), 8.

47. Edward Burnett Tylor, *Religion in Primitive Culture* (1871; reprint, New York: Harper & Bros., 1958), 12.

48. Irvin, *Christian Histories*, 25.

49. Functionalism is not as central in anthropological thinking as it once was. However, I use it in this book because it is the anthropological concept that influences development projects and challenges of management of change across cultures.

dividually or communally, to the people who engage in them. Functionalism postulates that cultures are "stable and self-correcting,"[50] affirming that "anything one group of people is inclined toward doing is worthy of respect by another"[51] group of people. Functionalism "can make almost anything right, and prevents condemnation of anything."[52]

Functionalism moves toward making individual cultures morally absolute with its assumption that "human affairs are explained . . . by the perfectly natural process of cultural evolution."[53] Donald T. Campbell, a past president of the American Psychological Association, demonstrated the similarities between natural and cultural evolution in the following way:

> [W]hen an evolutionary biologist encounters some ludicrous and puzzling form of animal life, he approaches it with a kind of awe, certain that behind the bizarre form lies a functional wisdom that he has yet to understand. I believe the case for socio-cultural evolution is strong enough so that psychologists and other social scientists when considering an apparently bizarre incomprehensible feature of their social tradition, or that of another culture, should approach it with a similar awe, expecting that when eventually understood, when our theories have caught up with it, that seemingly bizarre superstition will turn out to make adaptive sense.[54]

Marvin Harris uses functionalism to solve many cultural riddles by analyzing the roles of particular cultural practices in balancing ecological factors. His explanation of why Christians eat pork, but Muslims and Jews don't, is that pigs are hazardous to a fragile ecosystem because they don't graze. For this reason, apparently, the Levitical law, which Muslims and Jews observe, forbade raising and eating pigs. Christians don't observe this aspect of the Levitical law, evidently because they lived in urban environments and were less dependent on the pastoral ecosystem.[55] While Harris's theory on the dietary restrictions of the Levitical law is harmless, his efforts to justify warfare as an "ecologically adaptive life-

50. J. M. Blaut, *The Colonizer's Model of the World: Geographical Diffusionism and Eurocentric History* (New York: Guilford, 1993), 27.

51. Clifford Geertz, *The Interpretation of Cultures: Selected Essays* (New York: Basic Books, 1973), 44.

52. Robert B. Edgerton, *Sick Societies: Challenging the Myth of Primitive Harmony* (New York: Free Press, 1992), 25.

53. Elvin Hatch, *Culture and Morality: The Relativity of Values in Anthropology* (New York: Columbia University Press, 1983), 14.

54. Donald T. Campbell, "On the Conflicts between Biological and Social Evolution and between Psychology and Moral Tradition," *American Psychologist* (December 1975): 1121.

55. Marvin Harris, *Cows, Pigs, Wars and Witches: The Riddles of Culture* (New York: Vantage, 1974), 34.

style among primitive peoples"[56] fail to recognize the value and dignity of human life. Some anthropologists use functionalism to defend female genital mutilation, thus insulting the dignity of human life. And there is an apocryphal story about the anthropologist who said missionaries should not feed starving people because it will disrupt the cycle of nature; dead bodies participate in this cycle by fertilizing trees.

Functionalism fails to make a distinction between the inherent worth of people and their ability to create destructive cultural practices. These points will be further developed in chapter 4; it is sufficient here to say that functionalism is misguided because it assumes that the value of cultural practices are equal to the value of the people who participate in them. It makes truth relative to culture and creates a legion of ethical problems in the management of cultural change.

Narrative ethicists do not endorse cultural relativism; they do, however, believe that no particular culture has a monopoly on truth. Therefore, they relativize all cultures by affirming the need for a multicultural community to interpret truth. They recognize, though, that these interpretations are influenced through media that are culturally influenced.

Troeltsch believed that "Christianity and Western culture are so inextricably intertwined that a Christian can say little about his faith to members of other civilizations, and the latter in turn cannot encounter Christ save as a member of the Western world."[57] This belief is the problem that narrative ethicists want to solve. People need not become a member of the Western world to become Christian; all cultures, to differing degrees, are distant from Christ, but the truth of Christ can be expressed in all cultures.

Absolute Truth in Relative Cultures

As we shall see in chapter 4, cultures bear the image of their human creators, and because human beings are fallen, so are the cultures they create. Hence, cultures as well as human beings need to participate in the redemptive work of Christ. How then can people know the absolute truth in Jesus Christ, which, while transcultural, is revealed through fallen cultural media? One difficulty of the human predicament is that people "can't somehow leap out of culture and history and gaze directly into . . . the mind of God."[58]

56. Ibid., 57.
57. H. Richard Niebuhr, *Christ and Culture* (New York: Harper & Row, 1951), 30.
58. Jeffrey Stout, *Ethics after Babel: The Languages of Morals and Their Discontents* (Boston: Beacon, 1988), 23.

Paul Hiebert offers four philosophical positions from which Christians can help people navigate through this predicament: *absolute idealism, critical idealism, naive realism,* and *critical realism.*[59] The first three positions do not acknowledge the cultural nature of perceptions and are, therefore, less conducive to the discernment of truth across cultures than the fourth position is. Absolute idealism assumes that reality is a cognitive construct existing only in the minds of individuals or groups. The Bible, for idealists, can mean whatever they think it means; there is no need to acknowledge cultural influences. Critical idealism assumes that truth can be obtained through a rational reading of the Bible, also making cultural influences incidental to truth. It postulates that reality is in the mind, which in turn imposes order on the environment. Critical idealism assumes that human rationality is the same for all human beings.[60] Naive realism also fails to foster the importance of truth across cultures but improves on the previous positions by acknowledging external influences, including human cultures, on the perception of truth. It assumes that truth can be known without bias, so that people who hold this position study the Bible without acknowledging the influences of the biases through which they interpret it.

The fourth position, critical realism, is the most conducive to discerning truth cross-culturally. It affirms that truth exists but recognizes that a person's perceptions of truth will be only partial because "humans can only see it through their cultural lenses."[61] Truth exists; it is known by faith, and it can be discerned through cultural media. This statement sounds insubstantial in scientific cultures, especially those in which faith is perceived as though it were a science. However, the belief in any expression of truth is based on faith in the assumptions through which the expression of truth is perceived. Christians who are critical realists believe the universal church is the steward of an absolute truth, revealed through Jesus Christ and recorded in the Bible through narrative via the contexts of several first-century cultures. Critical realists recognize that "there can never be a culture-free gospel."[62]

---

59. Paul G. Hiebert, *Anthropological Reflections on Missiological Issues* (Grand Rapids: Baker, 1994), 23. Hiebert actually has six positions. However, only four are conducive to discerning biblical truths. The other two positions, *instrumentalism* and *determinism,* postulate that truth cannot be discerned.

60. Ibid.

61. Charles H. Kraft, *Anthropology for Christian Witness* (Maryknoll, N.Y.: Orbis, 1996), 418.

62. Hunsberger, *Bearing the Witness of the Spirit,* 239.

Revelation is perceived through cultural narratives, and the perception of it might change within different cultures, but the truth of Christ does not change from one culture to another. Narrative ethicists realize that the gospel has a cultural setting, that "There is no cultureless gospel . . . Nor is it the case that the gospel can be reduced to a set of cultureless principles."[63] The vitality of Christian ethics, cross-cultural and otherwise, emerges from the reality that the truth of Christ is not relative to any one particular culture. It is perceived through the media of at least two cultures. The first medium is the culture from which it came; the second is the culture into which we want to integrate it. We cannot begin to perceive how the truth of Christ applies to our lives unless we begin to integrate it into our cultural narratives. However, we must first discern this truth from the cultures that are delivering it to us.

This integrative effort certainly transforms our narratives, but it also transforms our perceptions of what we are accepting as truth. The following examples are only a few of the many ethical issues that challenge us to discern how the expression of truth translates from one culture to another.

Many Christians supported slavery during the American Civil War because they thought it had a biblical precedent in the Book of Philemon. No competent ethicist today would use Philemon's story to support slavery; the narratives of contemporary cultures have influenced us to reinterpret the meaning of the revealed truth in this inspired work. The roles of women in churches have been redefined as theologians understand the truth of women's issues in light of the cultures where biblical revelation transpired. The traditional positions that churches have taken on homosexuality are currently being examined in light of biblical and cultural teachings on sexual ethics. These teachings are challenging Christians to shift and defend the narratives they use to discern the moral values of homosexual behavior.

Each of these issues illustrates that our cultural narratives inform the way in which we perceive and construct our view of how the redemptive work of God through Christ influences us. If we want our theology and ethics to transform our cultural narratives, we have to start with narratives rather than with the propositions. The narratives define the context from which propositions are written; they define the issues that the propositions address and the questions we ask in developing them.

63. Lois Barrett, "The Church as Apostle to the World," in *Missional Church: A Vision for the Sending of the Church in North America,* ed. Darrell L. Guder (Grand Rapids: Eerdmans, 1998), 114.

2

Scripture:
From Narrative to Metanarrative

Wealth creates poverty. Wealth and poverty lie together. Where there is no wealth, there is no poverty.

African proverb

You take out what you did not put in and reap what you did not sow.

The third slave, Luke 19:21

If you don't have a sword, sell your cloak and buy one.

Jesus, Luke 22:36

Puzzled over the shortage of houses in an Indonesian village, Christian development facilitators discovered that even though there was enough land and building materials to provide adequate housing, the people were hindered from building because of their burial and ancestral customs. The villagers explained that their traditions forbade men to live in their own houses until they had provided honorable funerals for their parents. Since funerals were very expensive, often requiring fifteen to twenty years of saving after the parents' deaths, all the sons and their families were obligated to live in their parents' houses for many years after their parents had died. The traditions dictated that caring for ancestors was as important as caring for the living. Such customs, however, threatened the general welfare of the village, causing crowded living conditions, poor health, and a tense social atmosphere.

The development practitioners believed the villagers could improve their living conditions by transforming their burial and ancestral customs. However, the villagers, assuming their decision supported the values that permeated the narrative of their culture, did not believe housing was a major issue in the physical or social development of their village. Instead, they believed that any neglect of the ancestors could cause even worse conditions, such as birth defects, accidents, and a number of other misfortunes. Therefore, they struggled with the tension of caring for the ancestors and providing adequate housing for the community, believing that the ancestors governed the welfare of present and future generations.

The development facilitators tried to find the proper biblical response to the dilemma of the village, but they disagreed about what Scripture to use and how to interpret it. One facilitator cited Matthew 8:21–22, where a disciple wishing to follow Jesus asked permission to bury his father first. Jesus responded, "Follow me, and let the dead bury their own dead" (v. 22). The facilitator who cited the passage believed that Christians have minimal responsibility to their ancestors. He thought people who have new life in Christ should let the people who are dead in their traditions bury those who die in the traditions. The group, however, disagreed; burying the dead is a basic human responsibility. They thought the passage had more to do with discipleship than with allegiance to ancestors. However, they could not produce an adequate biblical response to the villagers' ancestral traditions.

The Need for a Metanarrative

According to Bernard T. Adeney, the "most significant problem in ethics is biblical interpretation."[1] As we saw with the Tower of Babel story, Christians can interpret the Bible from any number of assumptions, making the Bible mean anything they want it to mean, causing various interpretations to clash and conflict.

1. *Strange Virtues: Ethics in a Multi-cultural World* (Downers Grove, Ill: InterVarsity, 1995), 34.

The lack of a common reference point from which to interpret Scripture makes Christians vulnerable to *emotivism,* "the doctrine that all evaluative judgments . . . are *nothing but* expressions of preference, expressions of attitude or feeling."[2] An emotive exegesis of Scripture, like an emotive ethic, interprets the Bible through feelings. It is often prefaced with such statements as "I feel that this passage means . . ." or "to me, this passage means. . . ." Emotivism, also called noncognitivism,[3] has become one of the most popular methods of Bible study, making biblical interpretation difficult in Christian ethics because it promotes a subjective interpretation. It emerges when cultural narratives legitimize interpretations of Scripture, shifting the central question of a passage from "What was the author's intention?" to "What does this text mean to me or my community?"[4]

The problem of emotivism becomes particularly controversial in managing cultural change, because the multiplicity of cultures increases the number of feelings that can influence the interpretation of any scriptural reference. This chapter will attempt to solve the problem by exploring the role of the Bible as a metanarrative of redemption. Metanarratives are the grand stories that offer "interpretations of history that explain and justify the rise, success and fall of given cultures."[5] They contain themes "such as Progress, Emancipation, or Enlightenment that establish the values of the society."[6]

The Bible, as a metanarrative, offers redemption as an explanation for the rise and fall of cultures. It starts with God and unfolds the grand themes of the story of his eternal plan, moving from the creation and the fall to final rehabilitation.[7] It traces God's relationship with creation through history by way of the Jewish and the Christian communities. The Bible, as a metanarrative, is a series of stories embedded within the larger narrative of "a universal purpose carried out through a continuous

---

2. Alasdair MacIntyre, *After Virtue: A Study in Moral Theory,* 2d ed. (South Bend, Ind.: University of Notre Dame Press, 1984), 11–12.

3. Stanley J. Grenz, *The Moral Quest: Foundations of Christian Ethics* (Downers Grove, Ill.: InterVarsity, 1997), 51.

4. Roy Clements, "Expository Preaching in a Postmodern World," *Evangelical Review of Theology* 23 (April 1999): 179.

5. Thomas N. Finger, *Self, Earth, and Society: Alienation and Trinitarian Transformation* (Downers Grove, Ill.: InterVarsity, 1997), 116.

6. Ibid.

7. Douglas Groothuis, *Truth Decay: Defending Christianity against the Challenges of Postmodernism* (Downers Grove, Ill.: InterVarsity, 2000), 75.

series of particular choices."[8] That purpose is the redemptive hope that Christians have in Christ Jesus.

The development facilitators in the Indonesian village, after considering the Matthew 8 passage about burying the dead, realized that the disciple who made the request would not have followed Jesus even after burying his father. He, like the people in the Indonesian village, wanted to become like his father, who lived in the traditions of his ancestors. Jesus challenged the disciple to leave his father's dead traditions. While this interpretation eliminated a misapplication of Scripture, it did not offer an alternative interpretation.

The development facilitators failed to define the major themes of Scripture to provide a framework for their ministry, which they needed to do before extrapolating meaning from individual biblical passages to apply to particular cultural conditions. Hence, the group became distracted from focusing on the broader purpose of their ministry and let a minor issue drain their energy.

The broader purpose of the development facilitators was to implement a community development project; reducing the influence of the ancestors might be a by-product of their ministry. Meeting the greater purpose, the project facilitators needed to discern how the biblical theme of redemption had a positive expression in their work. They needed to answer the following questions: "How can we address the influence of the ancestors in a manner that complements the redemptive themes of Scripture?" "Are there expressions of redemption in Scripture that address our problem with the ancestors, either directly or indirectly?"

One central principle of the New Testament that speaks to the ancestor issue in the Indonesian village is the liberation from traditions. This principle is central to many of the New Testament teachings. In saying that "the Sabbath was made for man, not man for the Sabbath" (Mark 2:27), Jesus subjected tradition to the welfare of the community. The writings of Paul, likewise, emphasize that traditions are useful only to the point of facilitating the redemption of humankind. Paul emphatically taught that the Jewish Christians in Rome should not nullify the law, their traditions, but uphold the law because of their faith in Christ (Rom. 3:31). The law, however, was to serve them, not the other way around. In the Jewish community the law is part of the elements of the

8. George R. Hunsberger, *Bearing the Witness of the Spirit: Lesslie Newbigin's Theology of Cultural Plurality* (Grand Rapids: Eerdmans, 1998), 72.

kosmos, or the socially constructed elements of reality that distract people from God.

The biblical theme of liberating people, such as the Indonesian villagers, from traditions does not imply that they should discard their traditions but that people can transform their traditions and celebrate them as expressions of faith rather than of fear. Christians celebrate a variety of cultural traditions to honor the memories of their ancestors; those in my culture decorate graves with flowers on Memorial Day. They do not celebrate out of fear, but because they want to recognize the contributions their ancestors made to their lives and to their culture. The Hebrews brought Joseph's bones out of Egypt (Gen. 50:25) not because they feared him, but because they were liberated to honor their oath to him.

The Biblical Emphasis on Redemption

Redemption, a central theme in Scripture, is embodied in Colossians 1:15–20, the fourth biblical account of creation. The emphasis of this account is the redemptive hope of God's reconciling all elements of creation to himself through Christ, bringing peace to a fallen world. It serves well both as the framework for managing cross-cultural change and as the basis for ethical inquiry, not only for a personal ethic but also for environmental and social concerns:

> [Christ] is the image of the invisible God, the firstborn over all creation. For by him all things were created: things in heaven and on earth, visible and invisible, whether thrones or powers or rulers or authorities; all things were created by him and for him. He is before all things, and in him all things hold together. And he is the head of the body, the church; he is the beginning and the firstborn from the dead, so that in everything he might have the supremacy. For God was pleased to have all his fullness dwell in him, and through him to reconcile to himself all things, whether things on earth or things in heaven, by making peace through his blood, shed on the cross.

This passage has three key points applicable to establishing redemption as an ethical basis for managing cultural change. The first point, the supremacy of Christ (v. 15), affirms that the redemptive work of God, through Christ, is the foundation of the ethical management of cultural change. This truth helps us to discern whether any ethical decision supports God's redemption of creation through the salvific work of Christ, such as the decision to give food to starving people, even if the food is not accompanied by Scripture verses or a salvation tract.[9]

The second point, God's reconciliation of both the visible and invisible elements of creation (v. 16), has three parts. The first part concerns the apostle Paul's response to Gnostic teaching. The Western church tends to interpret visible and invisible as physical and spiritual, which limits Christian ministries to the spiritual realm and prevents them from grasping the comprehensive ethical nature of managing cultural change. A proper interpretation of the passage includes God's reconciling work, which embraces social, cultural, political, and economic structures.

The second part focuses on the meaning of reconciliation. The Greek term in the passage, *apokatallasso*, a unique use of *katallasso*, is commonly translated "to reconcile"; however, it is not the best translation. "Catalyst" is better, since *katallasso* is the cognate of catalyst and communicates the idea of an agent bringing together two or more unrelated elements. The elements change when they are brought together, but the catalytic agent remains unchanged. In this situation, God is the catalytic agent who reconciles the elements of creation, changing their nature but not changing his nature.

The apostle Paul, in affirming that God catalyzes the elements of creation and reconciles them to himself through Christ, emphasized that Christ is the head of the church. He recognized that "since its break with the Jewish national community the Christian movement had considered itself the 'church' and thus *the true Israel*. He knew that the infant church understood itself as *a new people* composed of Jews and Gentiles."[10] In Christ, the church becomes the new community of Israel, the steward of God's covenanted relationship with creation. It "received the task of representing symbolically what really should have taken place in Israel as a whole: complete dedication to the gospel of the reign of God, radical conversion to a new way of life."[11] Through Christ, God made "one new humanity in place of the two, thus making peace" (Eph. 2:15 NRSV).

The church, as God's catalytic and reconciling community, universalizes the particularities of the Torah, transforming the cultural mores of

9. The interpretation of any ethical action as bearing witness to the redemptive work of God through Christ is the theological basis of evangelism through development work. Christians who engage in such work can give it an evangelistic intent by interpreting their work as part of God's overall redemptive work in creation.

10. Gerhard Lohfink, *Jesus and Community: The Social Dimension of Christian Faith*, trans. John P. Galvin (Philadelphia: Fortress, 1984), 2.

11. Ibid., 34.

the Jewish community from the particular expressions of that community to the universal expressions of a global, multicultural church. In this transformation, the church reconstructs the bloody rite of circumcising the flesh, the central initiatory rite of the Jewish community, to the bloodless rite of baptism, the central initiatory rite symbolizing new life in Christ. Also, the practice of offering dead animals as sacrifices to God becomes the practice of faithful people offering themselves as living sacrifices (Rom. 12:1–2).

The theme of transformation, central to many of the Pauline epistles, is the main topic of his Letter to the Galatians. It addresses the influence of the Judaizers, people who wanted to apply the Jewish law to the churches in Galatia. The Judaizers' refusal to accept Paul's teachings about the church as the transformed Israel created two communities. He emphasized the transformation by directing the closing blessing of the epistle to the "Israel of God" (Gal. 6:16). In Romans, a later epistle, Paul expatiated on this theme by affirming that "not all who are descended from Israel are Israel" (Rom. 9:6). Israel, God's redemptive community through Christ, is the church. Paul is interpreting the church as the fulfillment of Zephaniah 3:11–13, which focuses on "the restoration of a righteous remnant as the true people of Israel . . . a people humble and lowly, who seek refuge in the name of Yahweh."[12]

The third part of the second point of Colossians 1:15–20 clarifies the definition of reconciliation. A common misinterpretation of reconciliation is used to support universal salvation. However, reconciliation and salvation are not synonymous. Reconciliation, as it is used in this passage, has the sense of restoration. It assumes creation's fall and God's commitment to its restoration, so that it can fulfill his purposes. Because of the fall, creation can no longer support life, including that of plants, animals, and humans, as effectively as God intended. This inability introduced suffering into creation, such as hunger, sickness, and social and cultural disintegration, as well as other problems. Reconciliation focuses on the conviction that the "most basic thing about man is not his sin but his restoration."[13]

Through reconciliation God reclaims and frees creation by his redemptive work through Christ:

12. Duane L. Christensen, *Transformations of the War Oracle in Old Testament Prophecy* (Missoula, Mont.: Scholars, 1975), 160.

13. Harvey G. Cox, "The Responsibility of the Christian in a World of Technology," in *Economic Growth in World Perspective,* ed. Denys Munby (New York: Associated Press, 1966), 177.

[Reconciliation] consists in Spirited actions, often very ordinary everyday ones, against the anti-creational forces that violate creation's integrity and degrade and destroy. . . . [It] means freeing Israel (and all creation) from whatever oppresses or victimizes. It reaches from inner spirit to sociopolitical and economic spheres to cosmic realms. It means realizing the life potential of all things. . . . Redemption is to free people and the rest of nature to become what all was created to be.[14]

Reconciliation gives human beings the hope that "the creation itself will be liberated from its bondage to decay and brought into the glorious freedom of the glory of the children of God" (Rom. 8:21). It affirms that "creation is so good that God intends to purge it from evil and bring it to perfection."[15]

Salvation, in contrast to reconciliation, is a narrower concept that has several dimensions. In the Hebrew Scriptures, it "is clearly social and corporate and includes every aspect of life."[16] In the New Testament, "Jesus links salvation inseparably with the Kingdom of God. . . . [It] refers to the past, present and future redeeming activity of God in Christ."[17] Yet, it does not imply universalism. To believe "that God plans a cosmic salvation in which eventually all things will be reconciled to God does *not* mean that every person will be saved. Rather it means that all parts of the created order—'persons, human civilization and even the non-human creation'—will participate in God's ultimate salvation."[18]

Efforts to manage cultural change participate in God's restorative efforts to bring salvation to the world by rehabilitating the elements of creation to fulfill their intended purposes. The natural environment of the Indonesian community, for example, had plenty of resources to support the health of the community. However, the religious and cultural traditions prevented the people from using these resources effectively. If the people transform their spirituality by integrating the truth about God's reconciling work into their cultural narrative, they can empower themselves to use their resources to support their communal well-being.

The third point of Colossians 1:15–20 concerns peace as the result of God's reconciling work through Christ, which should be the central goal of community development work; however, contemporary Christians

14. Larry L. Rasmussen, *Earth Community, Earth Ethics* (Geneva: WCC, 1996), 256.
15. Ronald J. Sider, *One-Sided Christianity: Uniting the Church to Heal a Lost and Broken World* (Grand Rapids: Zondervan, 1993), 92.
16. Ibid., 84.
17. Ibid., 87.
18. Ibid., 91.

neglect it. I've asked workshop participants in North America, Asia, and Africa to identify the values in this passage that are relevant to creating a narrative for community development. Rarely, however, does anyone choose peace, and the few who do, limit its definition to the absence of war.

The biblical concept that Christ is our peace, that peace is "the sphere within which all creation takes place; all the laws and purposes which guide creation and government of the universe reside in Him,"[19] comes from the vision of the new heavens and the new earth in Isaiah 65:17–25. Isaiah's description of the ultimate harmony of creation is the proper theological meaning of peace, and it is realized in a survival strategy[20] that is fully functioning. Isaiah's vision enumerates the true ingredients of peace, including the eradication of infant mortality and the early death of adults (v. 20). No longer will people work for the pleasure of others (v. 22), but they will live in the houses they build and eat the fruit of their vineyards (v. 21). Their children will not be doomed to misfortune, but they and their descendants will be blessed by God (v. 23). In that harmony, the "wolf and the lamb will feed together" (v. 25).

The people with whom Christian community development facilitators work are all too familiar with the conditions that Isaiah was addressing. They watch helplessly as their children die from preventable diseases, and they toil for the comfort of others. They build, clean, and guard houses that they can never live in, and they prepare food that they will never afford to eat. Isaiah's vision gives them hope for a better life for themselves and for their children.

Isaiah's vision offers a theological and ethical basis for Christians who believe they can work toward transforming cultural values that jeopardize human welfare. I discovered the pertinence of this passage, especially of the wolf and lamb eating together, when I conducted a workshop in Uganda, where development practitioners were reconciling families with children who had been kidnapped by the Lord's Resistance Army, a rebel group that brainwashes children to fight against their governments. Many of these children are as young as eight years of age. The people who work with them say the children are worse than wolves with no fear of people or death. Isaiah's vision inspires the development practitioners to transform these wolves into lambs and have them eat with other children

19. Fritz Rienicker, *A Linguistic Key to the Greek New Testament* (Grand Rapids: Zondervan, 1980), 567.

20. A survival strategy is the combination of activities that a community engages in to ensure its continued existence. This point will be addressed more fully in chapter 12.

in the village. The success of the development practitioners is attributed to the hope they received from this passage.

The final element of redemption as a biblical meta-theme is the vision of creation in the last chapter of Revelation, where the leaves of a tree are healing the nations of the world, which is the profound reversal of the destruction caused by the fall; "Creation in the beginning started with nature and ended with the human being."[21] Genesis 3 records how humankind brought sin into the world, bringing a curse on the land by eating the fruit of a tree. The vision in Revelation 22:2–3, however, "started with the liberation of the human being and ends with the redemption of nature."[22] It communicates the hope of a tree that heals the nations, removing the curse.

The biblical meta-theme of creation, fall, and reconciliation reflects the values of the kingdom of God that empower people throughout the world to shape their cultural narratives redemptively. The Bible offers a metanarrative rather than a narrative because reconciliation is not an attempt to make all cultures look alike. Instead, it is an effort to offer to all people in all cultures values that will empower them to enhance their lives by transforming the values that shape their cultural narratives.

Redemptive Interpretations of Luke 19:11–27

Since biblical interpretation is a central activity in the ethical inquiry necessary to manage cross-cultural change, it deserves considerable attention. The central problem, as we saw, is that people tend to interpret Scripture according to the themes of their own cultural narratives. Most of these interpretations do not pose an ethical threat to Christianity, but some do. I want to explore the interpretations of some passages of Scripture that have significant implications for managing change across cultures and to examine some of the themes in cultural narratives that give legitimacy to these interpretations.

There are a variety of biblical passages whose interpretations change within different cultural narratives. For instance, Jesus' instruction to his disciples to sell their cloaks to buy a sword (Luke 22:36) lends itself to the support of just war and other violent engagements. However, it will have an opposite interpretation if we determine how its context supports the redemptive theme of Scripture. Jesus' teaching comes immediately before the Roman soldiers arrest him, presumably for insurrection, not

21. Jürgen Moltmann, *God in Creation* (Minneapolis: Fortress, 1993), 68.
22. Ibid.

because he has any illusions that swords are adequate to defend him or his disciples from the Romans. It could be that Jesus wants to lampoon the powers of Rome by giving the soldiers, in a satirical fashion, enough evidence to convict him.[23]

Another passage that suffers from popular misinterpretations is the parable of the Ten Minas (Luke 19:11–27). This passage is quite complex, and its contrasting interpretations have significant implications for managing change across cultures. This study will seek to identify some of the themes in the cultural narratives that influence the different interpretations of the parable.

Jesus tells the story after eating in the house of Zacchaeus, a very wealthy tax collector. That he was willing to eat with sinners drew complaints from the crowd. Zacchaeus, however, responded to Jesus' visit by saying that he would give half of his possessions to the poor and would repay anyone whom he defrauded by four times the defrauded amount (Luke 19:8). Jesus then proclaimed that salvation had come to Zacchaeus's house because Zacchaeus was a son of Abraham and because he had come to seek and to save the lost (Luke 19:10). The crowd interpreted Zacchaeus's repentance as evidence that the kingdom of God was near; Jesus told the parable to challenge their understanding of the kingdom.

The parable is about a nobleman who went to a distant country to get royal power for himself. He summoned ten of his slaves, giving them each a mina and instructing them to invest the mina in a business while he was away. The citizens of the community hated the nobleman, wishing him not to return. Nevertheless, he returned with royal power and held his slaves accountable for their use of the mina he had given them, rewarding them according to their success in multiplying his wealth. The first slave turned one mina into ten and was rewarded by being put in charge of ten cities. The second slave turned one mina into five and was rewarded with five cities. The third slave wrapped the mina in a cloth and returned it as he received it, saying "I was afraid of you, because you are a harsh man; you take what you did not deposit, and reap what you did not sow" (v. 21 NRSV).

The third slave's response exposed the nobleman's view of himself. The nobleman, in response to the slave, said "I will judge you by your own words, you wicked slave! You knew, did you, that I was a harsh man, taking what I did not deposit, and reaping what I did not sow?

23. Nancey Murphy and George F. R. Ellis, *On the Moral Nature of the Universe: Theology, Cosmology, and Ethics* (Minneapolis: Fortress, 1996), 200.

Why then did you not put my money into the bank? Then when I returned, I could have collected it with interest." (v. 22 NRSV). At the protest of the crowd, the nobleman ordered the bystanders to strip the third slave of his one mina and give it to the slave who had ten. The parable ends with an observation that people who have will get more, while those who have nothing will lose what little they might have. The final passage of the parable records that nobleman's ordering the slaughter of his enemies.

Contemporary scholarship supports two interpretations of the parable that are diametrically opposed to each other. I will call one the traditional and the other the transformed; they result from different cultural narratives. The traditional interpretation, which focuses on obedience to a master, emerges from a cultural narrative that emphasizes the value of personal piety in religious devotion and practice. The second interpretation, which focuses on empowering people who are oppressed by unjust social and economic systems, emerges from a cultural narrative that seeks to encourage people to transform their social structures.

The Traditional Interpretation

The traditional interpretation sees Luke 19:11–27 as an allegory of the kingdom of God and identifies Jesus as the rich man who leaves the country, just as Jesus will go to heaven to return in judgment. The slaves are the disciples of Jesus, who are to use his gifts wisely; it teaches his followers to be good managers of the resources that God entrusted to them. This interpretation focuses on stewardship, whether the wealth is allegorical—representing either management or evangelism—or actual. From either point of view, the slaves have the responsibility to return to the nobleman, Jesus, more than they received from him.

This interpretation is considered traditional because it affirms the efficacy of economics and militarism, the two factors that have the most influence in shaping the narratives of modern cultures. Economics, at one time, was the study of household management; now it is an aspect of human nature, because it defines the "person-in-community."[24] The global economic metaculture has made humans not only social but also economic beings. As Harvey Cox maintains, the "religion and culture of a society cannot be studied apart from its economic and social context."[25]

---

24. Herman E. Daly and John B. Cobb Jr., *For the Common Good: Redirecting the Economy toward Community, the Environment, and a Sustainable Future* (Boston: Beacon, 1989), 7.

25. *The Secular City: Secularization and Urbanization in Theological Perspective* (New York: Macmillan, 1965), 8.

Similarly, the pervasive presence of the military-industrial complex throughout the world has redefined the nature of warfare to the point where we do not see a contradiction between Jesus' teaching his disciples to love their enemies and his ordering the slaughter of his enemies. The traditional interpretation is a product of the narrative of modern culture.

Some commentators who support the traditional interpretation ironically expose the flaws in it. Commentator I. Howard Marshall mentions the difficulty of using this violent imagery to communicate the coming of Jesus. He gives it an evangelistic slant and resigns himself to the validity of it, believing this interpretation, because of its evangelistic perspective, would have made sense to Jesus' audience. It "conveys to them the seriousness of their position."[26] Similarly, Craig L. Blomberg, while recognizing the economic implications of the parable, concludes that it violates the Levitical prohibition of charging interest by containing "at least a tacit endorsement of the rudimentary form of capitalism practiced by banks and moneylenders in the ancient Greco-Roman world."[27]

Donald B. Kraybill also supports the traditional interpretation, arguing that "the actual objects in a parable are usually not literal prescriptions for Christian behavior" and proposing that the "commodity in the story is our knowledge of Christian faith."[28] The significance of Luke's placement of the parable after the story of Zacchaeus is that "Luke is suggesting *we* are responsible for the stewardship of the ideas of the Zacchaeus story. . . . Those who invest and multiply their kingdom knowledge will be given more. Those who waste it may lose the kingdom completely."[29]

Joachim Jeremias also dislikes the traditional interpretation, but he does not resign himself to it. He writes, "It is hardly conceivable that Jesus would have compared himself, either with a man 'who drew out where he had not paid in, or reaped where he had not sown' . . . or with a brutal oriental despot, gloating over the sight of his enemies slaughtered before his eyes. . . ."[30] Jeremias rejects the authenticity of the parable as Luke presents it, claiming that "Luke is certainly wrong."[31]

26. *The Gospel of Luke: A Commentary on the Greek Text* (Exeter, U.K.: Paternoster, 1978), 709.
27. *Neither Poverty nor Riches: A Biblical Theology of Material Possessions* (Grand Rapids: Eerdmans, 1999), 124–25.
28. *The Upside-Down Kingdom*, rev. ed. (Scottdale, Pa.: Herald, 1990), 131.
29. Ibid., 132.
30. *The Parables of Jesus*, rev. ed. (London: SCM, 1963), 59–60.
31. Ibid., 59.

R. Paul Stevens, while affirming the validity of the traditional interpretation, also dislikes the parable's image of God but believes that many
of Jesus' parables present a ridiculous picture of God for the purpose of
shocking people into "converting to the real God."[32] According to Stevens,
a ridiculous view of God can serve a redemptive purpose. He believes the
parable challenges people to believe in a God who makes outrageous
demands:

> Believe in a God who will squeeze everything he can out of you, who will
> never forgive a mistake, who will swat you down to hell if you mess
> things up even once, and this is what you get: a pinched, unimaginative,
> no-risk-taking and utterly deadly life. Believe in the God and Father of the
> Lord Jesus, and you will be inspired to try things out, to experiment, to
> take risks and to flourish.[33]

Stevens's view of the parable illustrates the problem of attempting to salvage the integrity of the traditional interpretation. Within the contexts
of modern cultures, the parable does not provide a ridiculous view of
God; it describes the world that people live in. The traditional interpretation of the parable, in depicting the first slave as the hero of the story,
presents a view of God that is consistent with the behavior of that slave.
People do not respond to the parable by changing their view of God;
they consider how they can serve God by becoming more like the first
slave, whether they interpret the parable literally or allegorically.

If Christians want to interpret the parable as a challenge to their view
of God, the hero of the parable has to change. In contrast to the traditional point of view, the transformed interpretation of the parable presents the third slave as the hero of the story, which assumes a just view
of God in an unjust political and economic environment. It does not provoke people into examining their view of God; it challenges them to
overcome the political and economic conditions that victimize them.

The Transformed Interpretation

The transformed interpretation is intimately tied to its setting. It neither portrays the parable as an allegory of the kingdom of God nor does
it depict Jesus as the nobleman. Instead, it describes the political and economic life of the community and sees the third slave as the hero of the

32. "Investment," in *The Complete Book of Everyday Christianity*, ed. R. Paul Stevens and
Robert Banks (Downers Grove, Ill.: InterVarsity, 1997), 540.
33. Ibid.

story; he illustrates Jesus' point by confronting the power of the noble-man by taking the nobleman's money out of circulation. Jesus recognized that the crowd interpreted Zacchaeus's repentance as a sign that the kingdom of God was going to be established in their midst, delivering them from the political and economic oppression they were suffering. Jesus' use of the parable was an effort to challenge the people to stop using their hope for a Messiah to anesthetize the pain of their oppression and to inspire them to do something about transforming the oppressive conditions in which they lived. They were like many Christians throughout the world who continue to live in oppressive social and economic conditions, which they believe they are powerless to change. Such Christians comprise congregations with names that emphasize the power and deliverance of the second coming, hoping that the second coming will save them from their bondage. They are vulnerable to making powerlessness a virtue, believing they can do nothing to transform their lives apart from expressing their hope in the coming of the kingdom of God.

Jesus told the parable to imply that things would get worse before they got better; the people could not continue to tolerate economic and political oppression, believing the kingdom of God was at hand simply because one tax collector repented. To the contrary, they were to consider what they were going to do about an economic system that continued to oppress them. The purpose of the parable is not to make people better stewards of wealth or to inspire them to become evangelists but to challenge them to consider how Jesus empowers them to transform their political and economic structures. The hope that Jesus offered them stood in stark contrast to their understanding of the coming kingdom. He discouraged them from passively waiting for the kingdom, believing they would be happy when the Messiah came. Instead, they had to act passively to overcome the powers that were oppressing them.

John Dominic Crossan notes, "The normal strategy of the traditional peasantry is passivity. . . . A communally organized traditional peasantry, reinforced by a functionally useful slowness, imperviousness and stupidity—apparent or real—is a formidable force."[34] The transformed interpretation depicts the third slave as expressing the power of passivity, a method of sabotage through which peasants can transform the social structures that oppress them. The third slave recognized the injustice

34. *The Historical Jesus: The Life of a Mediterranean Jewish Peasant* (New York: Harper Collins, 1992), 126.

of the rich man, who takes what does not belong to him and reaps what he does not sow, and stopped the injustice by taking his money out of circulation, preventing the injustices from continuing. Through his brutal honesty—admitting his fear of the rich man—and by appearing somewhat stupid and lazy, the third slave gained power over the rich man and publicly shamed him by exposing his greedy, malicious nature. The third slave's discourse is a rhetorical masterpiece; he "cuts through the mystifying rhetoric that has dominated the exchange between the elite and his first two retainers, and he identifies the aristocrat for what he is: strict, cruel, harsh and merciless."[35]

The nobleman might have resolved the struggle by justifying his actions, or he might have repented, admitting his wrong. However, he attempted to reinforce his public image by admitting the validity of the slave's observation and asserting his power by commanding the slaughter of his enemies. The third slave, in standing up to the nobleman, took the first step toward subverting a system that would eventually destroy the community. His actions illustrate one of the points of the parable: that truth is a subversive weapon of the powerless. The parable challenged the crowd to confront their oppressors with truth-telling.

Theological support for the transformed interpretation comes from R. Alan Culpepper's commentary on Luke. He appreciates the importance of Luke's use of the cultural setting, which "incorporates such familiar elements that the audience recognizes the pattern and anticipates the outcome."[36] Culpepper interprets the throne claimant as Archelaus, Herod's son. According to Josephus, Archelaus traveled from Judea to Rome to appeal to Caesar to rule Jerusalem. While he was gone, a Jewish delegation opposed his return because of his cruelty and greed. He slaughtered three thousand citizens near the Jerusalem temple and pirated the nation's wealth, reducing the people to poverty.[37] The identity of the nobleman as Archelaus, according to Culpepper, discourages an allegorical interpretation of the parable in which the nobleman represents either God or Jesus and shifts its focus from responsibility and stewardship to greed and vengeance.[38]

35. William R. Herzog II, *Parables as Subversive Speech: Jesus as Pedagogue of the Oppressed* (Louisville: Westminster/John Knox, 1994), 164.

36. *The New Interpreter's Bible* (Nashville: Abingdon, 1995), 9:362.

37. Ibid.

38. Ibid.

Factors of the Interpretation of Luke 19:11–27

The transformed interpretation of the parable is critically important to cross-cultural ethics because it affirms the nature of how the world works for the poor and powerless, and because many Christians throughout the world use this parable to justify their participation in business practices that are ethically questionable. Let me share a story to illustrate this point.

A visit to any major city in the world exposes travelers to the economic disparities that cause impoverished people to lose hope of ever meeting their basic survival needs. During a visit to a rural Asian village, I met several women who wove baskets to earn less than a dollar a day. They lived in houses that made their village look like a rural slum, and their malnourished children chewed on sugar cane. Their meager incomes could not meet their everyday needs, and they had no hope of providing a decent living for their families.

When I returned to the capital city, a leader of a Christian fellowship for business people invited me to dinner at the modern hotel where he was staying. The stark contrast of cultures that existed in that country became evident as I strolled through the lobby, whose elegance contrasted sharply with the poverty of the bamboo huts I had just visited. Tall fluted columns supported coffered ceilings with red trimmings and gold moldings, and a chamber orchestra filled the lobby with the sounds of Vivaldi's *Four Seasons* as ushers accompanied me to the restaurant. The hotel was only a short drive—but a world away—from the village I had visited that afternoon.

The initial stages of our dinner conversation focused on the significant numbers of Asian businesspeople who were converting to Christianity. My host attributed this growth to the compatibility of Christianity and business. "Unlike Confucianism," he said, "which resists a business ethos, Christianity provides the moral principles to make businesses successful." He supported his statement by citing figures that bore witness to the growth of Christianity in Asian countries where the economies were maturing.

My host intended this statement to be a compliment to Christianity, which he expected me to affirm. However, I directed his attention toward defining the Christian principles that make businesses successful. My concern was twofold. First, I wanted to learn whether the moral principles he had in mind were unique to Christianity. Samuel P. Huntington believes, "Religion, indigenous or imported, provides meaning and direction for the rising elites in modernizing societies."[39] If Huntington is right, Christianity is the beneficiary of economic growth rather than the impetus for it.

My second concern was to determine if the principles my host had in mind were as beneficial to the local economy as they were to the businesses. Many businesspeople, Christian and otherwise, purchased baskets from village women and exported them to North America and Europe. My interest was whether their successes made a valuable contribution to the village economies or resulted in furthering the economic impoverishment of these villages.

My host affirmed that Christian businessmen are successful because they are effective stewards of the resources that God had blessed them with. While this point might be valid, it can be contradicted by the belief that a central tenet of evaluating the role of Christian principles in business is not necessarily measuring the monetary success of the businesspeople. Instead, the ethical value of a business especially lies in assessing how its transactions affect the poorest participants. Do these transactions, for example, empower the village basket weavers to liberate themselves from the impoverished conditions that shackle them? I asked my host how the Christians in the business community understood the success of businesses when the women who served as the foundation of these businesses were so poorly compensated.

My host pondered my question, perhaps wondering how I could be so rude. I expected his reply to address the ways Christian ethics influenced him to contend with the laws of risk as well as the laws of supply and demand. The conversation, however, took a different turn. My host responded by comparing himself and his business associates to the first slave in the parable of the minas in Luke 19:11–27. He considered that the first slave in the parable set an example for the Christian business community to justify their business transactions with the villagers. They can turn one unit of currency into ten units by purchasing baskets from the women and selling them to exporters. The businessmen believed these transactions indicated that the businesses are successful because the business people are faithfully investing the money that God entrusted to them. The transformed interpretation of the parable, however, indicates that the businessmen were missing the point of the parable.

39. *The Clash of Civilizations and the Remaking of World Order* (New York: Simon & Schuster, 1996), 101.

Before we can fully understand the potential impact of the transformed interpretation of the parable, we must first examine the hermeneutical as well as economic and political factors that support it. We must then use these factors to explore why this interpretation is so foreign to the modern church. The purpose of this exploration is not only to justify the transformed interpretation but also to illustrate some principles of interpreting Scripture.

The Hermeneutical Factor

The primary task in understanding this parable, as in all biblical texts, is to discover the author's original intent, which is necessary because *"a text cannot mean what it never meant."*[40] While applications of biblical texts can vary, the meaning of a biblical text cannot be foreign to the intentions of the original author.

Many theologians cannot accept the transformed interpretation of Luke 19:11–27 because it does not correspond to Matthew's account of the same parable, which refers to talents instead of minas (Matt. 25:14–30). The similarity between Matthew 25:14–30 and Luke 19:11–27 leads many people to believe that these two passages of Scripture have the same meaning. This belief, however, is based on the idea that the Gospels are modern journalistic accounts of the life of Jesus. The Bible is journalistic to the extent that it is concerned with interpreting the meaning of such events as "wars, revolutions, enslavements and liberations, migrants and refugees, famines and epidemics."[41] However, it does not conform to the central values of modern journalism, uniformity and objectivity, which require accounts of any event to be similar and imply that stories written from the same source should have the same meaning. The writers of the Bible, however, were often inspired to apply different meanings to the same stories.

My proposal is that Matthew and Luke used similar—if not the same—source material[42] to make different statements, so that Matthew's use of the material reflects the traditional interpretation of the parable while Luke's reflects the transformed interpretation. This proposal avoids a journalistic view of the Gospels that influences Christians to at-

40. Gordon D. Fee and Douglas Stuart, *How to Read the Bible for All Its Worth: A Guide to Understanding the Bible* (Grand Rapids: Zondervan, 1993), 26. Italics in the original.

41. Lesslie Newbigin, *Honest Religion for Secular Man* (Philadelphia: Westminster, 1966), 20.

42. It is widely agreed that the common sources that Matthew and Luke used to write their Gospel accounts are the Gospel of Mark and one or more documents commonly referred to as Q, the initial for *Quelle,* the German word for "source."

tempt to harmonize and objectify the meaning of texts that are similar in content, often at the expense of understanding the differing intents of the authors. For instance, Matthew's Sermon on the Mount records Christ as saying "blessed are the poor in spirit" and "blessed are those who hunger and thirst for righteousness" (Matt. 5:3, 6). Luke's sermon, often referred to as the sermon on the plain, however, records "blessed are you who are poor" and "blessed are you who are hungry" (Luke 6:20, 21). Similarly, Luke focuses on one demoniac in the region of the Gerasenes (Luke 8:26–39), while Matthew concentrates on two demon-possessed men (Matt. 8:28–34).

While many of the teachings from Luke and Matthew came from the same source, each Gospel writer was inspired by the Holy Spirit to put a different emphasis on the teachings. In his sermon on the plain, Luke puts an economic emphasis on Christ's teaching about the poor and an individual emphasis on his ministry to the demoniac. Matthew, in turn, put a spiritual emphasis on Christ's teaching about the poor in spirit and a community emphasis on Jesus' response to the demoniacs.

Even if we interpret the differences in Matthew's and Luke's accounts of the parable as being two separate discourses and Jesus' exorcism of demons as two different events, we are still influenced by journalistic principles. However, there is no reason why we should read the Gospels as objective accounts of Jesus' life and teachings. The result of such a reading would be a harmonization of the Gospels that would miss the individual points of view that are unique to the separate Gospel writers, and we would still be without an objective view of the Gospels. An exegetical process that appeals to a "mechanistic, tape-recorder mentality"[43] defies the interpretive nature of the Gospels. Each of the four Gospels interprets the teachings of Jesus and the events of his life to make particular theological statements. In this sense, the Gospel teachings are both accurate and interpretive.

Textual differences do not cast doubt on the belief that Matthew and Luke constructed their parables from the same source of material. The differences, however, illustrate how each author crafted the material to communicate a different message to a different audience. For example, Luke's account is about a nobleman who goes to a distant land to get power; Matthew's is about a rich man who goes on a journey. Fittingly, Luke's nobleman gives the successful slaves power over cities while Matthew's account has the slaves sharing their master's happiness. Fi-

43. Fee and Stuart, *How to Read the Bible for All Its Worth*, 163.

nally, and quite significantly, Luke concludes his story with the nobleman's slaughter of his enemies, while Matthew excludes it.

The Context of the Parable in Matthew

Matthew located the parable among a series of teachings on the coming of Christ and rewrote his material to fit that context,[44] which agrees with the allegorical meaning of the traditional interpretation of the Luke passage. He tucked the parable of talents between the parable of the ten virgins and a descriptive narrative on sheep and goats, all of which follow a discourse on the end of the age. Because Matthew wrote to a Jewish audience, he crafted the material to make an eschatological point. In his Gospel, Jesus had an encounter with people in the Jewish community who did not affirm his messianic role. He told this parable to assert himself as the rich man and to portray his followers as having stewardship over his kingdom.

The Jewish context of Matthew's version of the parable resolves some of the interpretive difficulties that make the traditional interpretation offensive in Luke's Gospel. This audience included pious Jews who wanted everyone to believe they followed the law, whether or not they did. It also included common people, oppressed by the pious Jews because they failed to keep the law, as well as early Christians who were defining their faith in the context of their Jewish roots.

The pious Jews, as the most vocal people in the community, were also Jesus' primary audience. In believing that Jesus was a charlatan, they naturally believed he was reaping where he did not sow. In using that statement, Jesus was challenging the implications of their own beliefs, liberating them to consider the truth of his identity. Likewise, the condemnation of the third slave suggested that they, like the slave, were lazy and worthless. Rhetoric of this nature, confronting people with truth of their own self-deception, was a common element in the dramatic discourses between Jesus and this segment of the Jewish population. For example, he declared that the Pharisees, who were abusing the temple, were turning it into a "den of robbers" (Matt. 21:13).

Matthew's context of the parable, however, is troubling because it implies that Jesus acquiesced to the practice of charging interest on loans, despite the prohibition of this practice in the Levitical law. The practice of charging interest, or raising prices to absorb prohibitive interest rates, was not uncommon in the first-century Jewish community. While Jesus

44. M. Eugene Boring, "The Gospel of Matthew," in *The New Interpreter's Bible* (Nashville: Abingdon, 1994), 8:453.

used interest in this parable as an illustration with which his audience was familiar, this use was incidental to the eschatological point of the parable. It does not imply that Jesus endorsed the practice.

The Context of the Parable in Luke

While the social and theological contexts of Matthew's Gospel corroborate the traditional interpretation of the parable, these contexts do the opposite in Luke's Gospel. Luke gives the material in his parable a different twist because he wants to communicate a different message to his audience.

Luke addresses his Gospel to the "most excellent Theophilus" (1:3). We don't know exactly who Theophilus was; he was a Gentile and his description as "excellent" suggests that he may have been a nobleman with political and economic power. Luke's focus on the poor and oppressed in his Gospel suggests that he believed that Theophilus had the influence to seek justice for them. He shows interest in the dispossessed by his choice of parables. Only Luke includes the parables of the rich fool (12:13–21), the lost coin (15:8–10), the prodigal (15:11–32), the dishonest manager (16:1–12), the widow and the judge (18:1–8), and the Pharisee and the tax collector (18:9–14). Luke narrates the stories of the shepherd's visit to the manger (2:8–20), Jesus' raising of the widow's son (7:11–17), the rich man and Lazarus (16:19–31), Jesus and Zacchaeus (19:1–10), and the criminals crucified with Jesus (23:32–33). We cannot read Luke's Gospel without being impressed with his concern for the downtrodden. His references to poverty and oppression were not metaphorical, allegorical, or symbolic of other issues; he focuses on the plights of real people in real-life situations. His intent was to reveal how the gospel could liberate them from wealth as well as from poverty and oppression.

Unlike Matthew, who placed the parable in an eschatological context, Luke placed it after the story about Zacchaeus, the rich tax collector, which suggests that Jesus was calling for "a reversal of values"[45] and gives it an economic and political nature. Luke, in writing to a titled Gentile, turns Matthew's rich man into a nobleman, who gives his slaves power over cities and orders his enemies to be slaughtered. The parable does not point to an eschatological truth but illustrates the corrupting and oppressive influences of money and power; it depicts the

45. Willard M. Swartley, "Luke's Transforming of Tradition: Eirene and Love of Enemy," in *The Love of Enemy and Nonretaliation in the New Testament* (Louisville: Westminster/ John Knox, 1992), 158.

third slave as the hero because he empowered himself to stand up to the nobleman.

Comprehending the meaning of this parable is difficult "because we are accustomed to reading it as having the same sense as the parable of the talents in Matthew."[46] However, unless we read the Gospels with a tape-recorder mentality, under the influence of objectivity, ignoring their interpretative natures, we have no exegetical reason to believe that Luke and Matthew intended to make the same point.

The Economic Factor

While the hermeneutical factors can be used to validate both the traditional and the transformed interpretations, the economic and political factors of the first century support only the transformed interpretation of Luke's parable. The most important economic concept is that of the "image of limited good," which was coined by George M. Foster, who wrote the following about the attitudes of people in peasant societies:

> [They] view their social, economic, and natural universes—their total environment—as one in which all of the desired things in life, such as land, wealth, health and love . . . status, power and influence, security and safety, *exist in finite quantities and are always in short supply*. . . . In addition *there is no way directly within peasant power to increase the available quantities*. . . . It follows that *an individual or a family can improve a position only at the expense of others*.[47]

The image of limited good, a pervasive concept in traditional economies, denies that wealth can be created, a concept that provides the vitality of modern economies. It assumes that people acquire it only at the expense of the people who lose it. The African proverb cited at the beginning of this chapter bears witness to the influence of this concept. In economies where the supply of resources is fixed, wealth and poverty need each other. The prohibition of interest in Deuteronomy 23:19–20 reflects the Israelites' belief in the image of limited good. Other biblical teachings also reflect this assumption. For instance, "Wealth is described in terms of land (Ruth 2:1–3; 4:34–5:3), herds (Gen. 13:2; Job 1:3; 42:12) and natural products (Matt. 13:45–46)."[48]

46. Boring, "Gospel of Matthew," 364.

47. "Peasant Society and the Image of Limited Good," *American Anthropologist* 67 (1965): 297. Italics are in the original.

48. Martin LaBar, "A Biblical Perspective on Nonhuman Organisms," in *Religion and Environmental Crisis*, ed. Eugene C. Hargrove (Athens: University of Georgia Press, 1986), 78–79.

The image of limited good served as the defining factor of economics until 1776, when Adam Smith determined that "labor, not nature, was the source of wealth."[49] Prior to that, the church, assuming the image of limited good, struggled to discipline people who charged interest on loans. The Third Lateran Council in 1279 refused usurers both communion and a Christian burial, and the Council of Vienna in 1312 advocated that people who sanction interest and those who charge it are to be punished as heretics.[50] Smith's realization that the growth of any economy is more dependent on managing labor than on utilizing natural resources was the economic equivalent of discovering that the earth revolves around the sun. It destroyed the validity of the image of limited good[51] and created the basis of modern economics, a system that thrives on interest, the time value of money.

Since the validity of the image of limited good was not challenged prior to Adam Smith, we must assume that Jesus' audience would have used this economic concept to interpret the meaning of the parable. In the economics of limited good the rich get richer and the poor get poorer, which happens in Luke's parable; the first and second slaves increased their master's wealth at the expense of the greater good of the community. The good news of the parable for the people was that they did not have to be victims of economic tyranny. They could be like the third slave, who exposed the master's greed and refused to participate in his efforts to gain wealth by depriving the poor. The parable discouraged the people from their passivity toward political and economic structures that disempowered them by seeking signs that the coming Messiah will rescue them. It also contends that life is going to get worse before its gets better; therefore, the people have to change their images of the Messiah and create a system that empowers them to be who they are.

The Military Factor

Warfare has a powerful influence on the narratives of Western cultures. People construct cultures according to ideas they deem plausible, and these structures reflect their cultural narratives. Soldiers fight and die to protect the values that are embedded in the narratives of their na-

49. Robert L. Heilbroner, *The Worldly Philosophers* (New York: Simon & Schuster, 1986), 49.

50. R. H. Tawney, *Religion and the Rise of Capitalism* (1922; reprint, London: Penguin, 1990), 59.

51. In light of environmental concerns, economists in recent decades are reconsidering the low regard modern economics has paid to the stewardship of economic resources, creating the need to manage wealth in terms of managing labor and valuing nature.

tions; in turn their deaths shape the narratives of their nations, raising their deaths as well as the narratives of warfare to a religious status.

In cultures where Christianity is dominant, particularly in the United States, the belief that God through Christ is on either one side or the other of a conflict is assumed as a self-evident truth. Many Americans believe that they are a chosen people, a new Israel.[52] Woodrow Wilson illustrated this point well when he said that "when men [Americans] take up arms . . . there is something sacred and holy in the warfare."[53] Similarly in 1912, Theodore Roosevelt used biblical images to characterize the war cry of the twentieth century, saying that "we stand at Armageddon and we battle for the Lord."[54] I was in the Philippines on October 20, 1994, during the celebrations of the landing of General MacArthur and the United States military on the beaches of Leyte. While watching the reenactment, I was struck by the religious nature of the language MacArthur used when he told the Filipinos that their day of redemption had arrived. As Georges Khodr notes, "All war is metaphysical; one can only go to war religiously."[55] People fight to defend the values embedded in their cultural narratives.

The idea of religious warfare gives an eschatological interpretation to the killing of the nobleman's enemies in Luke 19:27. According to this popular interpretation, at his second coming Jesus will slaughter his enemies who resist the establishment of his kingdom. The problem with this interpretation, however, is that it assumes a crusade ethic that was not part of Christianity until the ninth century. An examination of the development of this ethic in the Christian church is illuminating.

The Christian church, having had an ambiguous relationship with political entities throughout its history, has embraced three positions toward warfare. The first position, pacifism, was the prevailing ethic of the church from Pentecost to the conversion of Constantine in A.D. 313. All major Christian theologians prior to Constantine advocated nonviolence. The early Christians evidently believed Jesus transformed the concept of

52. Paul Boyer, *When Time Shall Be No More: Prophecy Belief in Modern American Culture* (Cambridge, Mass.: Harvard University Press, 1992), 238.

53. Loren Baritz, *Backfire: A History of How American Culture Led Us into Vietnam and Made Us Fight the Way We Did* (New York: Morrow, 1985), 4.

54. Dale Aukerman, *Reckoning with Apocalypse: Terminal Politics and Christian Hope* (New York: Crossroad, 1993), 161.

55. Walter Wink, *Engaging the Powers: Discernment and Resistance in a World of Domination* (Minneapolis: Fortress, 1992), 26. Georges Khodr served as Metropolitan of Mount Lebanon, a diocese of the Greek Orthodox Patriarchate of Antioch.

"God as a 'Divine Warrior' leading his hosts in battle against foes in both human and cosmic spheres"[56] into an ethic where God loves his enemies and beckons the faithful to do likewise. Unlike many modern Christians, the first-century Christians did not attempt to harmonize the models of warfare in the Old Testament with Jesus' teachings to love one's enemies (Matt 5:44). Instead, they believed that the Old Testament practices of warfare highlighted the radical nature of Jesus' teachings.[57]

Just war is the second position concerning warfare that the Christian church embraced. After Constantine's conversion to Christianity in A.D. 313, participation in warfare became normative for Christians. However, the church did not unconditionally endorse Rome's war campaigns. Augustine developed the criteria for a just war to make warfare more palatable to the church; these criteria, with some modifications, serve the church to this day.

Augustine established the principles of just war, however, without using biblical support. Christian theologians have frequently cited Romans 13:1–7 and 1 Peter 3 as the foundations for the just war ethic. However, Augustine never mentioned these passages in his writings. He evidently believed that a war ethic was not compatible with Christianity and did not attempt to use the Bible to legitimize the Roman interest in warfare. He justified his efforts to develop a war ethic for the Roman Empire by importing ethics from Plato and Cicero, modifying them by adding that "love should be the motive in war; justice should lie on one side only, and it should be done in 'a mournful mood.' "[58]

Under the influence of the Islamic conquests during the seventh and eighth centuries, the church developed the ethic of the crusade, the third position it has embraced toward war. When Charlemagne imported the crusade ethic into Christianity from Islam on Christmas Day, A.D. 800, he redefined the Christian ethic of warfare by introducing "war as a means of

56. Christensen, *Transformations of the War Oracle in Old Testament Prophecy,* 17.

57. Ethicists offer a second reason for the pacifist ethic in the early church. They suggest that early Christians were not opposed to warfare as such, but they opposed military service because it required them to participate in the idolatrous practices of the Roman Empire. This argument postulates that Christians could participate in the military when the idolatrous practices of Roman began to decline with the increased acceptance of Christianity in the Roman Empire. Edward A. Ryan, S.J., makes this argument in "The Rejection of Military Service by the Early Christians," *Theological Studies* 13 (1952): 1–32. This argument gives some theological rationale for the absence of Christians in the Roman army during the first and second centuries and for their presence during the third and fourth centuries. However, the early *Christus Victor* view of the atonement renders it unpersuasive.

58. Roland Bainton, *Christian Attitudes toward War and Peace* (Nashville: Abingdon, 1960), 90, 98.

spreading the faith,"[59] with the purpose of meeting Mohammed on Mohammed's terms.[60] In so doing, Charlemagne shifted the narrative of Christianity from one of redemption to one of conquest, with the following results: first, redemption was relegated to a minor role; second, the person of Christ became less central and Christian interests more prevalent; and third, the church became a political construct that had to be defended.

The shift from redemption to conquest as a central ethic in the Christian narrative changed the way in which the Western church perceived and interpreted its history and purpose. The radical hope for a new heaven and new earth was transformed into support for the prevailing political structures, making the idea of a redeemed creation "trivial or socially inconsequential."[61] The church's purpose was reduced to caring for the immortal soul while it endorsed the political agenda of the state. A crusade narrative, for example, made Christopher Columbus a very spiritual man. A most jealous keeper of the honor of God, Columbus was "eager to convert the peoples and to see the seed of faith of Jesus Christ spread everywhere."[62] The crusade ethic changed the nature of his faith to the point where he would not have acted differently if he were Islamic or Jewish.[63]

The crusade ethic shifted the relationship between the Christian community and the *other* from one of loving enemies to destroying infidels. The enemies became not the ones loved or to be brought to faith but the "disregarded barbarians" and "the incarnation of anti-faith."[64] Christendom came to perceive itself as having a divine calling to rule the *others*, if not to destroy them. The morality of the ethic became self-evident.

If Luke's intention in his rendering of the parable was to compare the nobleman to Jesus, he would have been endorsing a crusade ethic, with the enemies being slaughtered for the purpose of establishing the kingdom of God. Since Matthew's version of the story has an eschatological intent, this verse would fit better in that Gospel than in Luke's. However, since Matthew chose not to include it, we can conclude that Luke did not have any eschatological intentions when he wrote the story.

59. Jacques Ellul, *The Subversion of Christianity,* trans. Geoffrey W. Bromiley (Grand Rapids: Eerdmans, 1986), 100.

60. Henri Pirenne, *Mohammed and Charlemagne* (New York: Norton, 1939), 234.

61. Harvey G. Cox, *Feast of Fools: A Theological Essay on Festivity and Fantasy* (Cambridge, Mass.: Harvard University Press, 1969), 105.

62. Tzvetan Todorov, *The Conquest of America: The Question of the Other,* trans. Richard Howard (New York: Harper & Row, 1984), 12.

63. Ibid., 15.

64. John Howard Yoder, *The Priestly Kingdom: Social Ethics as Gospel* (South Bend, Ind.: University of Notre Dame Press, 1984), 88.

The transition of the crusade ethic from a temporal to an eschatological event is seamless, depending on the interpretation of Christ's atonement and his defeat of evil. This subject will be examined more closely in chapter 5. For now it is sufficient to argue for the validity of the *Christus Victor* theory of the atonement, which makes Jesus' victory on the cross the only necessary battle for him to fight, since his death and resurrection were sufficient to defeat evil once and for all. To suggest otherwise is to diminish his victory on the cross.[65]

Revelation 19:13 suggests a crucade ethic by portraying Jesus' appearance with the armies of heaven, clothed in a blood-stained robe. However, while the verse sets the scene for a battle, there is no battle; the confrontation between the powers is nonviolent. The enemies of Christ are prepared for a battle but realize they have already been defeated when they see the blood on Jesus' robe. The powers disintegrate at the sight of the blood, realizing that they were defeated on Calvary.

Christ's victory at Calvary indicates that neither Luke nor his audience would have understood the nobleman's slaying of his enemies in Luke 19:27 as portraying Jesus as slaughtering his enemies. Such an interpretation is inconsistent with narratives of first-century Christians. The church was still to develop the crusade ethic. Therefore, the parable in Luke's Gospel cannot be interpreted eschatologically.

Interpreting the Bible is a difficult issue in ethical inquiry primarily because we tend to interpret it to reinforce the values of our cultural narratives. This leads us to make conclusions that might contradict the original meaning of biblical texts. Ethical inquiry, however, from a Christian perspective, must be done by approaching the biblical text reverently; it "involves 'stepping out of one's own frame of mind.'"[66] Christians should read the Bible, "not as a story about a community . . . [but as] a community which owns it as their shared story."[67] Ethical inquiry, therefore, cannot be done without the Bible; it provides the themes of God's relationship with creation that liberates people from fear of ancestors, economic oppression, and cultural myths.

---

65. Vernard Eller, *The Most Revealing Book of the Bible: Making Sense out of Revelation* (Grand Rapids: Eerdmans, 1974), 178.

66. Anthony C. Thiselton, *Interpreting God and the Postmodern Self: On Meaning, Manipulation, and Promise* (Grand Rapids: Eerdmans, 1995), 51.

67. John Howard Yoder, "The Bible and Civil Turmoil," in *For the Nations: Essays Public and Evangelical* (Grand Rapids: Eerdmans, 1997), 84.

3

Culture:
From Functionalism to Redemption

*For God did not send his Son into the world to condemn the world, but to
save the world through him.*

John 3:17

A team of agricultural facilitators encouraged the farmers[1] in an
East African village to try some innovations that would increase their
yields of sorghum and maize by 30 percent. The farmers listened atten-
tively as the agriculturalists told them about hybrid seeds, fertilizers, irrigation methods, and soil conditioning. The agriculturalists, however,
were disappointed that only one farmer agreed to try the new methods,
but they were content to begin their project with the one farmer, whose
name was Mdumbwa. They assumed that the other farmers would follow his example after they saw his success, but they did not anticipate

1. Development facilitators who work in agriculture use this "agriculturalist-farmer"
distinction. While it might carry negative connotations, it serves as a convenient linguistic
tool to distinguish the development facilitators who work in agriculture from the people
who cultivate plants in the village gardens.

the manner in which the people perceived the influence of the unseen realm on the seen realm.

As the agriculturalists expected, Mdumbwa's harvest increased, yielding six more bags of sorghum than in the previous year. The agriculturalists were delighted and expected the villagers to be also. Instead of approbation, however, the agriculturalists found suspicion. The other farmers suspected Mdumbwa of using a form of witchcraft called *bukuzi*, which is used to steal crops from other farms. It is a belief based on the image of limited good, which implies that all agricultural production exists in fixed amounts, even before it is produced, so that farmers should get equal harvests unless they do something to upset the natural balance of agricultural distribution. The villagers explained any disparity in the farmers' harvest by witchcraft.

Because witchcraft demands a sacrifice from the people who use it, the villagers watched Mdumbwa and his family in order to discover exactly what he had sacrificed to gain his harvest yield. When Mdumbwa's son became sick and subsequently died, the villagers believed they had found the true reason for his success. Some thought that Mdumbwa was aware of what he did; others believed he did not know that the foreigners used him to spread their witchcraft. In either case, Mdumbwa's son was dead, and the villagers decided that no amount of sorghum was equal to the lives of their children.

The villagers had nothing to say to the agriculturalists after the boy's funeral. The agriculturalists were perplexed to learn that the villagers made a connection between the boy's death and their work. They believed their work was ameliorating the impoverished conditions of the village. How, they wondered, could the villagers believe that their work was making a bad situation worse? While the agriculturalists had explained the technical details of increasing the yield of a harvest, they neglected to speak about the spiritual dimensions of the new farming methods. As a result, the villagers suspected them of actually propagating witchcraft, because witches are always secretive.

The Nature of Culture

C. S. Lewis compared the task of ethical inquiry to sailing a fleet of ships; the primary responsibility is avoiding collisions.[2] This comparison is particularly germane to the ethics of managing cultural change. In

2. C. S. Lewis, *Mere Christianity* (New York: Macmillan, 1960), 70.

managing change across cultures, the navigators are vulnerable to colliding because they are traveling through different realities.

Two Views of Causation

When the agriculturalists introduced Western farming methods to the East African villagers, two worldviews collided. The distrust of the farmers was aroused because the agriculturalists failed to explain the causes of the increase in Mdumbwa's harvest yield, which the agriculturalists attributed to science. Even though the agriculturalists were Christians, they separated their scientific knowledge from their religious beliefs because their cultural narrative dictated that science was objective fact while religion was subjective belief. They thought the integrity of their work would be compromised if they raised any unsolicited conversations about their religion. In contrast, the cultural narrative of the farmers integrated religion and science because they believed the spiritual realm governed the physical realm.

The two worldviews had different understandings of causation, agentive and empirical, which is a major factor in many cultural conflicts. In agentive causation, physical change has an agent,[3] such as spiritual beings or forces. It is characteristic of cultures where spiritual narratives have primacy, like that of the farmers in the East African village. The central concern for the village farmers was *who* caused the changes in Mdumbwa's harvest yield. They believed that one or more witches in the village had the power to do what the new farming methods could do, and they had to be persuaded that the changes promoted by the agriculturalists were different in nature from those produced by witchcraft.

In empirical causation science is the medium of change and its nature is systematic. Its central assumption is that the physical realm governs itself, and it postulates that physical change can be rationally verified. As proponents of empirical causation, the agriculturalists were concerned with *what*, not *who*, caused the changes in Mdumbwa's harvest yield, and they were oblivious to the need to explain the causes for the change to the villagers.

Because of the different emphases of their cultural narratives, the farmers looked for meaning in the innovations, and the agriculturalists focused on microbes. Narratives cannot explain causation. They can, however, bear witness to a tradition that provides a basis to interpret

3. I am limiting the use of the term to agents who are believed to have some moral efficacy.

causation; they are concerned with reasons instead of causes.[4] The redemptive narrative of the Christian faith, for example, assumes the existence of God and depicts him as the primary agent of causation; changes in the elements of the physical realm that result from interactions with each other are considered to be secondary. A central tenet of Christianity concerning God's relationship with the creation is that "God as *primary cause* uses *secondary causes* to effect his will."[5] These understandings of causation are central elements in understanding the nature of culture. Had the agriculturalists explained this to the village farmers, they would have better satisfied the curiosity of the village farmers.

The Definition of Culture

Anthropologists tend to understand the nature of culture by offering various definitions of the term, which range from "the total way of life of a people" to a "set of techniques for adjusting both to the external environment and to other [people.]"[6] Marvin Harris defined culture as "the socially learned ways of living found in human societies [that] embrace all aspects of social life, including both thought and behavior."[7] Clifford Geertz observed that cultures are the "webs of significance [that people] have spun."[8]

For the purposes of this book, culture is defined as a particular expression of the biblical concept of the *kosmos,* the socially constructed matrix that serves as the arena in which people live. It is a necessary response to the fall. The Garden of Eden contained everything that humankind needed to live harmoniously in the presence of God and with each other. However, after the fall, creation was no longer fully able to meet human needs. When Adam and Eve were expelled from Eden, they had to craft a culture out of nature to express the values that became central to humanity. Clothing, for example, was one of the first natural elements that humankind transformed into a cultural artifact. The *kosmos* is composed of individual cultures, which include the learned behaviors through which people provide themselves with the products, services, and rela-

4. Jerome Bruner, "The Narrative Construction of Reality," *Critical Inquiry* 18 (autumn 1991): 7.

5. Ian G. Barbour, *Science and Secularity: The Ethics of Technology* (New York: Harper & Row, 1970), 36.

6. Clifford Geertz, *The Interpretation of Cultures: Selected Essays* (New York: Basic Books, 1973), 4–5.

7. Marvin Harris, *Theories of Culture in Postmodern Times* (Walnut Creek, Calif.: AltaMira, 1999), 19.

8. *Interpretation of Cultures*, 5.

tionships they need to live in community with one another. These products and services pervade every aspect of human life, such as government, economics, education, religion, health care, food production and preparation, social relationships, all types of tools, and science and technology. Each of these elements of culture has one or more leading functions, or the purpose for which people create a social institution.[9]

While the *kosmos* is good, it is also fallen. It is good to the extent that it meets human needs, yet its fallenness prevents it from fulfilling the purposes for which people created it. Throughout the biblical writings, the *kosmos,* in reflecting the fallen nature of the people who created it, invariably estranges people from God. The author of 1 John instructed his audience "Do not love the world [*kosmos*] or anything in the world [*kosmos*]. If anyone loves the world [*kosmos*], the love of the Father is not in him" (1 John 2:15); God gave his son to redeem the *kosmos* (John 3:16–17).

Cultures reveal a people's interpretation of reality as well as their values, primarily what they esteem to be important in both the temporal and eternal realms. People who lived in the indigenous cultures of North America, for example, valued nature in a manner that prevented them from carving land into parcels that could be sold. Europeans, however, valued nature for the economic commodities that it produced, so that they could easily divide the land into individual parcels. Hence, the exchange of land between the Europeans and the Native Americans was a result of a clash of cultural values that emerged from different narratives concerning nature.

The eternal realm, such as heaven, is also perceived according to the values of a culture. The belief that the streets of heaven are paved with gold reflects the values of the early Christians who struggled to survive in ancient economies. They envisioned their hope in Christ as culminating in an eternal existence where there was no economic scarcity. The early Muslims, in contrast, who lived in the pastoral cultures of the Arabian desert, had no interest in a heaven with streets of gold. The experience of spending their temporal lives following camels, sheep, and goats through a parched desert led them to envision heaven as a place with green pastures, springs of cool water, and virgin women. The experience of heaven will undoubtedly redeem the values inherent in both perceptions.

9. For a discussion of leading functions, see Roy A. Clouser, *The Myth of Religious Neutrality: An Essay on the Hidden Role of Religious Belief in Theories* (South Bend, Ind.: University of Notre Dame Press, 1991).

The Nature of Cultural Redemption

The redemption of the *kosmos,* embracing the cultures that comprise it, raises questions concerning its secular nature. In contrast to the popular definition as that which is temporal and not religious or sacred, *secular,* in the context of this book, refers to "a system of thought and practice which lies . . . outside of the direct responsibility of religion, but in which the will of God is to be done."[10] It is the conviction that God realizes his will when social institutions fulfill their respective leading functions, rejecting the idea that the creation and any socially constructed entity is beyond the redemptive power of God.

Lesslie Newbigin was one of the major proponents of the secular nature of redemption. While serving as an Anglican Bishop in India, he distinguished between secularism, which removes God from the temporal realm, and secularization, which makes God's redemptive work the central hope of the temporal realm. Newbigin defined the temporal as the medium through which human beings realize God's redemptive work through Christ. He writes that "the very idea of a secular order . . . 'is a Christian idea.' . . . The global process of secularization is 'rooted in the biblical faith which understands human history in terms of the mighty acts of God for the fulfilment of his purpose.' "[11] In the Christian concept of secularization, God gets his hands dirty as he redeems the *kosmos.*

The Good News for the *kosmos* is that it participates in redemption; the elements of the *kosmos* are among all things that God reconciles to himself through Christ (Col. 1:15–20). This participation in redemption enables the *kosmos* to fulfill its leading function of providing the context in which people live their lives. The consummation of the redeemed *kosmos* is the realization of the kingdom of God when the nations bring their splendor into the New Jerusalem (Rev. 21:26). "When the *kosmos* is redeemed, it ceases to be the *kosmos.*"[12]

Meaning as the Central Element of Culture

Meaning gives culture authority because people create it according to the way they construct and perceive reality. To focus on meaning in the study of cultures challenges the popular notion that cultures should be

10. George R. Hunsberger, *Bearing the Witness of the Spirit: Lesslie Newbigin's Theology of Cultural Plurality* (Grand Rapids: Eerdmans, 1998), 143.

11. Ibid.

12. Hermann Sasse, "κόσμος," *Theological Dictionary of the New Testament*, ed. Gerhard Kittel (Grand Rapids: Eerdmans, 1965), 3:893.

viewed apart from values, but values establish standards for action.[13] No cultural form or function can be value-free or morally neutral. All basic human functions, such as eating, drinking, or working, have value because they have meaning. The abilities of people to produce and to buy food, for example, are not neutral but are either good or bad expressions of culture, depending on how they are done. Producing food and drink by sacrificing animals, or even humans, to appease the spirits expresses a culture's moral standards; they are not value-free. "Culture is never neutral; it is always a strange complex of truth and error, beauty and ugliness, good and evil, seeking God and rebelling against him."[14] Cultural change, therefore, "cannot be a matter of ethical indifference."[15]

This focus on the ethical construction and, hence, the meaning of culture emphasizes the need for people who manage cultural change to hold agentive and empirical causation together as primary and secondary causes of change. The Ghanaian philosopher, Kwame Gyekye, explained why agentive causation took precedence over empirical causation in African cultures, preventing them from experiencing the positive benefits of technological progress:

> Our cultures appreciated the notion of causality very well. But for a reason which must be linked to the alleged intense religiosity of the cultures, causality was generally understood in terms of spirits, or metaphysical power. The consequence of this was that purely scientific or empirical causal explanations, of which the users of our culture were somehow aware, were often not regarded as profound enough to offer complete satisfaction.[16]

Agentive causation, in contrast to empirical causation, is central to the African cultural narrative, which gives their lives meaning. The East African farmers were expressing a central value of their culture by interpreting the agriculturists' innovations as expressions of witchcraft. They had no understanding of scientific farming techniques. The agriculturalists should have taken the farmers' understanding of agentive causation seriously, guiding them to reinterpret their worldview. They could have salvaged their project had they learned the positive relationship that exists between agentive and empirical causation. God, as Creator, Re-

13. Willie E. Hopkins, *Ethical Dimensions of Diversity* (Thousand Oaks, Calif.: Sage, 1997), 25.

14. Hunsberger, *Bearing the Witness of the Spirit*, 56.

15. Lesslie Newbigin, *The Open Secret* (Grand Rapids: Eerdmans, 1981), 161.

16. "Philosophy, Culture and Technology," in *Postcolonial African Philosophy: A Critical Reader*, ed. Emmanuel Chukwudi Eze (Oxford: Blackwell, 1997), 28.

deemer, and Sustainer of the world, was the agent of the changes they were striving to realize. Their empirically verifiable methods were the media through which God worked.

The Influence of Plausibility Structures

The East African farmers could not accept the new agricultural methods because these methods had no support from their society. The clash between agentive and empirical causation results from different perspectives of reality, which are intimately connected to the social constructs of a culture; "ideas do not succeed in history by virtue of their truth but [by virtue] of their relationship to specific social processes."[17] Plausibility structures determine what kind of knowledge is valued in a culture and provide a framework to evaluate the continued usefulness of that knowledge. They imply that people's understanding of reality is dependent upon social support.[18] Lucien Levy-Bruhl was one of the first anthropologists to recognize that plausibility structures influenced the development of logic and reasoning in a culture. Unlike Kant and Hegel, who believed people living in traditional cultures were pre-logical, Levy-Bruhl insisted that their alleged rejection of discursive reasoning was attributable to "highly selective standards of relevance," not to an "intellectual incapacity." These standards of relevance produce in them an "insuperable indifference to matters bearing no apparent relation to those which interest them."[19]

Plausibility structures exist because people develop and maintain ideas that have cultural relevance, which is embedded in their cultural narratives; a void in a narrative creates the need for innovative ideas, and these ideas change the narrative. For example, the Associated Press reported that four Lao Buddharan monks who lived in Portland, Oregon, went into a railway tunnel to appease spirits, who were angry about a commuter railway built beneath a cemetery, by burning incense and chanting. The monks believed that a recent transit center mishap and earlier construction deaths pointed to the need for harmony between the physical and the spiritual worlds. Vanhlang Khamsouk, secretary general of the Lao Buddharan temple in Portland, recognized that the ritual

---

17. Peter L. Berger, *Facing Up to Modernity: Excursions in Society, Politics, and Religion* (New York: Basic Books, 1977), 27.

18. Peter L. Berger, *The Rumor of Angels: Modern Society and the Rediscovery of the Supernatural* (Garden City, N.Y.: Doubleday, 1969), 43.

19. Mary Douglas, *Purity and Danger: An Analysis of Concepts of Pollution and Taboo* (London: Routledge & K. Paul, 1966), 76.

defied the plausibility structures of their neighbors, but he believed the gesture was important.[20] The reporter, apparently aware that the ritual did not fit the plausibility structures of the community, undoubtedly perceived it as an amusing story that would entertain his audience. However, if this religious community has any influence on the greater society in which it is located, the plausibility structures of the society might change, making agentive causation a viable understanding of change in that culture.

Brilliant ideas often fail to get integrated into particular cultures because the plausibility structures of those cultures cannot absorb them. For instance, Kenneth Olsen, the former president of Digital Equipment Corporation, once declared that there was no market for home computers. At that time, personal computers did not have the social support to make them plausible in the homes of American people. Bits, buses, and mice had different places in our narratives: eight bits equaled one dollar rather than one byte, buses transported people rather than data, and mice preferred to occupy kitchen cupboards rather than desktops. Likewise, the agriculturalists introduced farming innovations that did not fit into the plausibility structures of the East African village, which held witchcraft, not chemical fertilizers or hybrid seeds, as the plausible cause of change. The agriculturalists failed to manage change effectively because they introduced ideas that were based on empirical causation into a culture where agentive causation was primary.

The Problem of Reification

A development practitioner working in a refugee camp asked a woman if she had any plans for her future. She replied, "How can I plan for anything? My future is in the hands of God, the government, and the United Nations." She seemed to be expressing a fatalistic sense of powerlessness; however, she did not really believe this trinity of powers influenced her future but that it rested with the spirits who reside in the trees outside of the camp. Each Thursday afternoon just hours before sunset, the beginning of the Islamic holy day, she joined a group of women under the trees who prayed, burned incense, and discerned the future by interpreting the vision that the spirits gave them. These meetings under the trees were central expressions of the women's subculture. They believed they could

20. Associated Press, "Monks Try to Make Peace with Spirits Angered by Train," 19 September 1998.

tell the future from the visions, and they sold their knowledge to other women in the refugee camp. They were genuine information entrepreneurs.

A sociologist of religion might argue that these women were frustrated by the powerlessness they experienced in the structures of their formal religion as well as within the bureaucratic confines of the governmental and international agencies. They found power in the ceremony under the trees only because they believed the ceremony had power over them. They could not have been empowered by their interpretations of the visions had they acknowledged them as their own creation.

The women lived in a world that was possibly reified. Reification occurs when social institutions become bigger than and gain control over the people who created them. The creators lose their freedom and their moral agency, becoming subjugated to their own creations instead of nurtured by them.[21] Reification implies that people can forget their authorship of the human world and that the "dialectic between [people], the producers, and [their] products is lost to consciousness."[22] Albert Schweitzer saw the loss of control over human institutions as a consequence of modernity. He observed that "the man of to-day . . . has no freedom, no mental collectedness, no all-round development. . . . [He] surrenders his spiritual independence and his moral judgment to the organized society in which he lives."[23] Hendrikus Berkhof saw it as a result of the world alienated from God by human powers; "it is life improperly so-called, a life under the guardians, in slavery, within which man falls short of his destined end."[24]

Ethical Tensions as Obstacles to Cultural Change

The central question in managing cultural change is, How do Christians understand the nature of cultural conflict? It receives two different answers. I have divided the two sides of the debate between the spiritual warfare advocates and the institutional transformation advocates.

---

21. Bruce G. Brander, *Staring into Chaos: Explorations in the Decline of Western Civilization* (Dallas: Spence, 1998), 75.
22. Peter L. Berger and Thomas Luckmann, *The Social Construction of Reality: A Treatise on the Sociology of Knowledge* (New York: Anchor, 1966), 89.
23. Ibid., 76.
24. Hendrikus Berkhof, *Christ and the Powers,* trans. John H. Yoder (Scottdale, Pa.: Herald, 1962), 34.

Spiritual Warfare Advocates

The spiritual warfare advocates believe that territorial spirits, or demonic powers, control cultures. The popular understanding of territorial spirits is that they are unembodied beings who influence particular geographical regions.[25] This emphasis on demonic control raises the question of whether people live in a reified world. George Otis introduced this possibility by suggesting that territorial spirits are cultural reifications. He explained that they are "real because millions of people over the centuries have believed them to be real. They thrive because entire communities have shaped their spiritual and material environments to accommodate this reality."[26] The nature of reification, however, casts doubt on the ontological truth of Otis's statement. The power of popular belief can reify any perception, but it cannot make that perception true. The power of popular belief can embed territorial spirits in a cultural narrative, but it cannot make these spirits ontological realities. Reification renders people powerless to change their culture, particularly because they believe themselves to be powerless in the presence of a spiritual force or a social institution. This sense of powerlessness is the vitality of the contemporary theological emphasis on spiritual warfare, it emerges from the conviction that conflicts with evil are personal rather than institutional. This conviction is often true.

George Otis recounts several stories that indicate how territorial spirits manipulate human behavior. Missionaries have suggested that territorial spirits influenced the genocide in Rwanda in 1994. Some missionaries have told me that the killings in Rwanda began after the Rwandan government imported a monument from another country and erected it in Kigali. The monument, evidently, brought a host of demons that instigated the slaughter.

The credibility the missionaries gave to the territorial spirits suggests that the people surrendered their moral agency and became victims of a spiritual realm that destroyed their welfare. It means they believed that "human beings are little more than puppets tugged and jerked by transcendental forces."[27] Having lost moral control, their only hope for change was to engage in various expressions of spiritual warfare. Because the advocates of spiritual warfare see cultures as inhabited by such entities as

25. This understanding is apparent in the writings of C. Peter Wagner, George Otis Jr., and others.

26. George Otis Jr., *The Twilight Labyrinth: Why Does Spiritual Darkness Linger Where It Does?* (Grand Rapids: Chosen, 1997), 197.

27. Harvey Cox, *Fire from Heaven: The Rise of Pentecostal Spirituality and the Reshaping of Religion in the Twenty-First Century* (New York: Addison-Wesley, 1995), 282.

territorial spirits, they see the spiritual ethos of a society as composed of independent moral agents, who influence people to behave in ways that are beyond human control. They contend that Christians should pray to exorcise spiritual entities from the regions of the host cultures.

Institutional Transformation Advocates

The institutional transformation advocates believe that reification also has institutional expressions, which emerge when people think of them as having spirits. They might say, for example, that Harvard University has a different spirit than Stanford University. The people who make these comparisons are not implying that spiritual entities are hovering over these institutions, governing the behavior of the people within them—although this thought is gaining popularity through the writings of Frank Peretti and other authors. Instead, they are defining the character of each institution. Similarly, we can say the spirit of Amsterdam is different from that of Johannesburg. The statement suggests that each city has a different "collective ethos." The character of a culture becomes reified when people do not feel that they have the power to behave apart from its influence.

Advocates of institutional transformation do not ignore the power of prayer, but they locate the essence of the problem, not in spiritual entities, but in the nature of cultural institutions. For them, cultural change requires a transformation of the institutions that govern the culture. They recognize that cultures and their narratives have a mutually transforming relationship, and they can make changes in each part by changing the plausibility structures. For example, a short visit to Amsterdam may lead people to think that sex has a central place in its narrative. Many tourists who visit Amsterdam wonder why the Dutch government does not outlaw the sex industry; the plausibility structures of the tourists support the belief that morality can be legislated. My Dutch friends have told me that laws that prohibit immorality do not conform to the plausibility structures of their culture. They view the sex industry, not as morally acceptable, but as occupying a zone of immorality within the boundaries of morality. Governing the industry, they say, controls immoral behavior more effectively than attempting to prohibit it.

Resolving the Tensions

The terms of this debate resemble those of evangelism and social action. While the two sides are not necessarily mutually exclusive, they tend to become polarized around the spiritual commitment of each side. One side defines its approach as strictly spiritual while the other side believes that the spiritual must be complemented by relevant action. The debate is also clouded by different understandings of economic, political, and social theologies. I recall participating in a development seminar when a respected Christian leader emphatically stated that the gospel of Jesus Christ had nothing to do with political or economic transformation. He defined the gospel as addressing only the liminal nature of life.

The inability of the Christian community to recognize the roles of agentive and empirical causation in their efforts to manage cultural change exacerbates the tension between advocates of institutional transformation and those of spiritual warfare. It creates an either/or approach to managing cultural change when it should be a both/and approach; both sides are essential to empowering people to experience the redemptive power of Christ. People who are managing cultural change can hold effectively both agentive and empirical causation together. My purpose is to explore how our different understandings of causality might help us do this. Holding agentive and empirical causation together, under the redemptive ministry of God through Christ, can prevent either side of the tension from getting reified.

Functionalism as an Obstacle to Cultural Change

I once participated in a discussion with development facilitators in East Africa about cultural practices that foster the spread of HIV. The premise of this discussion was that HIV/AIDS was as much a social as a viral problem. The development facilitators knew that some cultural practices needed to change if they were going to influence the reduction of AIDS-related illnesses and deaths. The problem they faced was overcoming the obstacles to managing the necessary cultural changes.

We attempted to address this issue by identifying some of the customs in the culture that facilitate the transmission of HIV. After an uncomfortable silence, one participant said the people in the community where he worked view marriage as a relationship within the clan. Therefore, a woman is not considered married until she has had sexual intercourse with all of her husband's brothers and cousins. The terms "husband-in-law" and "wife-in-law" rather than "brother-in-law" or "sister-in-law" characterize the relationship men and their brothers' wives have with each other. In a culture where HIV is rampant, this custom is a potential death sentence for everyone who participates in it. The development facilitators cited two obstacles to changing this custom. The first was the myth of traditional, or primitive, harmony, and the second was the myth that cultural development is a value-free activity. Both myths are products of functionalism.

The Myth of Traditional Harmony

The myth of traditional harmony is a belief that people who live in traditional cultures have harmonious lives because their values, beliefs, customs, and behaviors foster their individual welfare and ensure their corporate survival. The essence of this belief is the assumption that people do not engage in behavior that can jeopardize their individual or communal welfare; it also implies that people will change any particular behavior if they learn that this behavior is hazardous to their welfare. The myth of traditional harmony is the source of the belief that truth is relative to cultures; it implies that beliefs are true and behavior is good if the people in a particular culture believe them to be so.

The development project that sought to prevent the spread of HIV in East Africa was funded by an international agency that permitted Christians to educate the public about the transmission of viruses, but Christians could not work to change any religious or social values. In most traditional cultures, the religious values are the social values; the same narrative produces them. The funding agency prohibited the Christians from addressing any moral issues because they wanted to preserve the culture and protect the indigenous people from becoming victims of religious imperialism. However, in their efforts to protect the people from these maladies, they were actually victimizing them. The prohibitions denied that the people had the moral maturity to choose alternatives to their way of life.

The myth of traditional harmony emerges from a narrative where rationalism is a supreme value. People who live in traditional cultures would not affirm it; they are too busy trying to survive in cultures that contain many practices that do not foster their social or individual welfare. However, the myth does make sense to people who can extract particular cultural practices and analyze their value in environments outside their immediate contexts, such as classrooms or writers' studies. The myth of traditional harmony has been a major obstacle to development ministries because it assumes that change is basically destructive to a culture and that traditional people will accept change only when it is imposed on them. It also depicts missionaries and other agents of cultural change as "not only illegitimate, but morally offensive."[28]

28. Wolfhart Pannenberg, "How to Think about Secularism," *First Things* 64 (June–July 1996): 27–32.

The foundation of the myth of traditional harmony is functionalism, which is useful in preventing people from evaluating the behavior in one culture against the standards of another. It also challenges outsiders to learn the functions of certain practices within the context of a given culture. For example, Levirate marriage, the practice of a widow marrying the brother of a deceased spouse, makes sense in cultures that do not offer life insurance and pension plans. However, traditional harmony does not account for the important factors that generate the need to manage cultural change by transforming many cultural practices. The central value of functionalism is efficiency; it assumes that human cultures, like nature, abhor vacuums, so that they, like nature, fill space efficiently.

There are at least three challenges to the validity of the myth of traditional harmony. First, cultural traditions perpetuate many obsolete customs. The presence of HIV, for example, causes the practice of consummating a marriage through one or more spouses to be culturally destructive regardless of what functional value it might have had at one time. The second challenge is the insupportable assumption that traditional cultures are immune to corruption. All cultures reflect the fallen state of humankind; they are characterized by practices that embody its propensity toward greed, selfishness, dishonesty, lust, promiscuity, envy, covetousness, pride, and other expressions of sin. People do not always make deliberate efforts to change behaviors that are destructive; instead, they often support behaviors that are individually but not communally beneficial. A major factor in the spread of AIDS, for example, is the powerlessness of women to insist that men wear condoms. As David S. Lanxdes writes, the men don't like to wear them, and the women have so many other problems they haven't time to think about something that will kill them in ten years.[29]

The third challenge to the myth of traditional harmony is reification. When people forget that they constructed their culture, their customs begin to control them, so that they do not believe they have the power to change them, even if they wanted to. People in every culture need liberation from traditions that jeopardize their welfare, but their traditions have been reified. When the health educators asked the village elders about stopping their practice of consummating a marriage

29. *The Wealth and Poverty of Nations: Why Some Are So Rich and Some So Poor* (New York: Norton, 1999), 501.

through multiple sexual partners, the village elders responded with resignation. Their tradition had become reified in that it was taking control of them to the point of killing them. Their culture will not end when this practice is stopped; it will end when HIV puts an end to their history.

The Myth of Value-Free Development

The myth of value-free development, an offspring of the myth of traditional harmony, implies that religious beliefs, cultural traditions, and community values should not be changed, particularly by innovations foreign to a culture.

The role of values in development work across cultures creates the need for development practitioners to define and defend the values that are inherent in their ministries. The agriculturalists working with the East African farmers and the health educators dealing with HIV both believed they were introducing value-free innovations into the cultures because they thought they were based on scientific fact. However, they were simply attempting to universalize values that they did not define or defend. The health educators taught the people who lived in the community about virus transmission. However, their respect for the myth of traditional harmony prevented these educators from addressing the methods through which the people consummated marriages, which, in their view, fell under the realm of religious traditions or community values, a realm where science fears to tread.

Contrary to popular thought, scientific facts are not value-free. They, like all cultural phenomena, are created through values and must be interpreted for meaning. Facts are not culturally abstract; they emerge from cultures and will change the values in a culture when transported from one to another, resulting in the change of cultures. Modern agricultural innovations, for example, influence the way traditional farmers view witchcraft, and knowledge about virus transmission changes the way people in traditional cultures view sexually transmitted diseases. The people within a culture will either accept the knowledge and change their traditions, or they will reject the knowledge and continue living with their values. In either situation, the innovations are not value-free; their effectiveness depends on their ability to produce cultural changes. They must be integrated into the cultural narratives if they are going to be implemented in any sustainable way.

Cracks in the Foundation

The myth of traditional harmony does not imply that development can be value-free; instead, it specifies that development innovations have profound implications for managing cultural change. It also challenges cross-cultural ethicists to reexamine the validity of functionalism. A superficial glance at any culture in the world casts doubt on its truth and the myths that are associated with it. People in every culture of the world are suffering and dying from cultural practices that have lost their rationale.

The realization that traditional practices do not necessarily foster the welfare of a community has created the need for cross-cultural ethicists to define the basis of managing cultural change. This task is formidable, primarily because it has so many expressions. Robert B. Edgerton suggests that cultural change must have a scientific basis.[30] Science, evidently, is a central element in his cultural narrative; however, it might not be the most effective basis for cultural change. Elvin Hatch concluded that cultural relativism, the philosophical foundation of functionalism, "carries the obligation that one cannot be indifferent toward other ways of life; [this indifference] obligates us to approve what others do;" it puts people in the "morally awkward position of approving starvation, the rape of abducted women, [and] the massacre of whole villages."[31] Hatch attempts to solve the problem of functionalism by recognizing that tolerance, its central tenet, is a commitment, not to neutrality, but to the status quo.[32]

While Hatch recognizes the need to define a moral foundation for cross-cultural ethical inquiry, his solution is weak because it takes a sociopolitical approach to change in order to protect the freedom of a culture from the "deliberate coercion" of outsiders.[33] Freedom without coercion occupies a central position in the narratives of Western cultures, especially in democratic societies where the general welfare of people is highly valued. However, freedom without coercion does not serve as an adequate basis for establishing a viable basis for cross-cultural ethics, because with freedom comes the responsibility to protect it, and that protection often takes the form of coercion. For instance, the freedom of speech must concur with the laws against libel. To make freedom without coercion a valid cross-cultural ethic is only a half-step away from

---

30. *Sick Societies: Challenging the Myth of Primitive Harmony* (New York: Free Press, 1992), 2.

31. *Culture and Morality: The Relativity of Values in Anthropology* (New York: Columbia University Press, 1983), 92–93.

32. Ibid., 94.

33. Ibid., 96.

functionalism. While it recognizes the invalidity of functionalism, it does not transform the assumptions of functionalism that people are free and responsible to do what is good for them and for other people in their cultures on their own volition. Freedom, like many other values, is commendable to any culture. However, isolating it as a supreme cross-cultural ethic is an effort to salvage functionalism by elevating one of its elements over the others. Neither freedom nor any other element of functionalism can serve as an absolute for cross-cultural ethics.

A valid basis for cross-cultural ethics requires an alternative to functionalism that incorporates some of its elements without making them absolute. Redemption serves as such a value because it is the universal ethical proposition that can be integrated into cultural narratives. When I discussed the struggle to establish an adequate basis for cross-cultural ethics with a friend who is an anthropologist, she said that there was no single basis for cross-cultural ethical reflection but that the multicultural, postmodern world required an ethical foundation made up of several elements, such as economics, politics, gender, and ethnicity, among others. Even the weather, she said, could serve as an ethical basis for cultural change.

When I asked what she thought about redemption as the basis of cross-cultural ethics, she claimed it was inadequate because it cannot be defined or evaluated. Redemption, I argued, is the result of God's reconciling work in creation; it empowers the elements of creation to fulfill the purposes for which they were created. It includes economics, health, sanitation, education, agriculture, and a host of other enterprises as they contribute to the welfare of human life. None of them are adequate by themselves, but their value is determined by how they contribute to restoring the ability of creation to support life. Redemption points toward, and results in, *shalom*. It can be evaluated, and possibly measured, by defining the increase that a community experiences in the ingredients of redemption.

A functionalist can argue that the death of a child contributes to the welfare of a community by making more economic resources available to support the other people in the community. Christians who support redemption as the basis of cultural change could not support that argument, because economics is the basis of that decision, and economics might not be redemptive in that social situation. Efficiency is the central value of economics; life is the central value of redemption. Economic factors can be given consideration in redemptive decisions; however, to make economic efficiency the basis of ethical decisions becomes idolatrous. Redemptive solutions seek to manage economic resources to enhance the lives of all people.

My anthropologist friend responded to my arguments by saying that "redemption is a religious construct that cannot be verified; you can't prove it exists; you cannot measure it or validate it. You only know redemption by what you call redemption. If you call something redemption, you interpret what you see as redemptive, believing you are proving that it exists because you named it."

"Bruce," she continued, "You are caught in a vicious cycle because you can't find any evidence for your concept! Redemption is too subjective; you can find objective evidence for economics, politics, and the weather, but you can't research redemption. The construct has no more validity than the word you are using to name it. The word is not the object." Language does not produce reality.

From Functionalism to Redemption

The discussion did not influence me to abandon the idea of advocating redemption as the basis for ethics. Rather, it challenged me to define and substantiate redemption, which is a broad concept that has two factors to make it a valid ethic for managing cultural change. It is universally valid and culturally specific. It rests on the authority of a universal religious tradition and can be applied to particular cultures to affirm positive values and transform negative values. For instance, it can sanction the practice of not eating pork in many Islamic/Arabic cultures, noting that pigs are inefficient to raise because they have a destructive influence on a desert ecosystem. It can also inspire a social transformation that will prevent such practices as female genital mutilation.

The shift from functionalism to redemption can provide the foundation for a discussion about Western assumptions about logic. My anthropologist friend questioned my argument about redemption as a valid basis for managing cross-cultural change because it was logically circular, defying the tenets of Western reasoning. My argument's circular nature, however, is not a problem if we analyze the validity of a few assumptions about Western logic. First, as Lesslie Newbigin argued, Christians should not be concerned about shaping the theological tenets of Christianity to accommodate the logic of Western cultures. He observed that Christians defend Christianity as reasonable, but there is no suggestion that the "assumptions [of reason] themselves are to be challenged."[34]

34. Lesslie Newbigin, *The Gospel in a Pluralist Society* (Grand Rapids: Eerdmans, 1989), 17.

Newbigin's concern was the Christian attempt to make the truth of Christianity fit the plausibility structures of modern Western philosophical tradition. The presupposition of this effort is that Western philosophy with its emphasis on reason validates truth. The assumption that something isn't true if it isn't logical causes faith to become "objectified as a focus for the application of reason."[35] It creates a problem similar to the Cartesian circle,[36] which holds that something cannot be true if it is not logical, but there is no way of verifying logic as the ultimate measure of truth.

People who accept Western logic as the measure of truth are in danger of reifying Western logic, possibly forgetting that the rationality is a product of their own making. Phillip E. Johnson postulated a theory of the efficacy of prayer that comes close to reifying the logic of Western empiricism. He claimed that an author who opposed his view was "urging Christians to rely for their salvation on a theory derived from materialist philosophy, rather than from scientific testing."[37] Johnson's statement leaves his readers wondering why he thinks scientific testing, an expression of Western logic, is a valid measure of the efficacy of prayer.

There is no universal, rational, metacultural standard, such as reason, against which truth can be measured because "every society constructs its appropriate conceptions of reason."[38] If Christianity can complement this socially constructed logic, that is good. However, there is no justification to make logic absolute by using it to validate a religious faith, especially the biblical faith of both Judaism and Christianity, which rejects reason in favor of revelation as the authoritative means to truth.[39] Any effort to adduce a positive relationship between Christianity and Western rationality must recognize only that Western logic contains some constructs that can be used to communicate Christianity.

Nancey Murphy changed the name of logical circularity from vicious to virtuous in an effort to transform current perceptions of it. She compared the spiritual experiences of Catherine of Siena to scientific theories of instrumentation. Murphy noted that Saint Catherine claimed that God was the agent of her experience of gladness, virtue, humility, and

35. Robert Wuthnow, *Rediscovering the Sacred: Perspectives on Religion in Contemporary Society* (Grand Rapids: Eerdmans, 1992), 89.

36. Coined after Rene Descartes, the father of modern philosophy, who attempted to develop an objective view of reality.

37. Phillip E. Johnson, "To Whom or What Do We Pray? Overestimating the Power of Science," *Commonweal* (June 1998): 16.

38. Ross Poole, *Morality and Modernity* (London and New York: Routledge, 1991), 158.

39. Roy A. Clouser, *The Myth of Religious Neutrality: An Essay on the Hidden Role of Religious Belief in Theories* (South Bend, Ind.: University of Notre Dame Press, 1991), 79.

charity because God told her so, but she could not empirically verify it. When asked why she believed God, and not some other moral agent, was the source of her inspiration, she answered that "the experience produced gladness, humility, [and] charity,"[40] the qualities that God told her she would experience. Saint Catherine's logic begins by claiming God as the source of her inspiration, and her experiences of inspiration point her back to God. The circularity of her argument creates a contingent, not a necessary, relationship between her conclusion and assumptions.

Murphy observed that scientists face a similar, circular problem when they engage in an experiment as simple as affirming the validity and reliability of thermometers. The workings of thermometers depend on molecular-kinetic theory, which maintains that the mercury rises in response to heat. The theory makes perfect sense until we consider that the rise of the mercury explains the theory and the theory explains the rise, creating a logical circle in a culture where logical progress is supposed to be linear. Murphy calls circularity virtuous, rather than vicious, because of its reliability and consistency. The conclusion is contingent upon the assumptions, but the consistency of the results explains the reliability of the theory. Saint Catherine's experiences of God's inspiration are likewise reliable and consistent because the consistency of the experiences, while contingent upon the assumptions, explains the reliability of the source. While certain aspects of Christianity conform to the ideas of rationality and consistency, other elements defy it.

I was in a meeting when someone said that "God is purely logical; we know the nature of God because we know logic." The statement was applauded because it approved the narrative bias of the audience; however, it was reductionistic, if not idolatrous and ethnocentric. It reduced God to someone that could be understood by that group of people while disregarding many aspects of God's nature that do not conform to Western logic. It also ignored the different ways in which people in non-Western cultures relate to God. Victor Turner, for example, noted that the Ndembu (an ethnic group in central Africa) "are obsessively logical . . . though on the basis of mystical premises."[41] Yet, mysticism is defined as transrational or beyond logic in most Western cultures.

Religious phenomenology, as well, does not conform to logic. African shamans who convert to Christ frequently heal the sick and exorcize de-

40. *Anglo-American Postmodernity: Philosophical Perspectives on Science, Religion, and Ethics* (Boulder, Colo.: Westview, 1997), 157.
41. Quoted in Edward C. Green, *Indigenous Theories of Contagious Disease* (Walnut Creek, Calif.: AltaMira, 1999), 35.

mons in the name of Jesus. In these phenomenological expressions of faith, the shamans are exercising transrational expressions of Christianity. They are also importing Jesus into their mystical religious traditions.

Christianity is both rational and mystical, or transrational, but it is greater than either of these structures. The rejection of the supremacy of Western logic is shifting the criteria for ethical cross-cultural change from rationality to redemption because the substance of its ingredients make it viable. Isaiah's vision of peace (Isa. 65:17–25) contains several empirically verifiable and measurable factors that serve as indicators of redemption, including infant survival, long life spans, social and economic justice, and productive work. They imply adequate medical care, a competent judicial and educational system, and social harmony. Each of these factors can be further defined by smaller indicators to determine whether they are met.

The validity of these indicators, though, is not that they can be subdivided into smaller, measurable, and empirically verifiable units. The validity of redemption is that it is a unifying theory bearing witness to God as the agent of causation because it bears the meaning of its agent. Any elements of empirical causation are important indicators of redemption; however, they do not provide meaning. Instead, they create a world where scientists are becoming "incapable of explaining the significance of [their] own findings."[42] They create efficient means to undefined ends. Redemption as the foundation of cultural change defines the means and the ends by holding empirical and agentive causation together. It recognizes that empirical causation produces knowledge to understand creation and affirms that God provides meaning for this causation. It solves the problem that the agriculturalists and the East African farmers were unable to solve because it moves the agriculturalists from microbes to meaning and the farmers from meaning to microbes.

If we examine redemption as an ethical basis for changing the cultural practice of consummating marriages through husbands-in-law, we find that redemption contains the substance to serve as an adequate ethical basis for managing cultural change. Because redemption addresses both agentive and empirical causation, it teaches that God is the agent of changing the behaviors that transmit HIV because he inspired a religious tradition that leads people to practice monogamy and fidelity. This teaching reveals that AIDS is a cultural problem, though not unique to

42. William Irvin Thomson, *Imaginary Landscape: Making Worlds of Myth and Science* (New York: St. Martin's Press, 1989), 48.

that culture. The epidemic can be addressed by creating and implementing alternatives to the existing cultural traditions.

Redemption as the Ethical Basis of Cultural Change

The myth of traditional harmony causes Westerners to wince at the idea of resorting to any religious tradition as the moral authority of cultural change. The alternative, however, is cultural or individual preferences. Cultural change, and any expression of it, is not ethically or morally neutral but is motivated by some values, which can be religious, cultural, or personal.

The notion that development, or any other means of cultural change, can be value-free is a fallacious implication of functionalism. The change it produces is a mere veneer. In the example of the wives and husbands-in-law, the health educators could distribute condoms and information on virus transmission. But their actions could not effectively transform the culture, because they could not transform the customs that facilitate HIV transmission. The demise of functionalism, and its accompanying myths, does not give the health educators the privilege of choosing whether they want to address the cultural traditions that transmit HIV, but they must choose some ethical basis for their efforts. In order to make a choice, they must first ask why one ethical foundation is preferable to another. For example, if the health educators choose a personal or cultural preference over a religious one, they could argue that they are encouraging people to make their own decisions. This argument has some validity; however, their participation in the decision is not morally neutral or value-free.

I used this case study in a workshop with a group of health educators who concluded that they preferred to distribute condoms rather than influence the villagers to change their sexual customs. When I asked them to define the basic assumptions of this decision, they agreed that they were content to accept their personal and cultural preferences as the moral authority of their decision. They believed this decision was a morally superior alternative to making any efforts to change cultural traditions by resorting to a religion, such as Christianity. Individual liberty was a greater value in their narratives.

The question their choice raised, however, was whether distributing condoms had any redemptive value. The community identified hospitality and gender relationships as the central values that perpetuate the practice, and an adequate ethic of change had to address both issues. The men in the community defended the custom as an essential characteristic of their culture because it expressed hospitality. However, the women wanted to change it, but they were powerless to do so. This community will begin to realize some sense of redemption when women enable themselves to engage in conversation with the men about changing or maintaining the custom.

The basis of this conversation is appreciative inquiry, an approach to social change that empowers people to define and preserve the values that any cultural practice embodies after the behavior and customs change. There are three sequential steps to appreciative inquiry. The first is diagnosing the nature of the problem by asking the following questions: What is the behavior? Why does it persist in the community? And what values are sustaining it? The second step is identifying the people who benefit from the practice, what the benefits are, and what the community will lose if the practice ends. The third step of appreciative inquiry is defining the beliefs, values, and attitudes that influence the practice and determining how changing the custom will affect these issues.

The diagnostic questions of appreciative inquiry can have many answers. For instance, the obvious answer for ending the practice of consummating marriage through multiple partners is to stop the transmission of HIV. But the answers could include gender relationships and hospitality, which identify the stakeholders of the practice and define the values that influence them to sustain the practice. If hospitality and gender relationships are the central values that sustain this practice, an ethic of cultural change has to address both of these issues in a manner that is acceptable to everyone. It must express the male concerns for hospitality and the female concerns for equality—or at least the lack of subjugation. One redemptive possibility is having the community celebrate marriages by eating together. Sharing meals is steeped in the narrative of Christian tradition, and it is a universal expression of hospitality. The anonymous *Epistle to Diognetus,* a significant piece of ancient Christian literature, mentioned that Christians "share their food but not their wives."[43] The sharing of a meal can redeem the practice of consummating marriage through multiple partners.

Redemption is the central value of any event where Christ is proclaimed; it gives meaning to acts whose meaning might not be self-evident. The agriculturalists working with the East African farmers failed

43. *The Epistle to Diognetus* 5.7 (*The Apostolic Fathers: Greek Texts and English Translations,* updated ed., ed. and rev. Michael W. Holmes [Grand Rapids: Baker, 1999], 541).

to inspire confidence in their innovations because they assumed that the meaning of the events was self-evident. They did not realize that technology had transformed their culture and was becoming a central element in their symbolic reality. Their task, like that of Christians everywhere, was determining how their work contained a sense of redemption as it transformed the narrative of the community, moving the people closer to the kingdom of God and transforming their culture accordingly.

4

Environment:
From Gnosticism to Biblical Holism

God saw all that he had made, and it was very good.

Genesis 1:31

There remains, then, a Sabbath-rest for the people of God.

Hebrews 4:9

In a Malian village, a few women earn a living by scooping sand away from doorways in a "daily contest to prevent the Sahara from burying [their] ancient village."[1] The women, along with a few insects, barely survive; most animals have perished; plants are shriveled, and the majority of the people who continue to live in that region struggle to sustain themselves on land that is rapidly losing its ability to support life.

One farmer who lives in that arid region of the planet, known as the Sahel, the shore of the Sahara desert, lamented that his harvest, scratched

1. Normitsu Onishi, "Where Dwelling Is Kept from Dune, One Scoop at a Time," *Los Angeles Times*, 14 January 2000, sec. A1.

from parched land, was only one-seventh of his father's harvest of just forty years ago. His neighbors living in the fishing villages along the Niger River are not faring any better. They speak of days when their ancestors' huts were filled with fish, but the people who live there now harvest the fish before they mature, reducing their catch to fingerlings. The farmers and the fishermen, as they eke out an existence from a deteriorating environment, bear witness to the wisdom of the oriental proverb: Going to heaven is easy; living on earth takes courage.

The Sahel is one of many regions in the world suffering from environmental degradation. Ecological decay challenges people everywhere to cope with life on a planet distressed by human abuse. The environment is one of the most critical issues in the ethical task of managing change across cultures, and Christians must decide how the narrative of God's redemptive relationship with creation speaks to the issue. This became real to me when I was in the Sahel. While traveling along the dusty roads, I noticed a patch of lush forest in the midst of land that contained only a few straggly bushes. The forest intrigued me because it appeared to be out of place in a desert. My host explained that the forest was the sacred land of the traditional religion in the village and that no one dared to enter it. He quickly changed the subject, believing sacred forests and local spirits were not topics for public discussion. I filed the story for future use.

A few years later, I facilitated a workshop on managing cultural change in the Sahel; one workshop participant told a story about an indigenous religious belief that forbade people to cut trees during particular months of the year. The prevailing belief was that the forest was sacred, and anyone who cut any of its trees would die and bring down the wrath of the local spirits on the entire community. The workshop participant wanted me to suggest ways in which he could help liberate the people from the taboo, so that they could harvest trees when they needed firewood or building materials. My immediate response was admiration for his genuine concern for the people who lived in bondage to the taboo. However, I also suspected that he was influenced by a Christian understanding of environmental issues that has provoked considerable criticisms in recent decades.

Criticism of Christian Ecological Ethics

The most severe of these criticisms comes from Lynn White, who described Christianity as "the most anthropomorphic religion the world

94

has seen" because it insists that "it is God's will that man exploit nature for his proper ends."[2] White postulated that because Christians see the sacred grove as inhabited by spirits and therefore idolatrous, they have been chopping them down for over two millennia. He concludes that until we reject the Christian notion that nature exists to serve mankind, the ecological crisis will worsen.[3] The workshop participant's desire to liberate the community from the taboos seemed to affirm the validity of these statements.

The observations of Lynn White and other environmentalists emphasize the tension between religious and ecological ethics and imply that Christians fail to recognize the contributions that these two fields of ethics can make to each other. The irony of Lynn White's statements was that he had no intention of disparaging Christianity; they were included in an article to nominate "St. Francis of Assisi as the Patron Saint of Ecologists."[4]

White, like many ethicists, realized that ecological ethics cannot be void of religious conviction because they govern how people respond to the environment. Larry Sullivan, the director of the Harvard Center for the Study of World Religions, emphasized this point by postulating that "religious tradition is a powerful influence that has yet to be tapped in the environmental arena. . . . Change won't happen without religions because they are the touchstone of people's deepest motivations."[5]

Larry Rasmussen, a theologian who writes about environmental issues, affirmed this conviction by noting that "efforts to safeguard and cherish the environment need to be infused with a vision of the sacred."[6] Also, Carl Pope, the Executive Director of the Sierra Club, the largest environmental organization in the United States, wrote that "the environmental movement for the past quarter of a century has made no more profound error than to misunderstand the mission of religion and the churches in preserving the Creation."[7] The esteem people hold for the environment is directly related to how they perceive its place in the narrative that defines their relationship with the sacred.

2. "The Roots of the Ecological Crisis," *Science*, 10 March 1967, 1205.
3. Ibid., 1206–7.
4. Ibid., 1207.
5. "Faith and the Environment," *Christian Century*, November 1998, 1014.
6. "Cosmology and Ethics," in *Worldviews and Ecology: Religion, Philosophy, and the Environment*, ed. Mary Evelyn Tucker and John A. Grim (Maryknoll, N.Y.: Orbis, 1994), 175.
7. Quoted in Trebbe Johnson, "The Second Creation Story: Redefining the Bond between Religion and Ecology," *Sierra: Exploring, Enjoying and Protecting the Planet* (November–December 1998): 52.

The taboo that forbids cutting trees illustrates the need for Christians to infuse an ecological ethic into the religious beliefs and practices of the community. Taboos are artifacts of the social structures that govern personal behavior. The taboo in the village that forbids people to cut trees emerges from the fusion of the environment with the sacred realm, which leads people to believe they will bring the wrath of the local spirits on the entire community.

The taboo poses a tension about transforming the community for Christians who are attempting to manage cultural change. One side of this tension involves the personal spirituality of the villagers. The taboo, regardless of its value in protecting the environment, associates the people who observe it with the traditional religion. The other side of the tension is that Christians will defy the taboo in an effort to show that the God of Creation is not the same as the community's god of nature. Christians can resolve this tension by emphasizing how the biblical creation stories serve as the foundation for the narrative of God's redemptive relationship with creation. This, in turn, compels Christians to discern whether the prevailing theologies of creation throughout the global church are consistent with the biblical accounts or whether they have been influenced by other theological and philosophical traditions.

Since the Christian church has been influenced by beliefs foreign to biblical tradition, the biblical accounts of creation have not served as the foundation of Christianity's understanding of the environment. The ecological crisis of Christianity is rooted in Gnosticism, an Indo-European philosophy that has influenced Christians to be indifferent to environmental ethics, despite the value the Bible places on creation.

Global Ecological Crisis and Creation Stories

The literature about Saint Francis of Assisi includes a story about Saint Francis and his companions resting on a hill during a journey. As they sat, pondering the mysterious beauty of nature, a great multitude of birds surrounded Saint Francis, perching on his shoulders, arms, and feet. Being overjoyed with the birds, he said to his companions, "I believe, dearest brethren, that our Lord Jesus Christ is pleased that we should dwell on this solitary mount, inasmuch as our little brothers and sisters, the birds, show such joy at our coming."[8]

8. Brother Ugolino, "Of the Sacred and Holy Stigmata of St. Francis and Certain Considerations Thereon," in *Little Flowers of St. Francis of Assisi*, trans. Roger Hudleston (New York: Heritage, n.d.); readable online at www.ccel.org/u/ugolino/flowers/htm/iii.liv.htm#iii.liv.

The story of Saint Francis is reminiscent of the harmony between nature and humankind portrayed in the biblical creation stories, which place a high value on the environment, affirming that the creation is good because it is the product of God's creative work. It is his first choice as the dwelling place of humankind and participates in his redemptive work through Christ.

Creation stories, serving as the prefaces to many cultural narratives, indicate the value that people in a culture place on their natural surroundings. Not all creation stories, however, esteem the environment highly; some are hostile toward the creation, seeing it as God's second choice for the dwelling place of humankind. Islam, for example, acknowledges that creation has an evil character for which Satan is responsible. It emphasizes that God originally intended for humankind to live in heaven but relegated them to earth after they participated in Satan's rebellion in heaven.[9]

The Islamic story has a variety of interpretations in Muslim cultures. For instance, Indonesians blame women as responsible for the human expulsion from heaven for inciting violence. According to their story, a woman entered the world after she killed seven of her children.[10] Likewise, a Swahili tradition describes Adam as spending his time in prayer while Eve sought out "the shade of the Tree of Knowledge of the Procreation of Life."[11] After Eve succeeded in enticing Adam to eat the fruit of the forbidden tree, they fell asleep and woke up on earth, making earth a consequential dwelling place of humankind.

While Islam has a low view of the environment,[12] it has not fared better in pantheistic cultures, where people esteem the physical creation to be divine. The Rig Veda, a collection of sacred Hindu writings, regards natural forces as divinities worthy of worship. A typical Hindu creation story depicts the creation as born out of the image of a human being:

> The moon was born from his mind;
> His eyes gave birth to the sun;
> Indra and Agni came from his mouth

9. See "The Cow," in *The Qur'an Interpreted,* trans. A. J. Arberry (New York: Macmillan, 1955), 30–72.

10. Satyagraha Hurip, *Bisma: Warrior Priest of the Mahabharata,* trans. David Irvine (Jakarta, Indonesia: Pustaka Sinar Harapan, 1990), 6.

11. Jan Knappert, compiler, *Myths and Legends of the Swahili* (Nairobi: East African Educational Publishers, 1979), 28.

12. Christopher Key Chapple, "Hindu Environmentalism," in *Worldviews and Ecology,* ed. Tucker and Grim, 114.

And Vagu [the wind] from his breath was born.
From his navel the midair rose;
The sky arose from his head;
From feet, the earth;
From ears, the directions.
Thus, they form the worlds.[13]

It may appear that pantheism, by deifying nature, would serve as a good foundation for an environmental ethic because it suggests that people who esteem the creation as divine ought to be vigilant about caring for it. However, as John Grim and Mary Evelyn Tucker have observed, pantheistic societies do not have a better record of environmental issues than do other societies. For instance, the "Taoist wisdom regarding nature was not able to prevent the deforestation of many parts of China, nor was Buddhist sensitivity to the interconnection of all reality able to prevent destruction of natural resources in Southeast Asia."[14] People will revere creation only if they have a high view of the deity they associate with it. People, however, often have a pragmatic view of religion, and they value their relationship with the gods and spirits on the basis of how well they meet their human needs. Pantheists might view the world in relational, rather than objective, terms, but they value it according to its ability to deliver goods and services. They are capable of venerating the earth while they exploit it for their survival.

The tendency of humankind to manipulate their environment seems to be a human trait rather than a problem of any particular religion. Regardless of our religious beliefs, "our ethics have remained largely anthropocentric and indifferent to the fate of the natural world."[15] The struggle for Christians is to discern what creation stories have influenced the interpretations of their faith, preventing them from giving the welfare of the earth a central place in the expression of their faith.

Lynn White, who explored the roots of the ecological crisis and attributed it to Christianity, made a noble effort to make Christians aware of the decay of the natural world. His solution, however, was only partial. While he located the problem within Christianity, he did not explore the reasons the problem became embedded in the narrative of Christianity. The source of the problem penetrates the roots of the church, making it much deeper and more insidious than Christians, in recent decades, have

13. Ibid.
14. Introduction to *Worldviews and Ecology*, 12.
15. Ibid.

realized. A concern for the environment can be grafted into the narrative of Christianity only when Christians recognize why they, throughout the history of the church, have not given priority to ecological issues.

Historical Roots of the Christian Ecological Crisis

Do the biblical creation stories influence Christians to have a low view of the environment? This section will offer a negative answer to that question by exploring how Gnosticism, not the biblical account of creation, pervades the narratives of Western Christianity.

The historical roots of the ecological crisis are in Gnosticism, which is a family of philosophical and theological heresies that originated in the Indo-European cultures of the Middle East and found fertile ground in the classical cultures of the Mediterranean region. Its basic premise, that the physical world is evil, complemented the Greek perceptions of the nature god, Pan. A minor god and an embarrassment to the Greeks, Pan was the only god of the pantheon who died.

Pan's story sets the context from which Gnosticism influenced Greek cultures and grafted itself into the narrative of Christianity. His problems began at birth because he was so ugly "that his mother ran away from him in fear, and Hermes carried him up to Olympus for the gods' amusement."[16] The gods on Mount Olympus never accepted Pan, and he fled from Olympus to live in the forest of Arcadia, where he became the "hidden indwelling power of nature"[17] and "the ruler of universal material substance."[18]

Pan had a portfolio of responsibility that could have brought him some dignity and respect, but he never amounted to anything more than a "hoofed, horned, horny deity who took pleasure in playing pipes and pursuing nymphs."[19] The hunters beckoned Pan to guide them to their prey, but Pan frustrated them by cavorting with the females of all animal species, leaving the hunters to fend for themselves against the hostilities of nature. Pan's sexual exploits and his inability to provide any valuable services to his constituency caused the intelligentsia of Greece to lose interest in him. Only the peasants, who perceived a sacred pres-

16. Robert Graves, "Pan's Nature and Deeds," in *The Greek Myths* (New York: Braziller, 1955), 1:101.

17. J. Donald Hughes, "Pan: Environment Ethics in Classical Polytheism," in *Religion and Environmental Crisis,* ed. Eugene C. Hargrove (Athens: University of Georgia Press, 1986), 17.

18. Ibid., 9.

19. Ibid., 7.

ence in nature, sacrificed to him, believing they could hear his voice as it enchanted nature.

After his death, however, Pan's influence increased. He became the personification of evil—a "horned, goat-hoofed devil who represented nature now as a snare and a delusion to the faithful."[20] Nature continued to be Pan's abode, and people had to protect themselves from his evil influences by cutting the trees, which prevented ignorant peasants and other naïve people from offering sacrifices to him. The demise of Pan set the context for Gnosticism to graft itself, like a virus, into the Christian church. It "followed the church like a shadow"[21] by offering a simple but unorthodox answer to the question of why God, who is good, allows evil to exist.

Gnosticism offered a solution to the problem of a flawed creation by postulating that it was not the product of a sovereign, good God. Instead, its creator is the *Demiurgos,* or half-maker, who created the world in his imperfect image. Hence, the physical world became an embarrassment to both God and human beings, which was acutely felt by Marcion, a Gnostic who lived in the second century. He believed it was blasphemous that the God of all grace was "responsible among other things for the disgusting paraphernalia of reproduction and for all the nauseating defilements of the human flesh from birth to final putrescence."[22] Gnostic teachings affirmed that the flawed creation held people in bondage and that they could escape the evils of the material world through a plan of salvation that required people to have special knowledge, or *gnosis.* Salvation, according to Gnosticism, is through knowledge rather than through faith; it has no hope for the creation, and it affects only the human soul, leaving the physical creation to the hopelessness of its own ravages.

Gnostic Creation Stories

While Gnostic creation stories rely heavily on the biblical accounts, they are different in that they depict the physical world, not as good, but as "the homeland of evil" and the human body as the soul's prison house.[23] The following stories are representative of Gnostic philosophy.

20. Ibid., 21.
21. John Dominic Crossan, *The Birth of Christianity: Discovering What Happened in the Years Immediately after the Execution of Jesus* (San Francisco: Harper San Francisco, 1998), xiii.
22. H. Richard Niebuhr, *Christ and Culture* (New York: Harper & Row, 1951), 168.
23. Brian J. Walsh and J. Richard Middleton, *The Transforming Vision: Shaping a Christian World View* (Downers Grove, Ill.: InterVarsity, 1984), 108–9.

The consistent theme in each story is the effort to dissociate the flawed creation from the ultimate God.

The first one presents Eve as androgynous and in the purity of her created state before she had any notions of her own sexuality, which Gnostics believe to be the evil means through which the material substance of humanity is reproduced:

> When Sophia let fall a droplet of light, it flowed onto the water, and immediately a human being appeared, being androgynous. That droplet she [Sophia] molded first as a female body. . . . An androgynous human being was produced, whom the Greeks call Hermaphrodites; and whose mother the Hebrews call Eve of Life [Zoe], namely, the female instructor of life.[24]

The second story depicts Eve as the product of the thoughts of the virginal spirit, who, as a savior figure, takes on a body to liberate Adam from the chains of his bodily prison. Eve speaks the following:

> I entered into the midst of their prison, which is the prison of the body. And I said, 'He who hears, let him get up from their deep sleep.' And he wept and shed tears. Bitter tears he wiped from himself and he said, 'Who is it that calls my name, and from where has this hope come to me, while I am in the chains of this prison?' And I said, 'I am the Pronoia of the pure light; I am the thinking of the virginal Spirit, who raised you up to the honored place.'[25]

The third teaching relevant to our purpose is Adam's instruction to his son that the eternal God is not the god who created humankind. The creator of humankind is actually lower than the people who have *gnosis:*

> The disclosure given by Adam to his son Seth in his seven hundredth year. And he said: "Listen to my words, my son Seth. When God created me out of the earth, along with Eve your mother, I went along with her in a glory which she had seen in the aeon from which she came forth. She taught me the word of *Gnosis* of the eternal God. And we resembled the great eternal angels, for we were higher than the God who created us."[26]

24. Hans-Gebhard Bethge and Bentley Layton, trans., "On the Origin of the World," in *The Nag Hammadi Library,* ed. James M. Robinson (San Francisco: Harper Collins, 1990), 7; readable online at www.webcom.com/gnosis/naghamm/origin.html.

25. Frederik Wisse, trans., "The Apocryphon of John," in *Nag Hammadi Library,* 13.

26. George W. MacRae, trans., "The Apocalypse of Adam," in *Nag Hammadi Library,* 1.

While few people in Western cultures have had any exposure to the Gnostic creation stories, they had an insidious influence on Western cultures and were exported throughout the world by Christians. The church has been unable to purge them from popular Christian teachings. The legacy endures in Western culture, if not throughout the entire church.

Contemporary Legacy of Gnosticism

Gnosticism continues to have a pervasive influence on Western cultures. The most common evidence of this influence is the manner in which our language has absorbed Gnostic terms. Agnostic, meaning without knowledge, continues to be a statement of unbelief in our culture, indicating that knowledge, rather than faith, is the means of religious experience. Westerners also communicate some contempt for the environment by the derogatory way they use such terms as "earthy" or "dirty."

Another influence of Gnosticism was cited by Harvey Cox, who speculated that the "Gnostic hatred for the human body can be seen in our curious willingness as Americans to accept almost unlimited violence on the movie and television screen."[27] Gnosticism may have also influenced the violent eschatological interpretations that thrive in Western cultures. While the eschatological term "apocalypse" conjures violent images in the religious subcultures of Western society, the term does not need to be violent; it actually means "an unveiling of Jesus' Lordship over the rampages of history on to his triumph and the End. . . . [It] has its center and meaning in that Lordship, not in disasters."[28]

The religious narratives of Western religious cultures and subcultures, however, are replete with literature about the apocalypse as a grand ecological disaster in which the earth is destroyed. Popular religion of the West indicates that "nuclear cataclysm is a central part of God's plan for the near future of the earth."[29] People argue that they are justified in ravaging the earth, rationalizing that "God is planning to destroy the world. So when we blow it up, we are doing God's will."[30]

27. *Feast of Fools: A Theological Essay on Festivity and Fantasy* (Cambridge, Mass.: Harvard University Press, 1969), 48.
28. Dale Aukerman, *Reckoning with Apocalypse: Terminal Politics and Christian Hope* (New York: Crossroad, 1993), 26.
29. Ibid., 140.
30. Ibid., 141.

Gnosticism has also influenced the church's mission, which has become indifferent to environmental ethics. Few mission statements define a church's purpose as working for the restoration of creation or for the redemption of the *kosmos*. Certainly, this neglect stems from the liberal/conservative tensions in the church. However, the failure to create a theology comprehensive enough to include environmental issues causes the mission of the church to resemble that of Gnosticism. Typical mission statements include such assertions as "the principle objective of the church is to win converts for Jesus Christ and safeguard them against eternal hellfire and damnation in the life beyond the grave. . . . When Jesus comes, all material possessions, including matters to do with land, water, animals and vegetation, will no longer matter."[31]

The problem with mission statements of this nature is that they neglect the values inherent in the biblical narrative concerning the creation, causing them to take on a Gnostic character, if only by default. They portray Christianity as a religion that rescues people from a flawed creation and ignore that salvation has to do with the wholeness and well-being of the person in community, both temporally and eternally. Salvation, in the fullest sense of biblical theology, assumes that the creation is capable of supporting life in its fullness. For this reason, the Bible starts "with eternity and God, and the creation of everything else. In Revelation the story of this cosmos ends, and everything reenters eternity."[32] The creation is not incidental to the salvation of humankind; it is the context through which people work out their salvation. It cannot be removed from redemption because it grows out of redemption, creating a sense of wholeness that is characterized by the biblical concept of *shalom*.[33]

The tendency to remove salvation from redemption is one of the most pervasive influences of Gnosticism. This influence is realized most vividly in the development of worldviews, which are the building blocks of the social structures in a culture; they comprise the basic assumptions that people use to interpret and organize reality. They empower people to provide some sense of order in their world, revealing what they value. People transform the narratives of their cultures when they change their

31. Samson K. Gitau, *The Environmental Crisis: A Challenge for African Christianity* (Nairobi: Acton, 2000), 82.

32. Paul G. Hiebert, R. Daniel Shaw, and Tite Tienou, *Understanding Folk Religion: A Christian Response to Popular Beliefs and Practices* (Grand Rapids: Baker, 1999), 74.

33. *Shalom* is the sense of wholeness that pervades every aspect of human life. My previous book, *Bridging the Gap: Evangelism, Development, and Shalom* (Monrovia, Calif.: MARC, 1993), addressed this issue extensively.

worldview, which allows people to see the world differently and to tell a different story about themselves.

Worldviews are buried in cultures, and they need to be excavated before they can be managed. Among the many ways of doing this is by conducting the exercise suggested in table 4.1, in which participants are asked to arrange a list of nouns into two or more categories.[34] This sorting exercise gives people the opportunity to become aware of the assumptions of their worldview by examining the reasons they arrange the elements of creation as they do. Columns A, B, C, and D of table 4.2 represent the results of the survey of table 4.1. After conducting this exercise with several hundred people throughout the world who have been influenced by Christian missions from Western cultures, I am convinced that Gnostic creation stories have been more influential than the biblical creation stories in shaping the worldviews of Christians.

Table 4.1 Sort the Following Nouns into Two or More Categories

God	lawn	cow	sky	girl
rice	man	angel	boy	tree
earth	sea	woman	grass	land
economy	demon	bread	spirit	water
gender	garden	wheat	blood	house

Column A illustrates the categories of the majority of Christian development practitioners, particularly those educated in Western cultures. This arrangement of the elements of creation makes a clear distinction between the spiritual and physical elements of creation, exposing its Gnostic influence by creating a dichotomy between nonmaterial and material elements, dissociating God and other spiritual entities from the creation. In true Gnostic fashion, God, angels, demons, and spirits are perceived to have a nature different from the elements of creation, such as man, woman, earth, and so on.

Column B, which emerges in many workshops, is a clearer expression of the prevalence of Gnostic beliefs in Christian thought. This arrangement continues the spiritual-physical dichotomy, separating spiritual entities from physical ones. However, it extends this dichotomy by separating people who are saved from those who are not saved. This effort to portray the uniqueness of humankind results in a second dichotomy

34. The original version of this exercise, which was based on Genesis 1, is credited to Paul Hiebert while he taught at the School of World Mission at Fuller Theological Seminary, Pasadena, California.

Table 4.2 Four Arrangements of the Nouns

Column A	Column B	Column C	Column D
Spiritual	**Spiritual**	**Creator**	**Creator**
God	God	God	God
angel	angel		
demon	demon	**Created**	**Created**
spirit	spirit	angel	angel
	*man	demon	demon
Physical	*woman	spirit	spirit
man	*boy	man	man
woman	*girl	woman	woman
boy		boy	boy
girl	**Physical**	girl	girl
earth	man	earth	earth
sky	woman	sky	sky
wheat	boy	wheat	cow
bread	girl	bread	water
cow	earth	cow	tree
garden	sky	garden	blood
blood	wheat	blood	
water	bread	water	**Socially Constructed**
land	cow	land	wheat
tree	garden	tree	bread
rice	blood	rice	garden
economy	water	economy	blood
gender	land	gender	land
lawn	tree	lawn	tree
	rice		rice
	economy		economy
	gender		gender
	lawn		lawn

*Denotes those who are saved.

that is characteristic of a Gnostic worldview, a dichotomy that separates those who are spiritual from those who are not spiritual.

Christians who create this arrangement invariably suggest that they are attempting to illustrate that the nature of the human person is distinct from the nature of other created elements. Humankind, at least in the biblical tradition, participates in the resurrection, receiving life after death. However, dichotomies that separate physical and spiritual elements of creation or saved humans from unsaved humans violate the tenets of Colossians 1:15–

20 by suggesting that the human soul is the only recipient of God's redemptive work and completely ignoring the redemption of creation.

Column B, reflecting its Gnostic source, portrays the narrative of Christianity as having no hope of redemption for the creation; it replaces the Christian hope for a future when everything will be created anew with a longing for the "soul's escape from the body and from the earth."[35] Unfortunately, Gnostic influence "remains in most secular as well as theological cosmologies today."[36] Gnosticism's enduring legacy is the way in which Christians in Western cultures have shaped their response to the environment, a response that stands in contrast to the values inherent in the biblical creation stories. The people who want to portray a biblical worldview complete the exercise in a different manner; columns C and D represent the results of their arrangement of the elements of creation and will be discussed in the next section.

Pancreationism: The Biblical Creation Stories

The four creation accounts in the Bible, which serve as a synopsis of the biblical narrative of redemption, outline a theology of creation that is best characterized as pancreation, which is the belief that "everything other than God is his creation and nothing in creation, about creation, or true of creation is self-existent."[37] The four biblical creation accounts affirm that all of creation depends on God for its existence and sustainability.[38]

The first account of Genesis (Gen. 1:1–2:4) gives creation a moral nature by declaring that it is good. It depicts God as the creative agent who brought a formless and void earth into being by his word. It assumes God's existence and implies that he has an uncreated nature, which makes him distinct from the other elements of creation. The story also narrates the creation of every living being, including humankind in the image of God. It concludes by noting that God blessed and hallowed the seventh day by resting. While this account is unconcerned with the origins of God, it gives considerable attention to the definition of his "verbal

35. Anthony C. Thiselton, *Interpreting God and the Postmodern Self: On Meaning, Manipulation, and Promise* (Grand Rapids: Eerdmans, 1995), 126.

36. Jeffrey Burton Russell, "Glory in Time: A History of the Desire of the Cosmos to Return to God," Faculty Research Lecture 36 (University of California, Santa Barbara, 7 March 1991).

37. Roy A. Clouser, *The Myth of Religious Neutrality: An Essay on the Hidden Role of Religious Belief in Theories* (South Bend, Ind.: University of Notre Dame Press, 1991), 202.

38. Pancreation is distinguished from pantheism, which affirms that God *is* all things, and panentheism, the belief that God is *in* all things, in that pancreation affirms that God also *transcends* all things.

decree in giving order and structure to the world. . . . Creation consti-
tutes a pattern of obedient responses to his commanding word."[39]

The second creation story (Gen. 2:4–25), in contrast to the first, is concerned with the circumstances in which God created humankind. It
teaches that God created man from the dust of the ground and breathed
life into him, causing him to become a living being. God planted a garden for the man, which included every tree that is pleasant and fruitful.
The man's responsibility was to maintain the garden, but God prohibited him from eating the fruit of the tree of knowledge of good and evil,
saying that he would die if he did so. This account concludes with God's
creation of a woman, from a rib of the man, as helper and partner for
him. God declared that the two shall become one flesh and that they
were naked but not ashamed.

The next chapter of Genesis (3:1–24), which is a continuation of both
creation stories, bears witness to the moral responsibility God assigned
to Adam and Eve by narrating the story of the serpent, who tempts the
woman to eat the fruit from the forbidden tree. The story's meaning is
built on the premise that Adam and Eve, because they are created in the
image of God, have moral responsibility to submit to his demands. The
serpent tempted the woman to question God's moral integrity by assur
ing her that she would not die and reminding her that by eating the
fruit she would become like God, knowing good and evil. She not only
ate but also offered the fruit to her husband. Immediately after eating,
Adam and Eve realized they were naked and made clothes from fig
leaves. When God confronted them, the man blamed his wife, and the
woman admitted that the serpent tricked her. Neither the man nor the
woman accepted responsibility for their attempt to become morally autonomous from God.

At the end of the story, God curses the snake and then explains to the
man and woman the consequences of their disobedience: the woman
would bring forth children in pain; she would desire her husband, and
he would rule over her; and the man would till the land by the sweat of
his brow. God then makes garments of skin for the man and his wife and
sends them from the garden. The moral of the story is that by exercising
their moral autonomy, Adam and Eve had failed to glorify God, and
their disobedience brought sin and death into the world.

The third creation story (John 1:1–18) is a direct response to Gnostic
teachings. It focuses on the incarnation of the Word of God, the creator

39. Walsh and Middleton, *Transforming Vision*, 45.

and redeemer of creation. In the prologue, John makes clear that Christ was with God at creation, emphasizing that "in the beginning was the Word, and the Word was with God, and the Word was God. He was with God in the beginning. Through him all things were made. . . . The Word became flesh and lived for a while among us" (John 1:1–3, 14). These verses, indicating that Christ was with God from the beginning, are an effort to define the divine nature of Christ, who became flesh. Hebrew theology did not allow for two expressions of eternality; if Christ, who became flesh, is also eternal, Christ must be divine, possessing the same nature as God. John also makes unequivocal statements about the creation coming into being through God and transforms the Gnostic concern with light into life: "In him [Christ] was life, and that life was the light of men" (John 1:4). John clearly wants to emphasize that the creation is good and that it is not the product of an inferior deity.

The fourth creation story (Col. 1:15–20), which we examined closely in chapter 2, highlights God's commitment to reconcile the world to himself through the redemptive ministry of Christ. This story is also a direct response to Gnosticism. Paul's central concern in this story was to convince the Gnostics that Jesus, who came in the flesh, had the same eternal nature as God. The Gnostics, believing that Jesus was either spiritual or physical, could not hold the two natures together. They believed "when Jesus walked, he left no footprints."[40] God, however, through the incarnation, affirmed the goodness of the physical creation.

While there are many common themes that readers can garner from these stories, they clearly indicate that God is concerned about creation, which is good, and that he has a redemptive and sustaining relationship with it. Yet, God's nature is distinguished from that of creation in that he is uncreated. The being of God is not contingent on creation, but the power of God is displayed through the creation. The created elements are not divine in any sense, but they embody the glory of God (Psalm 19 and 104). Creation is not esteemed, in part or in total, as worthy of religious devotion, but it bears witness to God's worthiness for worship. The creation "is an expression of God's love for man; . . . the natural world exists, in a sense, for [humankind]."[41]

Human beings, however, are active, not passive, participants in the creation because they are its co-creators, co-redeemers, and co-sustainers.

40. Glen H. Stassen, D. M. Yeager, and John Howard Yoder, "A New Vision," in *Authentic Transformation: A New Vision of Christ and Culture* (Nashville: Abingdon, 1996), 215.
41. Harvey G. Cox, *The Secular City: Secularization and Urbanization in Theological Perspective* (New York: Macmillan, 1965), 178.

The creation is not finished until humankind accepts the divine gift of exercising stewardship over it. "God does not 'rest' until he has created man and enlisted [people] in the creating process."[42] We live in a fallen creation that groans for redemption, and its redemption "is not prior to man's [redemption] but takes place only as man is redeemed. The redemption of nature, in short, takes place as nature shares in what God has done for man in Jesus Christ."[43]

If we complete the sorting exercise under the influence of the biblical creation stories, the results would look like either column C or column D of table 4.2. Column C makes the biblical distinction between the creator and the elements of creation. God is separate from creation by virtue of his uncreated nature, and all elements of creation participate in his redemptive relationship with it. Column D makes the distinction between the natural elements of creation and the socially constructed elements that comprise the *kosmos*. All the elements of the *kosmos* participate in the redemptive work of God through Christ, empowering people to fulfill their leading function of bearing the image of God.

The Sabbath as an Environmental Ethic

Creation stories are central to the establishment of environmental ethics; they contain the values that empower people to infuse their view of the environment into their social structures. The key to building an environmental ethic on creation stories is identifying the values in them that are conducive to a proper appreciation of the environment.

The central value in the biblical creation stories that fosters an environmental ethic is the Sabbath. For Christians, as for Jews, "it is the Sabbath and the idea of the Sabbath that introduces the necessary restraint into stewardship,"[44] which helps people to recognize the limitations of creation, giving it the opportunity to regenerate itself in response to the taxing demands that human beings put on it. The Sabbath is a unifying symbol of both Hebrew and Jewish communities, through which they get a glimpse of God's redemptive work in creation. It is a redemptive response to the many taboos that prevent people from cutting trees and avoiding sacred forests. According to Moltmann, "It is the Sabbath which blesses, sanctifies and reveals the world as God's creation."[45] As a symbol of libera-

42. Ibid., 177.
43. Ibid., 179.
44. Eric Katz, "Judaism and the Ecological Crisis," in *Worldviews and Ecology,* 59.
45. Jürgen Moltmann, *God in Creation* (Minneapolis: Fortress, 1993), 6.

tion, it transforms oppressive taboos because it incorporates the need for rest that all created elements have. God modeled this need by resting on the seventh day of creation, and the Decalogue includes the command to keep the Sabbath holy (Exod. 20:10). This concept of the Sabbath was extended to include the need for fields to lie fallow every seven years (Exod. 23:11) and to restructure economic relationships every fifty years.

The taboos that are evident throughout every culture of the world are shadows of the Sabbath. They can be negative symbols that reflect the need for regeneration, and to a great extent they are motivated by fear, not celebration. The villagers in the Sahel refused to cut a tree during a particular season because they feared that some spiritual being or force would curse or destroy them. Likewise, villagers in rural Ghana refuse to harvest water on particular days of the week because of their fear of violating the well-being of the water source. Christians are called to live in freedom of such fears. However, this freedom gives us the responsibility to recognize that the sustainability of our environment—and our very lives—depends on our ability to perceive a redemptive relationship between God and creation, a relationship that is symbolized by the freedom to celebrate the Sabbath. God chose to rest; we discipline ourselves to rest, and, in our calling as stewards over creation, we must observe an environmental ethic that allows the creation to rest.

The designation of a day of rest is a transcultural value with culturally specific applications. Christians in Western cultures modified the tradition of rest on the seventh day by making the first day holy. We worship and celebrate the resurrection of Christ on Sunday, and we traditionally reserve Saturday as a day of rest, regeneration, and recreation. The first-century Christians, in contrast, observed the Sabbath on the seventh day (Acts 13:14, 42) and gathered on the first day to worship (Acts 20:7). The transformation of the holy day from Saturday to Sunday is a later development in the first-century church, and it met some resistance. The Epistle to the Colossians instructs its audience not to accept judgment over the Sabbath day (2:16). Similarly, the Epistle to the Hebrews affirms the validity of the Sabbath but emphasizes the need for rest, regardless of the day (4:1–11). The central issue is the principle of the Sabbath rather than the specific day of rest.[46]

46. The early Christians merged the day of rest and worship into Sunday, creating a transition from Saturday to Sunday as the day of rest and worship. The Synod of Laodicea in Phrygia Pacatiana made a formal separation between worship on the Sabbath and on the Lord's Day by decreeing "Christians must not judaize by resting on the Sabbath, but

The workshop participant who was concerned about the taboo that prevented the villagers of the Sahel from cutting the branches of the trees should not consider how he can rescind the taboo, which would result in destroying a central value of the indigenous culture. Rather, he should consider how he can transform the taboo from an expression of fear to a statement of faith. Taboos, like other cultural expressions, need to be evaluated according to their contributions to the community. This taboo offers a relationship between God, the people, and the environment; it is a symbol that organizes the people into an expression of community—they are unified through the belief that trees should not be cut during a particular season. The belief connects the community with the spiritual realm and stipulates the consequences of its violation. It also, if only by default, creates an ethic that protects the environment. The ethical response to the taboo should be the effort to empower the people to maintain the health of their environment for a redemptive reason. The Sabbath is the redemptive taboo that serves as the foundation of the environmental ethic. It was made for humankind, not to disempower them by reifying itself, but to facilitate the health of their physical environment.

The Sabbath celebration is a commitment on the part of Christians to affirm that they are stewards of God's creation. We express this stewardship through rest, which is a symbolic recognition that the creation needs restoration. In resting, we affirm "that the biblical vision of the future is a restoration of creation [and] of our creaturely life before the Lord."[47] The biblical narrative of redemption is not a story about our rescue from creation; it is a story that enlists us in the transformation of creation. Sin came into the world when humankind ate the fruit from the forbidden tree, and it will depart when the leaves of the tree heal the nations (Rev. 22:2).

---

must work on that day." The document makes an important distinction between the Sabbath and the Lord's Day and emphasizes that worship is on the Lord's day, not the Sabbath. See "The Canons of the Synod Held in the City of Laodicea, in Phrygia Pacatiana," in *The Seven Ecumenical Councils*, ed. Henry R. Percival, vol. 14 of *The Nicene and Post-Nicene Fathers*, 2d series, ed. Philip Schaff and Henry Wace (reprint, Grand Rapids: Eerdmans, n.d.), 148, canon 29 (readable online at http://www.ccel.org/fathers2/NPNF2-14/Npnf2-14-51 .htm#P3294_592503).

47. Walsh and Middleton, *Transforming Vision*, 104.

5

Religious Practices:
From Power to Truth

And the spirit of the sea is masculine and strong. . . . And the spirit of the hail is a good angel. . . . And the Spirit of the snow has forsaken his chambers on account of his strength.

1 Enoch 60:16–19

Then all the people of the region of the Gerasenes asked Jesus to leave them, because they were overcome with fear.

Luke 8:37

And having disarmed the powers and authorities, he made a public spectacle of them, triumphing over them.

Colossians 2:15

A Christian development agency built irrigation dams in a West African Islamic village that embraced a folk religion, hoping to empower the people to manage the natural resource that symbolized harmony between the physical and spiritual realms. The village farmers had high expectations for the project, believing it would result in a noticeable increase in their harvest. However, they were disappointed before the end of the first growing season; the rainfall was lower than expected, so that there was inadequate water for their crops and gardens. The villagers feared a food shortage and possibly death because they knew the harvests would be low. The village elders blamed the hydrologists for offending the spirits that control the rainfall because they refused to make sacrifices to them before building the dams.

When the hydrologists tried to decide what their response to the problem should be, it was suggested that they exorcise the spirits. Influenced by popular literature on missions, some team members thought a display of spiritual power in the village would show the elders that Christians can control spirits. They believed they could march around the field, pray against the spirits, cast them from the area, and ask God to send rain. They saw this crisis as an opportunity not only to correct the rain shortage but also to bear witness to the power of Christianity. Other team members, however, did not like the idea of a power encounter because they did not believe the local spirits had any influence over the rain. They also thought that such an encounter, if successful, would do nothing more than portray Jesus as a rainmaker, a strong one if rain came but weak without it.

From their discussion the team members learned that encounters with people of other faiths do not begin with discussions of doctrine. Instead, they begin when people express their faith through their efforts to cope with the struggles of daily life, such as producing food, bearing and raising children, healing illnesses, pursuing justice, and maintaining social harmony. These practices, which reveal the essence of religious beliefs in traditional cultures, comprise the content of popular religious practices, commonly called folk religions.

The Nature of Folk Religions

When the disciples of John the Baptist asked Jesus why his disciples did not fast while the Pharisees and the disciples of John did, Jesus answered:

> How can the guests of the bridegroom mourn while he is with them? . . .
> No one sews a patch of unshrunk cloth on an old garment, for the patch
> will pull away from the garment, making the tear worse. Neither do men
> pour new wine into old wineskins. If they do, the skins will burst, the

wine will run out and the wineskins will be ruined. No, they pour new
wine into new wineskins, and both are preserved.

Matthew 9:15–17

The failure to transform old religious practices in light of the new covenant created the nucleus of folk religions, which, like the orthodox ones,
are among the elements of the *kosmos* that provide order in society. The
difference between orthodox and folk religions, however, is the difference between truth and power.

Definition of Folk Religions

Orthodox religions, such as Christianity and Islam, are the means
through which people express their values and convictions about ultimate reality, and the implications of these beliefs are both eternal and
temporal. Discerning truth is their primary concern. For expressions of
Christianity influenced by Gnosticism, for example, it is true that creation is flawed, if not evil; it places little value on the environment. For
orthodox Christianity it is true that the creation is God's handiwork; it
values the dependent relationship that the temporal has on the eternal
realm. Jesus inaugurated his ministry by stating that he was anointed
"to preach good news to the poor . . . proclaim freedom for the prisoners
and recovery of sight for the blind, to release the oppressed, [and] to proclaim the year of the Lord's favor" (Luke 4:18). The content of Jesus' ministry had economic, political, legal, physical, social, and eschatological
implications, eternal values that emerge from the physical realm.

Folk religions, in contrast to orthodox religions, focus on power rather
than on truth. They are socially constructed beliefs and practices that enable people to cope with the struggles of life. They emerge when a new
religion does not adequately transform the structures of the former religion, often creating a tension between the truth and power of the two.
While the people accept the truth of the new religion, they continue to
rely on the power of the former through their religious practices. This
results in confused convictions because they fail to bear witness to the
validity of either religion. They become like unshrunk cloth on old garments or new wine in old wineskins; the cloth tears apart and the wineskins burst.

The temptation to believe that spirits control rain was a way the
Christian hydrologists could modify the truth of Christianity to embrace
the power of a folk religion. Neither the Bible nor Christian tradition
gives any reason to believe that spirits control rain, which indicates that

the belief is a socially constructed solution to the problem of rain shortage. It makes sense in a culture where spirits are esteemed to be powerful agents. However, the belief also has the power to distract people from truthful means of coping with the meager rainfall.

Writing about the way in which the democratic movement in the Philippines deposed its dictator in 1986, Raul S. Manglapus illustrates how folk religions reveal the bedrock faith of the community:

> When the revolutionaries needed a visible symbol around which to rally, they did not bring out statues of Jefferson or Lincoln, or of the nineteenth-century Filipino martyr Jose Rizal, or of the slain twentieth-century national hero Benigno Aquino, Jr. . . . They brought out, instead, an image of the Blessed Virgin Mary, for when a man is ready to stand to the death for freedom, his first thought is to return to his fundamental faith.[1]

The power of the movement toward democracy in the Philippines was not inspired by speeches from democratic leaders; "tank commanders were made, instead, to listen to prayers, 'Our Fathers,' 'Hail Marys' and 'Glory Bes.'"[2] The religion of the people inspired them to overcome oppression, not by abstract propositions concerning democratic ideals, but by the appropriation of symbols central to their cultural narrative. Folk religions have a wide range of expression, creating a fine line between folk religious practices, orthodox beliefs, and contextual preferences. People often legitimize their cultural practices by imposing them on their religion, as we have seen with female genital mutilation, which was justified by religious teaching.

In the United States, many people legitimize wealth, materialism, and warfare by attributing them to the will of God. They speak about these issues as though Jesus' teachings on them were irrelevant. One American family held their Bible as they proudly displayed the glut of their possessions on their front lawn, "apparently oblivious to the image their portrait communicated."[3] We live as though our lives consisted of the abundance of our possessions (see Luke 12:15). Likewise, we pray for God's blessing in warfare as though God were a domestic deity. To pray to "Our Father in Heaven," however, is counsel not to domesticate God.

1. *Will of the People: Original Democracy in Non-Western Societies* (Westport, Conn.: Greenwood, 1987), xxiii.
2. Ibid.
3. Tom Sine, *Mustard Seed versus McWorld: Reinventing Life and Faith for the Future* (Grand Rapids: Baker, 1999), 21.

Power in Folk Religions

Different expressions of folk religions develop when people adopt a religious practice from outside their culture without engaging in the theological reflection necessary to reinterpret the meaning of their worldview within the context of their religion. This can be illustrated by charting the West African folk Islamic religion of the Hausa and the Fulani, who failed to reinterpret their cultural symbols when they converted to Islam.

Table 5.1 West African Folk Islamic Worldview

Unseen Realm (Other World)	Allah
Middle Zone (Between Seen and Unseen Realms)	Boka (Magic, Amulets, and Charms)
	Jinn (Spirits); Bori (Spirit Possession); Arnanci (Spirit Worship)
	Kura (Soul; Double of the Person; Travels in Dreams; Never Dies; Goes to Heaven)
	Iska/Iskoki (Personal Spirits; Divided into Four Types: Fire, Wind, Earth, Water; Influences Marriages; Water Cannot Marry Fire; Water and Wind Work Well)
	Ancestors
Seen Realm (Physical World)	People, Animals, Plants, Earth

The table is divided horizontally into three zones.[4] The top zone, the unseen world, communicates the theological sphere of the formal religion, of which truth is the central value. For instance, the confession of Allah as One and Mohammed as his prophet is the central focus of truth for Islam. Any person who makes that confession can become a Muslim. The middle zone, between the unseen and seen worlds, is the realm of folk or popular religion and contains the elements of the culture that serve as its vitality. Power is the central value of this zone, which is inhabited by the agents of causation. In Islamic cultures of West Africa, these agents include magic, charms, and spirit possession as well as worship of ancestors. Some of these entities are among the elements of the *kosmos* that became reified. The middle zone can also contain autonomous powers, such as demons, who maintain their own moral agency, and are usually associated with evil. The lower zone, the seen world, is the realm of social and physical sciences; efficiency, not truth or power, is its central value. Truth in this realm primarily serves as an instrumental

4. The information in the diagram is based on George Foxall, "Folk Islam: The Case of the Hausa of Northern Nigeria," *African Journal of Evangelical Theology* 11.1 (1994): 24–33. Its structure is based on Paul G. Hiebert's ideas in "The Flaw of the Excluded Middle," in *Anthropological Reflections on Missiological Issues* (Grand Rapids: Baker, 1994), 194–96.

measure of efficiency because people concerned about managing the resources of the lower realm want to do so as effectively as possible.

Our concern is the primacy of the middle zone in folk religions. Its elements appeal to the common people because they are accessible; they empower people to cope with the struggles of daily life. Allah alone is in the high realm of truth and the people worship him as the source of truth. However, when they need medical treatment for their children or rain for their gardens, they seek the power of the middle zone by appealing to Allah through various types of magic, such as appeasing their ancestors or having their dreams interpreted.

The powers of the middle realm express themselves in numerous ways. In an Islamic book shop, I purchased a book that explained how to use the ninety-nine names of Allah to cure the ills of life. It instructed that a woman can resolve fertility problems if she "fasts for seven days, and each day at the breaking of the fast, she repeats three names [of Allah] twenty-one times, breathes into a glass of water, and then breaks the fast with this water."[5] A Hmong refugee, who was defending himself from the charge of sexual abuse in a United States court, "wanted to sacrifice [a] chicken and drink its blood to prove he was telling the truth. . . . [He] told the lawyer that the spirits would kill whoever drank the blood and lied."[6] During the war in Mozambique, soldiers were vaccinated against bullets through witchcraft.[7] A Nigerian man boasted that his bullet-proof charm protected him from harm. He died, however, when he tested the charm by asking someone to shoot him.[8] Similarly, the spirits the villagers believed controlled the rain are elements of the middle realm.

The centrality of the middle zone in folk religions creates the irony that causes it to be known as "the excluded middle."[9] Missionaries and people who manage change across cultures exclude it from their focus despite its importance to the accomplishment of change. Many mission-

5. Shems Friedlander and Al-Hajj Shaikh Muzaffereddin, *Ninety-Nine Names of Allah: The Beautiful Names* (Lagos, Nigeria: Islamic Publications Bureau, 1978), 32. This is an example of a folk Islamic practice in an animistic culture; it should not be interpreted as an orthodox Islamic belief or practice.

6. Brian Bonner, "More Hmong Children Willing to Use Court System," *Knight-Ridder News Service,* 26 November 1995.

7. John Schenk, "Drugs and Witchcraft Join Mozambique's Sorrows," *World Vision–Africa,* 20–24 April 1992.

8. "Man's Faith in Bullet Proof Charm Proves Fatal," *The (Johannesburg) Star,* 23 March 1999, 5.

9. Hiebert, "Flaw of the Excluded Middle," 196–98.

aries believe that people of traditional cultures do not have a religion because they do not practice what the missionaries believe is a formal religion. Charles Darwin, for example, observed that traditional people had neither religion nor religious impulses.[10] The informants of E. B. Tylor, who were also oblivious to the middle zone, made similar conclusions because they could find no apparent evidence of structured worship. The people they observed definitely believed in a high god, but the middle realm provided the vitality of their faith, not religious ceremony.

Until recently, the middle zone was not part of the cultural narratives of modern Western cultures. Missionaries addressed the top zone with truth and the bottom zone with efficiency, but they did not address the power of the middle zone. They excluded the middle because they did not realize that people understand "truth functionally rather than substantially."[11]

Folk religions are becoming increasingly normative in all the major religious of the world, including the Christian church. Christians throughout the world, in their struggle for survival, do not have the interest or the opportunity to develop the finer theological points of their faith, such as determining whether spirits control rain. Instead they assume that spirits control rain because they need a faith that works as well as one that empowers them to cope without rain when they need water. They exorcise spirits with the hope that rain will fall, while they are oblivious to any contradictions the practice might hold.

The pragmatic nature of folk religions creates the need for Christians to manage cultural change with truth and grace. Emile Durkheim, the sociologist of religion, said that "all religions are true"[12] simply because he believed religions were instruments through which anthropologists study cultures. He was correct only in an instrumental sense. Religions provide a framework through which to study cultures and understand how people survive in their environments. However, efforts to manage cultural change from the perspective of redemption create the need to discern how the work of Jesus Christ is expressed in particular cultures. One way of doing this is by examining how theologians through the history of the church have attempted to understand the nature of the atonement.

---

10. Alan Neely, *Christian Mission: A Case Study Approach* (Maryknoll, N.Y.: Orbis, 1995), 91.
11. William A. Dyrness, *Invitation to Cross-Cultural Theology: Case Studies in Vernacular Theologies* (Grand Rapids: Zondervan, 1992), 160.
12. Emile Durkheim, *The Elementary Forms of Religious Life,* trans. Karen E. Fields (New York: Free Press, 1995), 2.

The Truth of the Atonement

The interpretation of the atonement governs how Christians manage the religious aspects of cultural change. Christians are in broad agreement that we receive salvation through the crucifixion of Christ; the central question concerning salvation is why we do. From a legal or political perspective, the crucifixion of Jesus has no unique meaning; it was one of the thousands of executions that took place in Palestine during its Roman occupation. Why then do Christians believe that the death of Christ has salvific value?

Christians have answered this question with four major views of the atonement. It is considered to be a ransom, a substitution, a moral influence, or the victory of Christ (*Christus Victor*). In this section, I will define each of these theories and propose *Christus Victor* as the theory that is most conducive to addressing the religious aspects of managing cultural change.

Ransom Theory

The idea of the atonement as a ransom is based on several biblical passages, including Jesus' teaching in Matthew 20:28 that "the Son of Man did not come to be served, but to serve, and to give his life as a ransom for many." The original intent of this passage is that Christ redeemed or liberated people from the powers of the *kosmos*. The powers are not absolutely evil or demonic; they are necessary for people to live as human beings, and they participate in the redemptive work of Christ. Due to the influence of Gnosticism, however, this view is vulnerable to depicting the ransom of Christ as payment to Satan, or the devil, for the liberation of humankind, implying that the *kosmos* is the dominion of Satan. The ransom theory of the atonement, then, depicts Christ as the price paid, presumably to Satan, for the liberation of humankind. H. D. McDonald moves toward this notion by stating that through the atonement "death has been deprived of its sting and the devil stripped of his dominion."[13] He continues, "For Christ saw mankind held in captivity to sin, death and the devil."[14] J. Denny Weaver, while not affirming this position, observes its apex by noting that the ransom theory of the atonement is the "price paid to Satan for freeing the sinners Satan held captive. With his resurrection, Christ then escaped the clutches of Satan, and sinners were

13. H. D. McDonald, *The New Testament Concept of Atonement: The Gospel of the Calvary Event* (Cambridge: Lutterworth; Grand Rapids: Baker, 1994), 39.
14. Ibid., 90.

freed from Satan's power."[15] While this position has gained popularity in some contemporary evangelical communities, it has a few theological flaws. First, in paying a ransom to Satan, it assumes that Satan has rights that must be respected.[16] Second, it suggests that God used deception with Satan to liberate humankind. Orthodox theology, however, does not imply this since God is above the ways of his fallen creation.

The third flaw in the ransom theory is the implicit assumption that the work of Christ is limited to spiritual issues, such as salvation, but it does not extend atonement to social, political, or economic structures. The view detaches faith in Christ from ethics.[17] Yet, one major ethical premise of Christianity is that the death of Christ influences every aspect of life, and it governs the moral implications of how Christians proclaim the kingdom of God by engaging in the transformation of the *kosmos*. Colossians 1:19 affirms that "God was pleased to have all his fullness dwell in him, and through him to reconcile to himself all things, whether things on earth or things in heaven." The ransom theory, in its popular form, limits the work of Christ to the salvation of souls, rather than extending it to proclaim the redemption of the *kosmos*.

Substitution Theory

The substitution theory, the inverse of the ransom theory, portrays "Christ's death as an act performed on behalf of sinners to satisfy the honor of an offended God or as the payment of a penalty required of sinners by God's law."[18] It postulates that "sinners stand guilty before a Holy God,"[19] and "only a perfect Jesus who did not have to die as punishment for sin could use his death as a merit transferable to sinners."[20] This theory is an improvement over the ransom theory because it focuses on the moral purity of God. However, its weakness lies in affirming that the "work of Christ consists not in what *Christ shows to us*, but in what Christ *does for us*."[21] This view, like the ransom

---

15. J. Denny Weaver, *Keeping Salvation Ethical: Mennonite and Amish Theology in the Late Nineteenth Century* (Scottdale, Pa.: Herald, 1997), 35–36.

16. Ibid., 36.

17. Ibid., 46.

18. Ibid., 36.

19. Ronald J. Sider, *One-Sided Christianity: Uniting the Church to Heal a Lost and Broken World* (Grand Rapids: Zondervan, 1993), 95.

20. Gabriel Fackre, *The Christian Story: A Narrative Interpretation of Basic Christian Doctrine* (Grand Rapids: Eerdmans, 1996), 126.

21. Ibid., 124, italics in the original.

theory of the atonement, separates salvation from ethics and gives Christians little or no reason to participate in the conquest of evil or to transform the structures of the *kosmos* that are governed by these powers.

Moral Influence Theory

The moral influence theory, also known as the subjective theory, was developed by Peter Abelard (A.D. 1079–1142) because he disliked the emphasis on God's stern judgment in the satisfaction theory. Abelard affirmed that Jesus died to demonstrate God's love; however, he did not believe that the death of Christ influenced how God related to humankind. Instead, he believed the "change that results from that loving death is not on God but in the subjective consciousness of the sinners, who repent and cease their rebellion and running away from God."[22] This view of the atonement is implied in various models of reconciliation; it focuses "on changing the hearts and minds of human beings so that they may love God and love their neighbors."[23]

The moral influence view is conducive to managing change across cultures because it has a strong ethical focus. It takes seriously Jesus' emphasis on transforming the *kosmos* and proclaiming the kingdom of God. It accentuates the moral life and teachings of Jesus and beckons his followers to act on what Jesus showed to us as well as on what he did for us. While Christ died for humankind, he also demonstrated the moral behavior and ethical values that should characterize the people who call upon the name of Christ.

This theory addresses the need to unite atonement and ethics, connecting Jesus not only with Christian salvation but also with Christian behavior. However, this theory is also flawed. One major criticism is its suggestion that "the fundamental human problem is ignorance,"[24] not sin, and its "hope for changing human hearts seems pale and weak."[25] This theory suggests that "something more is needed for atonement than illumination and inspiration,"[26] which is an atonement theory that disempowers the force of evil by proclaiming Christ's victory over it.

22. Weaver, *Keeping Salvation Ethical,* 38.
23. Fackre, *Christian Story,* 123.
24. Sider, *One-Sided Christianity,* 94.
25. J. Denny Weaver, "Christus Victor, Nonviolence and Other Religions," in *Mennonite Theology in the Face of Modernity: Essays in Honor of Gordon D. Kaufman,* ed. Alain Epp Weaver (North Newton, Kans.: Bethel College, 1996), 180.
26. Fackre, *Christian Story,* 124.

Christus Victor Theory

The fourth view of the atonement, *Christus Victor,* is based on Colossians 2:15, that Christ "having disarmed the powers and authorities . . . made a public spectacle of them, triumphing over them by the cross." It sees the work of Christ as defeating and redeeming God's enemies, which can be spiritual beings or such things as the social, economic, and political structures that comprise the elements of the *kosmos* and estrange both people and societies from God. One increasingly popular view of this theory is that it is a description of a conflict between structures in the ancient world, first, between Jesus and the political and religious structures of his day and, second, between the church and the empire; the same powers that confronted and killed Jesus continued to challenge the church.[27] The *Christus Victor* view of the atonement recognizes that while the powers in Jerusalem and Rome were particular, Christ's victory over them at the crucifixion is universal. The primary strength of this theory is "the rightful place it gives to the resurrection of Christ"[28] and the importance it places on Christ's influence on social, political, and economic structures. It recognizes that "Christ is Lord over natural and supernatural powers as well as persons; his Kingdom is cosmic in scope."[29] This view, unlike the others, provides a christological rationale for Christians to believe that Christ can transform culture.

The primary weakness of the *Christus Victor* theory is its focus on the nonpersonal nature of sin.[30] Its critics suggest that it fosters a view of objective evil as something that exists in nature and history, not within the depths of the human soul, and they conclude that "a fuller understanding of [this theory] must include liberation from the sin of the self as well as from the powers and principalities of evil."[31] Parallel to this is the criticism that this theory of atonement is secular in nature; its vitality is located, not in some unembodied entity that we classify as spiritual, but in the physical elements of creation.

While the criticisms should be taken seriously, I want to propose two major strengths that commend this theory to managing change across cultures. First, it recognizes that sin is structural as well as personal, pre-

27. Weaver, "Christus Victor, Nonviolence and Other Religions," 188.
28. Fackre, *Christian Story,* 129.
29. Ibid., 130.
30. The weaknesses of each of these theories has influenced theologians to combine them. Some theologians have developed a Messianic model of the atonement by combining substitution, moral influence, and *Christus Victor.* See Sider, *One-Sided Christianity,* 97.
31. Fackre, *Christian Story,* 130–31.

venting people from separating salvation from ethics. Second, its secular nature enhances its validity. Secularization, the influence that religion has on all areas of life, is an affirmation that God works through all elements of the *kosmos* to redeem it. The incarnation affirms this truth. Christians cannot ignore the presence of sin in social structures, whether sacred or secular. This expression of sin beckons us to discern the nature of these powers and affirm that they do not exist beyond the redemptive power of God. The narrative of God's redemptive relationship allows people to transform the story of their relationship with the powers of sin by confronting them.

The Nature of Power Encounters

Power encounters have become central topics of interest in mission studies in recent years. They raise many questions about the nature of Christ's power as well as about the nature of evil. The major question concerning power encounters is whether they communicate the redemptive power of Christ. Do they connect the salvation of Christ with empowering people to have victory over their perceptions of the elements of the *kosmos?* Do they empower people to see that the power of Christ is not simply a greater power than that of local shamans but is the power of God's redemptive relationship with creation? My contention is that the *Christus Victor* view of the atonement is central to empowering Christians to engage in power encounters.

Power Encounters as Initiation Rites

The centrality of the *Christus Victor* view of the atonement in power encounters is illustrated in the writings of Alan R. Tippet, a former missionary to Polynesia, who coined the term and who encouraged converts to Christianity to engage in them. He observed that "most of the world's people are power-oriented"[32] and need "*a rite of separation* from the old ties and loyalties,"[33] and he believed that Christ had victory over the powers—the elements of the *kosmos*—and liberated people from them. He realized that people live under both the real and the imagined influences of the middle realm, and they "respond to Christ most readily through power demonstrations."[34] He thought that an "encounter had to take

32. Alan R. Tippett, *People Movements in Southern Polynesia: Studies in the Dynamics of Church-Planting and Growth in Tahiti, New Zealand, Tonga, and Samoa* (Chicago: Moody, 1971), 206.
33. Alan R. Tippett, "Trends in the Theology of Mission and Their Effects on the Missionary Church Today," in *Some Anthropological Aspects of Missiology, 1978–1979* (Pasadena: Fuller Theological Seminary, 1995), 80.
34. Tippett, *People Movements,* 206.

place on the level of daily life against those powers which dealt with the relevant problems of gardening, fishing, war, security, food supply and the personal life crises."[35] As initiation rites that liberated converts to Christianity from bondage to former religions, people had to engage in power encounters to exercise their moral responsibility over the aspects of their lives they previously attributed to the supernatural powers. While Tippet did not use Colossians 2:15 specifically in relation to power encounters, it serves to substantiate his practice. The power encounter certainly expresses the freedom the apostle Paul wrote about in Galatians 5:1, "It is for freedom that Christ has set us free. Stand firm, then, and do not let yourselves be burdened again by a yoke of slavery."

Tippet emphasized that the power encounter is to be not an exorcism of spirits by missionaries but a demonstration of converts' freedom from the fear of old gods. Converts did this by burning charms, refusing to participate in traditional rites, and breaking the taboos. For instance, a convert named Kapiolani did this by climbing a sacred fire mountain and defying the fire goddess, Pele.[36] According to Tippett, power encounters must be voluntary acts of faith that help converts to liberate themselves through Christ from the elements in their cultures that enslaved them and to serve as a witness to their community.[37] Because they are rites of passage from the old religion to Christianity, missionaries are not to participate in them. This would destroy their very purpose. For instance, Tippett cited one incident of a missionary in the Solomon Islands who chopped down a banyan tree, which had served as a symbol of spiritual power. After the tree was down, the missionary "claimed victory in the name of Jesus" and "erected a cross, which, in the eyes of the villagers, became a functional substitute for the tree, the symbol of power which claimed their allegiance."[38]

The villagers interpreted the meaning of the cross according to their worldview. They might have seen the cross, in contrast to the banyan tree, as a more powerful spiritual symbol, probably because they interpreted the white missionary as more powerful than they were. In that sense, however, the cross did not convey either the message of redemption through Christ or the moral nature of sin. The degree of allegiance the villagers committed to the cross as a symbol of power is debatable.

35. Alan R. Tippett, *Solomon Islands Christianity: A Study in Growth and Obstruction* (New York: Friendship, 1967), 5.
36. Tippett, "Trends in the Theology of Mission," 80.
37. Ibid., 82–83.
38. Tippett, *Solomon Islands Christianity,* 101.

When they practiced cannibalism, they put white people at the top of their food chain, believing that anyone who ate them received their *manna*, or spiritual power. The cross may have been just another symbol of that *manna*; they were in no way compelled to commit themselves to Jesus Christ and to reject another source of power.[39]

The power encounter became a dynamic equivalent to baptism as a public profession of faith. Through the power encounter, the converts were dying to their former ways and accepting new life in Christ. Many of their friends and relatives, watching them defy the old powers, expected them to die. Their survival, however, destroyed the old powers by enabling them to embrace the truth of God through Jesus Christ. The power encounters that Tippett advocated were informed by a theological conviction that Christians had accepted the truth, which had set them free from enslavement to their cultural elements.

Power Encounters as Development Projects

Development work itself can be a form of a power encounter. For instance, development practitioners are often faced with the dilemma of drilling wells or building roads on land believed to be cursed. The local villagers might think that anyone who walks on the cursed land will become ill or die. If the villagers, however, participate in drilling the wells or building the roads, they will be forced to confront the powers they believe have cursed the land.

The research project I was part of in Mozambique bears witness to the validity of this kind of power encounter. The goal of the research was to learn whether development activities had an evangelistic impact on a particular region. The villagers were given two sets of questions to answer. The first set of questions asked the villagers if the project had any impact on transforming the spirituality of the community. The villagers answered that people attended church more often, they prayed regularly, and the instances of witchcraft and drunkenness were fewer. The second set of questions asked the villagers to list the development activities that made the greatest contribution to the village. These activities included agricultural work, sanitation, road construction, church support, literacy training, and Bible distribution. While conventional evangelical wisdom might cite Bible distribution and church support as the main contribution to the spiritual transformation of the village, over

39. Charles H. Kraft, "What Kind of Encounters Do We Need in Our Christian Witness?" *Evangelical Missions Quarterly* 25.3 (July 1991): 260.

90 percent of the villagers cited road construction as having the greatest spiritual impact.

The researchers discovered several reasons for this. First, because many of the roads in the region were destroyed during the recent wars, the road-building project met an essential need in the community and showed that Christians—and God—cared about the elementary needs of the community. Second, the road building also gave the development practitioners the opportunity to witness to the villagers. Road building in most developing countries is a labor-intensive effort. Without modern equipment, hundreds and sometimes thousands of people participate in the construction. The road crews prayed and sang hymns each morning, bearing a powerful witness to the villagers who participated in the project.

The third reason is that many of the new roads went through cursed land, which gave the road crews—and the participants from the local villages—an opportunity to engage in a power encounter with the spiritual forces that cursed the land. The road crews not only transformed the elements of the villager's *kosmos* when they entered the land without dying but also empowered the villagers to address and overcome their fear of the old powers. The road-building project was an encounter with the cultural elements of the village, although incidental to it. The project participants did not affirm or deny the presence of any spiritual powers or forces on the land. However, they challenged the villagers to transform their worldview by building the roads on land thought to be cursed, hence displaying the redemptive power of God.

The Truth of Christ and Power Encounters

Without a theological foundation, power encounters can suggest that power produces truth. Power encounters are primarily expressions of faith, and while they don't produce truth, they are statements of truth. A demonstration of power has little significance and cannot be properly interpreted without "a knowledge of the source of, and the reason for, the power."[40] Cross-cultural workers are obliged to learn about the place of power in the cultures they serve as well as about the place of power encounters in Jesus' ministry. Jesus discerned the truth about reality before he displayed power over it. He was not able to do miracles in Nazareth,

40. Ibid., 261.

except for laying his hands on a few people, because prophets were not honored in their own hometown (Mark 6:4).

The power encounters that Alan Tippett encouraged had integrity because the converts who engaged in them had to separate themselves from the elements of their cultures. If Tippett himself had engaged in the encounters, the integrity of the act would have been suspect from the perspective of cross-cultural Christian ethics. The people would have thought that as a foreigner, he had power over the elements of their culture. A power encounter that begins with truth obligates Christians to clarify their beliefs.

From Spirits to Koinonia

While holding a workshop in a southern Africa culture, I used the case study of the West African Islamic village that believed spirits controlled the rainfall to explain the theology of power encounters. One astute participant gave a unique interpretation to the case study. He explained that even though he believed in demon possession, he found no evidence that spirits had power over the rain. He suggested that the Christian development managers should have provided a witness of their faith to the community by praying for rain and observing a limited fast, and he cited 2 Chronicles 7:14 as support for his idea: "If my people, who are called by my name, will humble themselves and pray and seek my face and turn from their wicked ways, then will I hear from heaven and will forgive their sin and will heal their land."

The workshop participant's biblical evidence for his solution to the predicament in the West African Islamic village came from an Old Testament narrative that took repentance, prayer, and fasting seriously. His own community also took them seriously, but its rituals straddled the line between magic and redemption by causing things to happen and preparing the people to accept the inevitable. The rituals bonded the community into a holy people, who could respond to God's gifts whether they be rainfall or communal solidarity.

His presentation, however, needed clarification. In the Old Testament the land was the unifying symbol of the community. Israel believed that the land belonged to God (Lev. 25:25); it was inseparable from their "consciousness of their unique covenant relationship with Yahweh."[41] The symbol of God's covenant relationship changed when the church replaced Israel as the covenant community, and fellowship, or *koinonia*, be-

41. Christopher J. H. Wright, *God's People in God's Land: Family, Land, and Property in the Old Testament* (Grand Rapids: Eerdmans, 1990), 22–23.

came the symbol of the new covenant. Christian fellowship in the New Testament fulfilled the theological and ethical functions that the land fulfilled in the Old Testament[42] because of its social, ethical, and economic implications. The ethos of the Christian faith is not simply to deliver people from suffering or even to avoid suffering but to bear each other's burden, in order to make the pains of life endurable. The health of a community facilitates the healing of the land. When functioning properly, the people of a community can effectively cope with their environment either directly or indirectly and bring healing to both themselves and the land.

The problem of the West African village and the spiritual control of rainfall elicits a response that has several layers of meaning. We could say that the place was occupied by territorial spirits, which needed merely to be exorcised like the Gerasene demoniac in Luke 8:26–39. This superficial solution ignores the complexity of evil. If territorial spirits are in control, they are not there accidentally. The community has been fragmented in some way, presumably by the sins of the people. As Charles H. Kraft points out, the word *territories* "refers more to *the people* than to the geography."[43] The problem, therefore, is in the community, not necessarily in the land or the territory. The people are not passive victims in the control of territorial spirits; they must take an active role in nurturing the welfare of both the community and the environment.

Jesus' healing of the Gerasene demoniac offers guidelines to solving the problem. After he ministered to the demoniac, the people responded with fear and asked him to leave the region. The man who was the demoniac, however, wanted to follow Jesus, but Jesus sent him back into the community so that his presence could serve as a symbol of the moral healing that the community would have to undergo to become whole. Their fear indicates that they were not ready to change. The demoniac, evidently, absorbed a legion of pathologies and fears within the community,[44] and once healed, the demoniac became a necessary part of its elements. The Gerasenes needed him in order to transform their *kosmos*, which, like all changes and transitions, was met with fear and trem-

42. See Christopher J. H. Wright, *An Eye for an Eye: The Place of Old Testament Ethics Today* (Downers Grove, Ill.: InterVarsity, 1983), 100.

43. Animism or Authority?" in *Spiritual Power and Missions: Raising the Issues,* ed. Edward Rommen, Evangelical Missiological Society Series, no. 3 (Pasadena: William Carey Library, 1995), 131.

44. The purpose of this analysis is not to speculate about the reality of the demons in the man. The name Legion is one of the many symbols in the story that need to be interpreted to grasp the full meaning of the text. That analysis is beyond the scope of this book.

bling. The healing of the demoniac challenged the community to heal it-self because it no longer had him to serve as a scapegoat. Jesus' act of healing the demoniac allowed him to encounter the powers in the community that demonized him. What took place between the Gerasenes and the healed demoniac was a true power encounter because his return insulted the integrity of its welfare. They had to transform the elements of their culture to maintain the balance of harmony that the demoniac previously provided by serving as a distraction for them.

The people in the community, having lost their scapegoat, were over-come with fear, a natural response of people required to transform and redefine their lives with a different story that is about *them*, not the *other*. When Desmond Tutu chaired the Truth and Reconciliation Commission of postapartheid South Africa, he noted that people found liberation in telling their story.[45] The hope for the healing of the Gerasene community also lay in their ability both to transform and to tell their stories.

Cultural Change and People of Other Faiths

Jesus' ministry in the region of the Gerasenes sets an example of how Christians are to relate to people who practice other faiths. The Gera-senes were Gentiles who lived in the Decapolis, Greek city-states located southeast of Galilee on the edge of the Syrian Desert. The presence of pigs in the community indicated that self-respecting Jews would avoid these cities. However, Jesus visited them and ministered to an immediate symptom of their unhealthy community by healing a deranged, naked man, who ran through the streets, greeting visitors and asking them not to torment him.

Modern people who read the Gospel accounts of this story focus on the demoniac.[46] However, these accounts reveal more information about the community than about the demoniac. The relationship between the two can be demonstrated by rephrasing an African definition of being: "I am because we are; he was because they were." The demoniac can be un-derstood only within the context of his community. His presence in the streets of the village indicate that the social harmony of the community was fragmented; for some reason, it could not create a place for him. An encounter with Jesus prevents the people from resorting to scapegoats;

45. Desmond Tutu, *No Future without Forgiveness* (Parktown, R.S.A.: Random House South Africa, 1999), 127.

46. The Gospel accounts differ about the number of demoniacs. Matthew 8:28–34 mentions two, while Mark 5:1–20 and Luke 8:26–39 each mention only one. I will follow the Luke rendition of the story.

instead they have to transform their social structures with the truth of Christ. By healing the man, Jesus initiated the transforming process for the community.

Transforming the structures of the culture is the central approach to addressing other religions in managing cultural change. This transformative effort is concerned with theological doctrine, but this alone is inadequate to foster sustainable change. Lasting change occurs only when people are empowered through the redemptive work of God through Christ to transform the elements of their cultures that disempower them. The Christians who worked with the West African village had the opportunity to lead the villagers through a process of discerning the nature of their beliefs about the spirits and of empowering them to transform their cultural elements by finding alternatives to living in an environment that suffered from inadequate rainfall. If the Christians had engaged in a power encounter with the spirits, the villagers would have been misled about its true intent. The central point of Jesus' healing of the demoniac was to illustrate his redemption, which was possible for everyone in the community.

The Christian encounter with people of other religions should be an effort to empower them to live in the freedom of Christ. Christ is redeeming them and their cultures, calling them to be free from the elements that distract them from realizing the fullness of their redemption and salvation through Christ, who gives people the freedom as well as the power to submit to the sovereignty of God, so that they can pray for rain, experiment with drought-resistant crops, develop another economic base, and find food relief, among other things.

The elements, in contrast, regardless of the forms they take, whether religions, philosophies, or ideologies, become absolutes in the context of cultures, claiming there is only one way to navigate through the struggles of life. Christ triumphed over the powers, making spectacles of them and giving people the freedom to explore alternative solutions to the challenges of life within the boundaries of redemption. The Christians who faced the challenge of the West African village had no reason to engage in a power encounter with the spirits. However, they had every reason to explain why they believed that the atonement of Christ, a central theme in the narrative of God's relationship with creation, gave them power over the spirits.

6

The Powers:
Transformation through Subordination

Submit yourselves for the Lord's sake to every authority instituted among men: whether to the king, as the supreme authority, or to governors.

1 Peter 2:13–14

Everyone must submit himself to the governing authorities, for there is no authority except that which God has established.

Romans 13:1

MALONE: *Me Father died of starvation in the black 47. Maybe you've heard of it?*
VIOLET: *The Famine?*
MALONE: *No, the starvation. When a country is full of food and exporting it, there can be no famine.*

George Bernard Shaw

Can the earth feed all its people? That, I'm afraid, is strictly a political question.

T. R. Reid

Political Transformation and Global Hunger

Droughts are divine and famines are fabricated. I first heard this pithy observation when I participated in a drought surveillance trip to East Africa in the late 1980s. During those years, the physical environment lost its ability to support life, causing thousands of people and animals to die. In 1984 the relief workers described the area as a "moonscape"; the land itself was smoking and dust was everywhere.[1] Many people, suffering from hunger, watched helplessly as their family members and animals succumbed to the unforgiving terms of nature. They did not, however, go without a struggle. I watched one farmer hoeing a plot of parched land, trying to cultivate a few stocks of sorghum. A family in the same village placed their goats in acacia trees, nourishing them on acacia leaves, the only vegetation in the land. Nearby, a famished woman, holding an emaciated child, shook her breast, protesting, "No milk; no milk." The breast, like the land, simply had nothing more to offer.

The drought generated an abundance of news reports, many of which were misleading. They portrayed the drought as the cause of the famine, suggesting that the lack of rain caused a crop failure. One journalist accused Africa of being an unsuccessful producer of food.[2] Reports of this nature, accompanied by pictures of farmers trying to farm their parched land, led television audiences to believe that Africans were starving because the land was unfit for agriculture.

The stories, however, are only half true. The people were starving during the drought, but the drought did not cause the famine; "a year's drought is within the capacity of the peasant to survive."[3] Modern famines are generally not caused by drought but by tyranny or violence.[4] As the Ethiopian Relief and Rehabilitation Commission discovered "the 1984–85 drought was a political crisis characterized more appropriately by war than by drought."[5] Ethiopia is one of many African governments that spend nearly eight bil-

1. Mulugeta Abebe, "Perspective on Hunger: Getting Ethiopia Back on Its Feet," *Los Angeles Times*, 27 November 1998, sec. B, p. 7.

2. Blaine Harden, *Africa: Dispatches from a Fragile Continent*, (London: Harper Collins, 1993), 15. This report is erroneous because the best agricultural land in Africa is used to grow tropical flowers, fruits, vegetables, tea, and coffee that are shipped to Europe.

3. Myles F. Harris, *Breakfast in Hell: A Doctor's Eyewitness Account of the Politics of Hunger in Ethiopia* (New York: Poseidon, 1987), 160.

4. David Beckmann and Arthur Simon, *Grace at the Table: Ending Hunger in God's World* (Downers Grove, Ill.: InterVarsity, 1999), 19.

5. "The Addis Ababa Statement on Famine in Ethiopia: Learning from the Past to Prepare for the Future," 18 March 1995. Online at http://www.sas.upenn.edu/African_Studies/Hornet/Ben_InterAF.html.

lion dollars a year on weapons and military maintenance,[6] which is more than they spend on housing, health, and social welfare.[7] They find, however, for all the expenditure, they are no more secure.[8]

While droughts reduce the availability of food, politicians with economic priorities actually decide who eats during times of scarcity. Ethiopians were starving, not because they could not produce food, but because they did not have the political power to have food sent to them. Dawit Wolde Giorgis, a former Ethiopian government official, wrote about the difficulty of convincing the leaders that there was a widespread famine; "it is still incredible to me that the RRC's [Relief and Rehabilitation Commission] most difficult task was convincing its own leaders of the very existence of a widespread famine."[9]

Our surveillance team became acutely aware that political alienation was a central factor in the East African drought when the provincial governor, our host, treated us every evening to the finest food in the region. His cordiality and hospitality, however, was for the purpose of acquiring foreign aid. The governor was in a tough spot because he had fallen out of political favor with the military commanders who occupied the area. Since he could not appeal to them to provide food to his constituents, he invited us to his region without their support. The cost of feeding us so well was an investment of a desperate man, who had taken the risk of catching the military's wrath. The provincial governor's efforts to relieve his constituents from the threats of starvation were successful for a time. We agreed to deliver several truckloads of wheat and vegetable oil to the region as a symbolic effort of concern, but we knew this would not solve the hunger problem. The sustainable solution was advocating political power for the people.

While waiting to deliver the commodities, I became keenly aware of a constant criticism of food aid—it always comes too late. I was confident, however, that our commodities would arrive in time to do some good. But on the day we were to deliver the food, we found soldiers surrounding the warehouse where it was stored. When they refused to move and even threatened me when I tried to reason with them, I decided to see the military general. He had invited me to his office several months ear-

6. George B. N. Ayittey, *Africa in Chaos* (London: Macmillan, 1998), 173.

7. George Kinoti, *Hope for Africa and What the Christian Can Do* (Nairobi: International Bible Society, Africa, 1994), 39.

8. Ayittey, *Africa in Chaos*, 173.

9. Dawit Wolde Giorgis, *Red Tears: War, Famine, and Revolution in Ethiopia* (Trenton, N.J.: Red Sea, 1989), 134–36.

lier, assuring me that he would personally take care of any problems that might arise during my visit to the area.

I explained the predicament to the general, under the watchful eye of guards armed with firearms that ranged from handguns to anti-aircraft weapons. He responded to my concern that his soldiers were withholding our commodities from starving people by explaining that he had purchased them from the citizens through the regional governor, so that they were no longer the people's but his. He continued that he and the governor established a credit plan whereby the governor would purchase the commodities from the citizens for whom they were intended and then sell them to the military. In return the citizens could get the money to buy the food they needed. I told him that I would appeal to the international aid community to examine his credit record. He assured me that the commodities woud be returned. I left thinking the story had a positive ending. The commodities were returned, and a crew of men loaded them onto trucks and delivered them. After several weeks, I tried to track the commodities to determine if they did any good. However, I never completed this task, because a war had started, and the military had looted the entire region. The project disintegrated.

Press coverage of global hunger invariably suggests that hunger is an agricultural problem that governments are powerless to solve. Many press reports maintain that too many people depend on local resources inadequate to meet their needs. But this is not true; the global food reserve is sufficient to supply every person on earth "with 3000 calories a day—equal to the consumption of an average American."[10] The food produced in the 1980s was more than enough to feed the six billion people anticipated by the year 2000.[11] The problem is not the amount but the inaccessibility of food, making the distribution of food a problem of justice rather than agriculture.[12]

Political transformation is central to addressing global hunger because of the inadequate means for justly distributing food throughout the world, a justice issue that affects the world's poor, not the rich.[13] The ma-

10. The Institute for Food and Development Policy, *Six Myths and Facts about Hunger* (1993).

11. Jon Bennet, *The Hunger Machine: The Politics of Food* (Yorkshire, England: Polity, 1987), 18.

12. My emphasis on hunger as a political problem does not ignore that many countries, such as Ethiopia, have worked toward achieving food security by supporting agricultural development. However, the nature of most famines in the world are political, not agricultural.

13. Ronald J. Sider, *Rich Christians in an Age of Hunger: Moving from Affluence to Generosity,* 20th anniversary ed. (Dallas: Word, 1997), 7.

jority of the people in the world eat adequately, not because of the agricultural production of their societies, but because their political structures are equipped to foster the delivery of food to them at affordable prices.[14] Myles Harris, who went to Ethiopia to participate in the family relief efforts of the International Red Cross in Addis Ababa, the capital city of Ethiopia, woke up one morning, asking where the famine was; he felt "as if people were describing events in another country, not here in Ethiopia. There were no signs of food shortages in the city."[15] Africa's food shortages, ironically, afflict rural farmers who produce food, not the urban dwellers who consume it.

Christians must address global hunger as a political issue because it is embodied in the structures of individual communities. It challenges us to transform social structures by shifting the way we view the relationship between church and state. The narratives of Western cultures, which have hegemony in the global church, have influenced Christians not only to accept a subservient role toward the state but also to support its policies, often at the expense of fulfilling its own ministry. Christians are eager to feed the hungry and clothe the naked, but the subordination of religion to politics has made them hesitant to engage in political advocacy. Such an engagement, however, will challenge Christians to redefine the relationships between church and state in a manner that empowers churches to fulfill their leading functions in a redemptive manner.

The Enduring Problem of the Church

In his classic work, *Christ and Culture*, H. Richard Niebuhr defined the relationship between Christ and culture as the enduring problem of Christianity.[16] Niebuhr understood that the relationship between the church and the state was the primary indicator of the relationship between Christ and culture. Before we consider Niebuhr's ideas, we must first explore the four positions governments take toward religion; in each situation, the church has a subordinate role toward the state.

Governments and Religion

The first of the four is the Marxist position of severing religious institutions from the state. For instance, the Marxist governments in Mo-

14. Amartya Sen took this point one step further, arguing that there was actually an increase in food production in Ethiopia during the famine of the 1970s (*Poverty and Famines: An Essay on Entitlement and Deprivation* [New York: Oxford University Press, 1981], 92).

15. *Breakfast in Hell*, 44.

16. New York: Harper & Row, 1951, 11.

zambique and Ethiopia banned most churches and mosques and persecuted many Christians and Muslims. This separation assumes that the principles of government are value-free. This pretense, however, is unsuccessful because governments still need to define the values of their policies and do so by grafting them into the narrative of a philosophical, religious, or moral tradition. Governments are not immune to the moral consequences of their policies and decisions. For example, when the Ethiopian government had a choice to purchase either food or military weapons during the famine of the mid-1980s, they chose weapons. This choice was not morally neutral. In contrast, the values of a religious narrative might have empowered a church to exercise its leading function by purchasing bread; it might have also given the government the moral foundation it needed to survive.

The second position is religious pluralism, which characterizes most democratic republics in the world. Its central value is to allow citizens the free choice of religious belief and practice. Religious pluralism seems effective. Its shortcomings, however, reveal themselves when religious groups of one sort believe the state is discriminating against them. The Nigerian democratic government, for example, has been accused of bias against Muslims in the north and against Christians in the south. The future stability of that government will depend on its ability to fulfill its leading function of providing order by balancing its allegiance between Muslims, Christians, and other religious groups.

The third position governments take toward religion is one of an unofficial tie between the state and a particular religious group, which is vulnerable to corrupting the leading function of churches. In this relationship, religious leaders receive favors for giving ecclesiastical endorsements to political policies. This loose association characterizes the state and church in Rwanda, where the church exchanged its moral and fiduciary functions for political prestige, rendering itself powerless to exercise its moral authority in the society. Since the genocide in Rwanda in 1994, politicians in other countries have reassessed their view of church-state relationships. For instance, Mr. Mwai Kibaki, the former vice president of Kenya, commented that "church leaders should not spend their time praising politicians; we have enough people to praise us. Your task is to correct us when we go wrong and need to be reminded of the justice of God, and to pray for us."[17] He asked the churches to exercise their

17. Laurent Mbanda, *Committed to Conflict: The Destruction of the Church in Rwanda* (London: SPCK, 1997), 116.

leading functions of discerning whether political institutions, or any political element of society, are trustworthy and moral.

The fourth position is a state religion. Many ancient Christian churches and older Protestant denominations function in this category, including the Coptic, Orthodox, Anglican, and Lutheran traditions. Islamic republics are also characterized by this relationship. Nations with a state religion are often intolerant toward people who practice other religions. The Sudanese government, for example, in favoring Islam as its state religion, "has forced Christians to choose between renouncing their faith or renouncing food, education, jobs, even life."[18] A school serving twelve hundred predominantly Christian children was destroyed by the government.[19]

Christ and Culture

While states have defined their relationship with churches, churches have also defined their relationships with states. While they are sometimes complementary, they can also be conflicting. Niebuhr's book identifies five positions that churches use to define their relationship with the state.

His first category, Christ of culture, is characteristic of liberal Protestants. From a global perspective, it represents many European and North American communities, where Christianity is embedded in cultural and political traditions. These churches often perceive that their function is to support the government and see little or no tension between their faith and their culture. For instance, church leaders become chaplains to the state; churches display national flags and pray for God's blessings on the nation's wars and political conflicts.

Niebuhr's second category, Christ above culture, is characteristic of the Roman Catholic and Anglican traditions and continues to be prevalent in many cultures where the majority of the citizens are Roman Catholic or Anglican. The Roman Catholic Church, perceiving its mandate to be above culture, prefers to refrain from engaging in the political conflicts of a nation, and it takes a dim view of its priests who do get involved in politics. The liberation theologian Leonardo Boff and the U.S. Congressman Robert J. Drinan are among many priests whom Rome held accountable for their political involvement. The Rev. Drinan resigned from the U.S. Congress to honor his calling as a priest, and Leonardo Boff resigned his ordination.

18. Margaret Larom, "Sudan's Church Is Flourishing amid Poverty and War," *Episcopal News Service*, 19 March 1998, 2.

19. "Christian Buildings Razed in Sudan," *The Christian Century,* 2–9 June 1999, 609.

Niebuhr's third position, Christ and culture in paradox, is characteristic of the Protestant church in the United States, where people pride themselves on maintaining a separation between state and church, but integrate many expressions of nationalism and patriotism in their worship. Many Protestant congregations in the United States sing patriotic hymns and their sanctuaries display the U.S. flag. The government pays Protestant clergy to minister in government institutions, and many churches are faithful about observing national holidays, especially those that commemorate the nation's wars.

Niebuhr characterized Tertullian, Tolstoy, and the Anabaptists as characteristic of Christ against culture, his fourth category, which explains his conviction that the church's relationship with politics is a proxy indicator of its relationship with culture. He characterized Christians in this group as having a low view of politics and concluded that this attitude must extend to culture. This position, however, is more characteristic of modern missionaries, who generally have a low view of culture, causing them to be against the values and practices of the indigenous people of the countries they serve, preferring to destroy rather than to transform them. This position fuels much of the contempt held by critics of missionaries. It also makes cross-cultural ethical reflection a primary task of contemporary missions, in order to determine how cultural practices that insult redemptive values can be transformed.

Niebuhr viewed Augustine and Calvin as the best advocates of his fifth category, Christ transforming culture. He had a high view of Augustine's role as resident theologian to the Roman Empire and Calvin's attempt to make Geneva a Christian state. Niebuhr's use of Colossians 1:15–20, the "Hymn of the Cosmic Christ," to support his theory makes transformation look like reconciliation. The passage teaches that God through Christ will reconcile political structures. While Niebuhr did not explicitly reveal the category he favored, he encouraged Christians to recognize their "incapacity to give *the* Christian answer."[20] However, the attention he gave to Christ as the transformer of culture indicates his preference for this position. In contrast to the other positions, he offered no criticism of this one. He would have undoubtedly agreed that culture represents the *kosmos*, which becomes the New Jerusalem when transformed, empowering people to live in fellowship with God. As Niebuhr concluded, "The Kingdom of God is transformed culture."[21]

20. Niebuhr, *Christ and Culture*, 232.
21. Ibid., 228.

Niebuhr's Critics and Contributions

Although Niebuhr's book became the standard work on Christian ethics for a generation of leaders, primarily because it offered a framework for Christians to understand the relationship between faith and culture, it has received considerable criticism in recent years. [22] However, Niebuhr made two contributions to the debate that continue to be relevant to managing change across cultures. His first contribution, that politics is the primary indicator of the relationship between Christ and culture, postulates that salvation cannot be separated from ethics; as Gordon Kaufmann wrote, "The church . . . can never afford to separate herself from the world, for her mission to the world is of her very essence."[23] Such a view affirms that the transformation of social structures is the medium of the church's mission to the world. Christians cannot accept the status quo of any culture but must prevent the reification of social structures by discerning how the church can participate in their transformation.

Niebuhr's second contribution is the belief that there is a distinction between biblical ethics and Christian ethics; as he wrote, "Christ's answers to the problem of human culture is one thing, Christian answers are another."[24] The belief that biblical and Christian ethics are synonymous lingers in the narratives of the Western church—which serves as an umbrella for the global church—creating a useful tension between Christian ethics and biblical teaching. In one sense, the belief is beneficial because it recognizes that the redemptive narrative of Christianity includes twenty centuries of history that separate us from the earthly ministry of Christ. We cannot pretend to live in the *kosmos* of the first century, appropriating biblical teachings without applying them to our life situations. In another sense, this assumption raises the question of

22. See Glen H. Stassen, D. M. Yeager, and John Howard Yoder, "A New Vision," in *Authentic Transformation: A New Vision of Christ and Culture* (Nashville: Abingdon, 1996). The recent criticism of Niebuhr's book is well-deserved; he addressed it primarily to a United States audience who perceived its culture to be monolithic. In recent years, however, the perception has lost its validity.

23. *Nonresistance and Responsibility, and Other Mennonite Essays* (Newton, Kans.: Faith and Life, 1979), 52.

24. Niebuhr, *Christ and Culture*, 2. This teaching was undoubtedly influenced by H. Richard Niebuhr's brother, Reinhold, who considered Jesus' teachings "as finally and ultimately normative, but as not immediately applicable to the task of securing justice in a sinful world;" they have relevance for an eschatological, not a contemporary, era. (See "The Christian Witness to the Social and National Order," in *The Essential Reinhold Niebuhr: Selected Essays and Addresses*, ed. Robert McAfee Brown ([New Haven, Conn.: Yale University Press, 1986], 103.)

whether societies are obligated to maintain the same moral standards as individual people; moral people often live in immoral societies.[25] The tension creates the need for the church to participate in the transformation of social structures because an immoral society has diverse influences on moral people, and social structures will either stand or fall according to their moral convictions.

From Subservience to Transformative Subordination[26]

The tension between the morality of a person and the immorality of a society is the vitality of the church's role in managing cultural change. Churches that ignore their responsibility to transform social structures will become victims of their own negligence, which happened in Rwanda. The question, however, is how churches engage their society in a transforming relationship.

One approach through which churches can exercise their leading function in relation to governments is transformative subordination, which recognizes that Christians influence social institutions by simultaneously submitting to the leading functions of those institutions and maintaining the integrity of their own moral agency. The leading function of governments is to maintain order in society, which churches are mandated to support as they fulfill their own purpose.

Transformative subordination characterizes Jesus' relationship with the Roman government; he accommodated Pilate's role in maintaining order in Jerusalem by submitting to the Roman and Jewish laws to the point of the crucifixion. Jesus was the moral person living in an immoral society, submitting to the government while refusing to surrender his moral agency. Transformative subordination is likewise the position of the early church, where "the *subordinate* person in the social order is *addressed as a moral agent.*"[27] In a transformative relationship with political structures neither the person nor the church ever relinquishes independent moral agency. The person and the church are subordinate to the government for the purposes of social organization, but never for moral or ethical reasons.

25. John Hart, *Ethics and Technology: Innovation and Transformation in Community Contexts* (Cleveland: Pilgrim, 1997), 32.

26. The term is based on John Howard Yoder's "revolutionary subordination." While there is no difference in meaning between the two terms, "transformative" better serves the purposes of this book. See John Howard Yoder, *The Politics of Jesus* (Grand Rapids: Eerdmans, 1972), 163.

27. Ibid., 174.

Jesus, the apostles, and the faithful early church maintained their moral integrity, despite the legal consequences. Their example implies that "it is precisely because the Christian rejects 'governmental domination' that he can be subordinate to such domination, accepting the obligations of 'the voluntary subordination of one who knows that another regime is normative.' "[28]

Biblical Support for Transformative Subordination

The subordinate relationship of the church to the state has biblical support. In Romans 13:1–7, Paul teaches that everyone must submit to governmental authorities because they receive authority from God. Paul's teaching, which recognizes that the state has purposes instituted by God for the welfare of its citizens, has two qualifications often neglected in the contemporary interpretations of the passage.

The first qualification is that submission does not mean obedience. Christians can submit to a state either by obeying its laws or by accepting the consequences of defying them. The history of the church is replete with stories about Christians who submitted to authority without compromising their moral agency, thus making a statement that had the potential to transform the morality of the state. The number of governments that have collapsed during the past decade bear witness to the truth that they are not at liberty to defy the moral laws by which they are to govern. Immorality, whether embodied in persons, communities, or governments, has consequences.

The second qualification of Paul's teaching in Romans 13:1–7 is that Christians cannot surrender their moral agency to the state.[29] The fiduciary role of the church calls Christians to ensure that the state is fulfilling its leading function of administering order with integrity. The state, in its fallen nature, has interests that will compromise the morality of Christians if they submit to the state unconditionally. Christians cannot justify participation in what the church esteems to be an immoral issue, such as abortion or capital punishment, even if governments sanction it. When the church exercises its leading function in relationship to the state, "it is not the master or the servant of the state, but rather the conscience of the state."[30]

---

28. Richard J. Mouw, *Politics and the Biblical Drama* (Grand Rapids: Eerdmans, 1976), 101.

29. Moral agency is the matrix of virtues and values that bear witness to the affirmation that people are created in the image of God.

30. "The Church's Role," *Christianity Today,* 9 August 1999, 66.

Toward the Transformation of the Powers

According to legend, when the second-century martyr Polycarp was burned at the stake, the flames refused to consume him because he was such a holy man. Reflecting on his impending death, he said that "we have been taught to show appropriate honor to the principalities and powers ordained by God."[31] His use of the phrase "principalities and powers" in reference to the government about to execute him suggests he understood that rulers, authorities, and principalities and powers have an intrinsic interrelationship, which Paul develops in Ephesians 6:12 and Colossians 1:15–17 and 2:14–16.

Our contemporary view of rulers, authorities, and powers emerges from a dichotomy between the sacred and secular, or physical and spiritual realms, and influences us to perceive these entities as existing in separate domains. We fail to see that governments and other elements of our social structures have a spiritual ethos. In some ancient cultures, people believed a spiritual agent of causation actually occupied social institutions, which is apparent in the Book of Revelation, where the letters are addressed to the angels of the churches. These angels possibly could be messengers or deacons. However, the lack of a distinction between an angel as a spiritual and a physical being indicates that this spiritual-physical distinction was not as important in the ancient world as it is in the modern world. John evidently believed that angels governed the spiritual ethos of the social structure, whether they were seen or unseen, physical or spiritual.

The spiritual ethos of a social institution is not dependent on an external agent of causation but is intrinsic to it. Social institutions have an "outer, visible structure and an inner, spiritual reality."[32] The visible elements of a social institution, such as buildings, furniture, and decorations, as well as the personal appearances of the people who comprise it, indicate their inner spiritual reality. A statue or a painting in the yard or the foyer of a building makes a statement about the ethos of the business or organization the building houses; it also influences how people behave in that building. The spiritual ethos of any social institution prevents it from being morally neutral. Like all elements of the *kosmos*, they

31. Quoted by Luise Schottroff, "'Give to Caesar What Belongs to Caesar and to God What Belongs to God': A Theological Response of the Early Christian Church to Its Social and Political Environment," in *The Love of Enemy and Nonretaliation in the New Testament*, ed. Willard M. Swartley (Louisville: Westminster/John Knox, 1992), 226.

32. Walter Wink, *Engaging the Powers: Discernment and Resistance in a World of Domination* (Minneapolis: Fortress, 1992), 3.

are good, fallen, and redeemable. They are good insofar as they fulfill their leading functions. They fall when they lose their ability to execute their leading functions—when they cease to be subject to a higher law and become that law themselves.

George B. N. Ayittey speaks to this issue by observing that a government is often "perceived by those running it as a vehicle not to serve but to fleece the people."[33] Government leaders in many of the poorest countries of the world have become among the wealthiest people in the world. They live in palaces while their constituents live in shacks, and their motorcades cruise along highways that run parallel to footpaths carved with bare feet. They display their piety by going to a local church or to a mosque, and they leave their countries when they need to receive the best medical care in the world. Unlike Christ, who did not seize equality with God, many government officials make themselves the absolute authority in matters of good and evil, declaring themselves to be principles, rather than agents, of morality.

Israel and the Secular Nature of Redemption

The political development of Israel illustrates the secular nature of redemption available to social institutions.

Theocracy and Secular Monarchy

Israel began as a theocracy, became a secular monarchy, and was eventually occupied by a foreign superpower. Israel's shifts in government began with the prophet Samuel (1 Sam. 8). Following the practices of his predecessors, he administered a theocracy, which provided spiritual and political leadership to Israel with the assumption that he was God's agent and that God sanctioned his decisions. In turn Israel accepted his leadership as inspired by God, whether or not it obeyed the laws. When Israel's elders told Samuel they wanted a king, he was disappointed, but the Lord told him that Israel was rejecting, not him, but the Lord God as a ruler (1 Sam. 8:7).

God instructed Samuel to warn the people about the moral implications of their desire by telling them about the behavior of kings. They would draft their sons into their personal services, such as driving their chariots and farming their lands. They would take their daughters to be cooks, bakers, and perfumers. Kings would build armies, tax the citizens, and take the best of their crops, slaves, cattle, and donkeys, finally driv-

33. Ayittey, *Africa in Chaos*, 173.

ing the people to despair. They would call out to God but have no sense that he heard them. The people, despite these warnings, insisted on having a king in order to be like the other nations (1 Sam. 8:19–20).

While God acquiesced to Israel's request for secular leadership, he in no way relinquished the obligations of the power he bestowed on their kings; they were still accountable to him for maintaining their moral integrity. The welfare of the community of Israel rose and fell according to the manner in which the kings exercised their moral obligations. The community benefited from leaders who did right in the sight of God and suffered from those who did not. Josiah, for example, purged the community from mediums, household gods, idols, and other detestable things (2 Kings 23:24). He also organized the greatest Passover celebration the community of Israel had experienced in almost five hundred years; it included thirty thousand sheep and goats and three thousand cattle from his own herds (2 Chron. 35:7). Josiah used his political power as a leader who feared God to protect Israel from political destruction. He had integrity. In contrast, Josiah's three major successors did what was evil in the sight of God. The community, under the leadership of Jehoiakim, Jehoiachin, and Zedekiah, mocked the prophets God sent to them; they scoffed at them and despised their words until God turned his wrath against Israel's immorality, and they were destroyed by the king of the Babylonians (2 Chron. 36:16–17). God's influence on the leaders of Israel was moral rather than mystical. He worked through a secular government and held it accountable to his moral standards. The monarchy rose and fell according to its obedience to God's moral laws.

Israel and Roman Rule

Secular leadership in Israel continued in the New Testament in the form of Roman rule. The Gospel accounts of Pilate's interaction with Jesus indicate that he was a free agent who had to make a political decision to appease the authorities of both Rome and Israel. Pilate's dilemma, however, was not only political but also moral. The writer of the Gospel of Matthew recorded that Pilate's wife advised him to have nothing to do with Jesus, who was an innocent man, because she had a dream about him (Matt. 27:19). The dream had authority, indicating the belief that an agent of causation in the unseen realm had influence on the seen. It influenced Pilate to negotiate with the crowds in Jerusalem to acquit Jesus. The negotiations, however, engaged Pilate in a discourse about truth with Jesus. The Gospel of John recounts that when Pilate asked Jesus if he were the king of the Jews, Jesus answered, "I am a King. In fact, for this reason I was born, and for this I came into the world, to testify to the truth. Everyone on the side of truth listens to me" (John 18:37).

Pilate responded by asking, "What is truth?" The question would have been worth pursuing, but he did not wait for an answer. Consequently, he appealed to the people in the crowd, hoping they would resolve his dilemma by choosing Jesus as the prisoner who was to be released on Passover, but they chose Barabbas instead.

Pilate then sought to address his moral predicament by threatening Jesus with his power, but Jesus submitted to his rule, not to endorse the Roman government, but to accomplish his mission. Jesus lived in an economy of truth, and Pilate lived in an economy of power. Pilate, perceiving Jesus as powerless, could not grasp the nature of his truth. Jesus, realizing that Pilate did not represent truth, would not affirm the value of his power. Jesus refused to subject the validity of truth to Pilate's power, and he accepted the cross as the "legally to be expected result of a moral clash with the powers."[34] The encounter between Pilate and Jesus illustrates that God works redemptively through secular structures.

God's commitment to the creation affirms that he can choose to work through the ruling governments of the *kosmos* to realize his will, regardless of how morally degenerate they may be. Jesus practiced transformative subordination by submitting to the powers in accepting crucifixion. However, in doing so, he reminded the powers that they are powerless, even in victory, to make their will sovereign. The apostle Paul interpreted Jesus' journey to the cross as a march to victory over the powers that was characteristic of a military leader who had triumphed over his enemies. The people watching Christ limp to Golgotha witnessed the political equivalent of a victorious Roman general entering Rome, disarming his enemies, and making a public spectacle of them (Col. 2:15).[35]

The death of Christ appeared to be the victory of both the Jewish and Roman authorities; it was, however, their demise. They fractured their moral agency by condemning an innocent victim, so that they could no longer claim to be moral. Christ conquered them, not through their humiliation and death, but through his. The restoration of their moral agency depended on their ability to realize their defeat and to accept the atoning death of Christ as the source of their moral integrity. He subordinated himself to their will for this purpose.

34. Yoder, *Politics of Jesus*, 132.
35. See D. G. Reid, "Triumph," in *Dictionary of Paul and His Letters*, ed. Gerald F. Hawthorne and Ralph P. Martin (Downers Grove, Ill.: InterVarsity, 1993), 948.

Change across Cultures

The people who watched Jesus' trek to Golgotha believed his death reinforced their values and virtues. Like contemporary people who not only support executions but also watch them, the pious in the crowd became more pious, the self-righteous more self-righteous, and the vindictive more vindictive. Yet, in supporting the death of an innocent person, they lost the foundation of their morality. The cross symbolized their moral impotence as well as their hope for redemption.

The Redemption of the Powers

The secular nature of redemption is a uniquely Christian concept and is illustrated throughout the Scriptures, particularly in the political development of Israel and by Jesus' encounter with the Roman Empire. The presupposition of redeeming the powers through transformative subordination is that the political structures, which "are not autonomous, not independent, not eternal, not utterly depraved . . . [but] are mortal, limited, [and] responsible to God,"[36] can serve the humanizing purposes of God, by creating order within the state to ensure the welfare of the people.

There is good reason to believe that people who hold political authority in many countries throughout the world have become morally bankrupt. When Dawit Wolde Giorgis confronted Megistu Haile Mariam, the former dictator of Ethiopia, about the mass starvation during the mid-1980s, Megistu replied that "your primary responsibility is to work toward political objectives. Don't let these petty human problems that always exist in transition periods consume you." Giorgis interpreted Megistu's statement to mean "Let nature take its toll."[37] Nature, however, is not to blame for the consequences of the decisions politicians make to ensure their own interests. Ethiopians starved not because of nature but because the government failed to fulfill its divinely constituted leading function of creating justice and order in the society. But the redemption of governments is possible, even if it is expressed by a passive consent to the good that people want to do by restoring their communities. Many parts of East Africa bloomed about a decade after the famines of the 1980s, primarily because the people had the political freedom to rebuild their lives. They were liberated to plant trees, terrace land, develop water sources, improve methods of preserving soil, and upgrade the roads, schools, and health clinics.

36. Wink, *Engaging the Powers*, 66.
37. Giorgis, *Red Tears*, 128.

Political structures can be transformed when Christians refuse to resign themselves fatalistically to their immoral policies. According to Edward C. Banfield, fatalism is often the basis of a politically exploited society because "to the peasants . . . the state is more distant than heaven and far more of a scourge, because it is always against them. . . . [The peasant] believes that the situation is hopeless and that the only sensible course is to accept patiently and resignedly the catastrophes that are in store."[38] Christians can act in a redemptive manner by refusing to resign and accepting the consequences. After the Ethiopian Marxist revolution in 1974, which was a major cause of the famine of the 1980s, the government closed many churches and arrested church leaders. One church leader reacted in a redemptive manner by saying that "we will obey what does not go against our religion. But if you go against our religion, we will not obey. . . . We are ready and happy to die for our faith."[39] He would not surrender his moral integrity to the government. The moral influence of the church in Ethiopia was not incidental to the collapse of the Marxist government in 1991. That government, too, had the moral responsibility to fulfill its divinely established leading function.

The powers are redeemed when Christians challenge their authority by exercising their moral agency and empower people to transform the narratives of their cultures to embody the redemptive work of Christ in creation. Research reveals that this redemption is evident in Ethiopia where "the proportion of the population that is hungry has decreased over the last 25 years from one-third to one-fifth."[40] The powers are moving closer to participating in the narrative of God's redemptive relationship with creation, and they are becoming more effective in fulfilling their leading functions.

38. *The Moral Basis of a Backward Society* (New York: Free Press, 1958), 36–37.
39. Nathan B. Hege, *Beyond Our Prayers: Anabaptist Church Growth in Ethiopia, 1948–1998* (Scottdale, Pa.: Herald, 1998), 173.
40. Beckmann and Simon, *Grace at the Table,* 4.

7

Gender Equality: From Participation to Leadership

On the Sabbath we went outside the city gate to the river, where we expected to find a place of prayer. We sat down and began to speak to the women who had gathered there.

Acts 16:13

For it is disgraceful for a woman to speak in the church.

1 Corinthians 14:35

Gender equality is among the most critical ethical issues of our day. In June 1999, over a million Americans were introduced to the tradition of Trokosi, a Ghanaian practice of offering female children as wives to the gods, in order to stop an array of misfortunes. The young girls actually become slaves who are "overworked, partially starved, barred from attending school, beaten and—from around the age of 12—raped," not by a god, but by the priests who perform the service on behalf of the gods.[1] The narratives of virtually every culture in the world

1. Ann M. Simmons, "'Wife of the Gods' Stirs Up Ghana," *Los Angeles Times*, 24 June 1999, sec. A1.

are blemished with customs and traditions that dehumanize women and place them in subservient positions. For example, when fearing a drought, the farmers in Mozambique strip an elderly woman of her clothing and send her into the fields for a night to beckon the spirits to send rain. Her probable death makes her a sacrifice.

Indignities against women are not limited to traditional cultures. They are prevalent in the industrial world, and they have apparent support in the major global religions. Many Christian denominations continue to withhold leadership roles from women, Islamic traditions value a woman's testimony at half the worth of a man's, and only a few women have been able to penetrate the hallowed scientific and technological research laboratories.[2]

The subordination of women to men raises the question of whether it is a cultural universal. Sherry B. Ortner proposed that "the secondary status of women is one of the true universals, a pan-cultural fact. . . . It exists within every type of social and economic arrangement and in societies of every degree of complexity."[3] However, John Dominic Crossan challenges Ortner's conclusion, citing a study by Martin King Whyte that indicated a positive relationship between the subordination of women and the complexity of culture. He argued that "the lot of women would seem to be somewhat better in the simpler societies . . . than in the more complex ones."[4]

Crossan's statement gives us a clue to understanding the apostle Paul's teaching concerning gender relationships. Paul attempted to enhance the status of women in their respective communities by integrating them into the Christian community. The irony of Paul's teachings on this issue is that they are often taken out of their cultural contexts and interpreted as universal values, which is contrary to his original purposes. He was concerned with counteracting the cultural norms concerning the status of women by empowering them to participate in worship. Paul's teachings on church leadership are not gender specific, and proper interpretations of them would transform the order of many cultures in which approximately half of the human population is marginalized.

2. See David F. Noble, *A World without Women: The Clerical Culture of Western Science* (New York: Knopf, 1992), for a historical analysis of why and how women have been excluded from the cultures of science and technology.

3. Sherry B. Ortner, "Is Female to Male as Nature Is to Culture?" in *Woman, Culture, and Society,* ed. Michelle Zimbalist Rosaldo and Louise Lamphere (Stanford, Calif.: Stanford University Press, 1974), 67.

4. John Dominic Crossan, *The Birth of Christianity: Discovering What Happened in the Years Immediately after the Execution of Jesus* (San Francisco: Harper San Francisco, 1998), 163.

Created in the Image of God

Any discussion of gender equality must begin by seeking the meaning of the statement that human beings are created in the image of God (Gen. 1:26). Its most unencumbered interpretation is that human beings bear God's image by sharing finite and imperfect expressions of God's infinite and perfect attributes, such as love, justice, goodness, and grace.[5] People of both genders possess these qualities but express them differently, and they bear the image of God more fully as they respect each other's humanity. The finite and fallen manner in which we embody the image of God undoubtedly influences us to value people because they resemble the idealized physical images of humanity, not because they bear the image of our Creator. Bearing the image of God, however, is the leading function of human beings. The narratives of virtually every culture contain values that insult the dignity of people, and Christians must accept the challenge to transform cultural narratives that contradict the belief that all people are created in the image of God.

The Redemption Narrative and Marginalized Women

There are several stories in the Gospels about Jesus' effort to empower women to overcome the cultural values that prevented their complete development as human beings. Jesus' decision to allow the prostitute to wash his feet with her tears (Luke 7:36–50) was an abomination to his host, who was careful to protect himself from being defiled by her. Jesus, however, saw her as a human being who extended a courtesy that his host was too arrogant to provide. He defined her person by the nature of her being, not by the moral legitimacy of her profession.

The Samaritan Woman at the Well

The story of Jesus and the Samaritan woman at the well, recounted in John 4:1–42, has the same import.

THE STORY

When Jesus and his disciples were traveling from Galilee to Jerusalem, Jesus chose to pass through Samaria. His disciples preferred to travel from Galilee to Jerusalem by avoiding Samaria because they held it in contempt for both social and religious reasons. Jews considered the

---

5. Roy A. Clouser, *The Myth of Religious Neutrality: An Essay on the Hidden Role of Religious Belief in Theories* (South Bend, Ind.: University of Notre Dame Press, 1991), 174.

Samaritans to be unclean. However, by choosing to pass through Samaria, Jesus neutralized those Jewish values.

As they journeyed, they came to a village called Sychar, near the plot of ground Jacob had given to his son Joseph; it is the location of Jacob's well. The disciples went into town to buy food, leaving Jesus at the well. Being tired and thirsty from the journey, Jesus asked the woman at the well for a drink. Had his disciples been there, they would have reminded him that Jews do not ask Samaritans, especially women, for anything. They believed that drinking with someone was an act of solidarity, and they did not want Jesus to get too close to this woman, not only because she was a woman, but also because she was a Samaritan.

The woman, while not keen to host a Jewish man, had other problems. She went to the well at noon, several hours after the other women in the village performed the daily task of drawing water, a time when they shared village news and gossip. This woman seemed to be making an intentional effort not to be among the other women of the community. Surprised that Jesus began talking to her, the woman asked him how a Jewish man could ask a Samaritan woman for a drink. Most Jewish men would have preferred to thirst.

Having already violated many religious, cultural, and social taboos, Jesus could have responded to the woman's question about drinking in any way he wanted. He chose, however, to talk about water, living water, and the gift of God. The woman ignored Jesus' metaphorical answer and asked the practical question of how he could draw water without a pot. She could not imagine that any Jew would drink from her pot; they would have considered it to be ritually profane.

The woman was not sure what Jesus meant by living water, but she was confident he could not improve on the water in Jacob's well. She asked Jesus if he were greater than Jacob, who gave the well to the Samaritans and who, along with his sons and flocks, drank from it. Jesus answered by continuing his metaphor about living water: "Everyone who drinks this water will be thirsty again, but whoever drinks the water I give him will never thirst. Indeed, the water I give him will become in him a spring of water welling up to eternal life" (John 4:13–14). When the woman asked for the living water, Jesus told her to first call her husband and return with him. When the woman said she had no husband, Jesus responded, "You are right when you say you have no husband. The fact is, you have had five husbands, and the man you now have is not your husband" (v. 18).

The Meaning of the Story

The story has been interpreted several ways, and each interpretation reflects a specific cultural narrative. The common interpretation in Western churches is that the woman was immoral because she was living with a man to whom she was not married; morality is a central theme in the narratives of Western Christians. They propose that Jesus asked the woman to call her husband to remind her that she needed to repent. Other Christians believe that the woman was seeking in marriage what she could find only in God, and some think that she'd given up on marriage, having been widowed five times, and preferred to live with a man instead of risking widowhood again. The theme of immorality, however, remains constant.

The problem with each of these interpretations is that they ignore the role of women in Samaritan culture. People of first-century Palestine rarely esteemed women to have achieved any moral maturity. These interpretations depict her as having lived with a man to whom she was not married out of personal choice. The Samaritan woman's predicament was caused, not because she had the personal liberty and economic independence to choose her way of life, but because she had no other choice. I propose that the woman was ostracized from her community because she was barren. Bearing a child was the foundation of a woman's worth in first-century Samaria, as it continues to be in many cultures today. Yet, because the woman at the well could not bear a child, she embodied one of the community's greatest fears. Her barrenness and the confines of her culture do not justify the moral choices she made, but they highlight the moral dilemmas she faced.

If we interpret this story from the perspective of the narrative of Christian redemption, we can shift its focal point. Jesus was not reproaching the woman for forsaking her moral responsibility for something over which she had limited control. Instead, he was attempting to empower the woman to exercise her moral responsibility to transform the circumstances that were victimizing her. The vitality of the story is that this woman was a powerless resident of a traditional community, who came to the well when no one else was there because her barren womb made her offensive to the community. The village women refused to associate with her, not because she was immoral, but because she was infertile. People did not fear immorality; they feared infertility, and her presence in the village reminded the women of this fear. The village residents could not accept her into their community until they had neutralized the value they placed on progeny. The woman was shocked when Jesus talked to her, not only because he was a Jewish man, but also because he affirmed her dignity by expressing concern for her regardless of her ability to fulfill a valued function in her culture.

The Samaritan woman's inability to bear children gave her former husbands ample reason to divorce her. Since this woman depended on men for economic support, she had to remarry after her divorces. However, because she was barren, she was not a viable marriage prospect, forcing her to live with a man who did not give her the dignity of marriage. Because her barrenness was an embarrassment to her, her family, and her community, she became the village outcast. In asking about her husbands, Jesus was exposing a social injustice of the community. The woman, feeling a sense of affirmation from Jesus, recognized him as a prophet. When she said she was waiting for the Messiah, he revealed himself to her.

The redemptive impact of this interpretation is expressed in the final verses of the story. The woman, leaving her jar at the well, ran back to the village to tell the people about the man who knew all about her. Since everyone in the village already knew the details of her life, we can imagine that they responded by saying, "What is prophetic about someone who recognizes a moral lowlife when he sees one?" Yet they went to see Jesus because of her transformation.

The people in the village took her seriously, not because they responded to someone who described the details of her life, but because they wanted to see the prophet who restored her dignity and empowered her to challenge the Samaritan community to rescind the social value that stigmatized her. The passage does not tell all that happened to the woman, but it hints that Jesus empowered her to return to her community, not on the basis of her function, but on the value of her humanity. Her encounter with the villagers empowered her to convince them—and herself—that she, too, bore the image of God and was worthy of inclusion in their community, regardless of her ability to fulfill a function that was central to the values of their cultural narrative. The Samaritan woman's encounter with Christ empowered her to take a significant step toward transforming the immoral aspects of her society as well as the values central to its narrative.

A Tale of Two Women

The Samaritan woman at the well has had her counterparts in other societies throughout history. Two of them are Amina and Lydia. Amina, an Oromo by ethnicity and a Muslim by religion, is an impoverished, illiterate peasant woman, a mother of two children, who currently lives in eastern Ethiopia. The only story about her, as far as I know, is in this chapter. Lydia, in contrast to Amina, was a Jewish woman who lived in Philippi during the first century. Her profession, a merchant of purple fabric, indicates that she had some education and economic status. Her story is recorded in Acts 16:13–15. Amina led a group of women who prayed under a tree at the edge of her village; Lydia led a group of women who prayed by the riverside outside of Philippi.

The two women, while separated by history, culture, and economic status as well as religions, were also separated by two contrasting kinds of power that caused them to be marginalized in their communities. Lydia had sensate power, a subtle kind of charisma that attracted people to her and enabled her to be a natural leader. Amina, in contrast, had sensual power, which was explicit and therefore attractive only to certain people. While people noticed Lydia—and wanted to be noticed by her—they pretended not to notice Amina, especially those who esteemed themselves to be decent and self-respecting. If Amina went to Lydia's group, she would have sat on the outside of it until either Lydia or another member welcomed her. Lydia would probably not have gone to Amina's group.

Amina's Story

Amina's group met under a tree at the edge of the village on Thursday evening, the beginning of the Islamic holy day. Amina believed she had access to the apex of the spiritual power in her village as soon as the darkness prevented her from seeing a white thread she held in front of her face. At that moment, she led the women in the prayers and chants that gave her the power to tell their fortunes, cure infertility, and cast spells on enemies.

Amina seemed to have had a lucrative business, giving prophecies for a considerable price. However, she had a contract with a local sheikh who took advantage of her ignorance. She believed she received her power from local spirits and paid the sheikh exorbitant fees to make sacrifices to the spirits on her behalf, in order to maintain her power. The sheikh forbade Amina from ever going near the mosque. He arranged to meet her at his home each week and threatened that she would be cursed if she disobeyed him.

Amina became concerned about the sheikh's rising prices. Each week, she took him a chicken to pay for his services. When Amina resisted the high fees, he suggested other ways to pay. Amina submitted to his suggestions and became involved in a vicious spiral of sacrifices, sex, and spirits. She hated her relationship with the sheikh and wanted out of it, but the sheikh threatened her with death if he stopped making sacrifices to the spirits on her behalf.

Amina had become a spiritual prostitute, giving her money and her body to the sheikh for protection from the spirits. She began as a moral person coping with life in an immoral society. Succumbing to its immorality, she began to hate herself, the sheikh, the spirit, and her customers. She felt that she was less than a human being and considered suicide, believing that death was the only alternative to her wretched life. Eventually she stopped giving prophecies, and the village women became furious with her because they thought she was withholding her power from them. They cursed her when they met her under the tree and scorned her if they saw her in the market.

Amina responded to their reproach by returning verbal floggings not only at the women but also at everyone she met in the market. Her whole life began to disintegrate; she neglected her children, and they began roaming the street. Amina became deranged and lost control, chasing people and throwing rocks at them. Like the Gerasene demoniac, she cursed everybody, shouting prophecies at people passing by and ranting at those who mocked her. While children laughed at her, adults tried to ignore her. Amina began to hope the spirit that held her in bondage would actually kill her.[6]

One night, while Amina was lying sleepless on her bed, she saw a bright light. She was not surprised because she expected her spirit to appear to her. This light, however, brought her tremendous comfort. She felt her fears and anxiety flow out of her as she experienced what she believed was the love of God. The light vanished, leaving her with instructions to visit the Christian mission.

The next day, Amina visited the only Christians she had ever heard about. She told them her story. They prayed with her, and she accepted Christ as her savior. She became a strong believer in the emerging Christian community, telling her story, introducing people to Christ, and delivering them from their fears of the local spirits. Amina integrated her life into the redemptive narrative of Christianity, and she invited other people to graft themselves into this story.

6. Amina's belief that her spirit might kill her can also be interpreted to mean that she contemplated suicide. The belief in agentive causation in that culture makes suicide logically impossible.

When Amina entered the village church for the first time, however, both the men and the women members became uncomfortable. The women knew she was formerly the prophetess under the tree; in fact, some of them were secretly among her customers. Amina noticed a few of them but pretended they were not there, knowing they would prefer it that way. The men were also uncomfortable with Amina's presence because they suspected that she not only practiced witchcraft but also drank the blood of the chickens the sheikh sacrificed. The church people wondered if they could worship with a woman like her in their presence, and Amina wondered if the church was a place for her; she felt more comfortable under the tree.

Amina's conversion challenged the people in the church to face the injustice of their judgments about her as a human being, which actually said more about them than about her. They believed that God did miracles in people's lives, but they could not believe Amina should be the recipient of one. The people in the church were forced to expand their view of grace and to reconcile their own faith with God's goodness. She represented everything they wished to hide from God. They considered themselves to be good and saw that as the means of their salvation. Amina made them see that salvation came by God's grace, not by their own goodness. They could also not cope with the tensions and ambiguities of female participation in the church, perhaps because they were influenced by al-Ghazalli, the Islamic theologian who taught that "had it not been for women, God would truly have been worshipped."

Lydia's Story

Lydia's life, in contrast to Amina's, was genteel. She met women at a prayer site near the side of a river on the Sabbath because Philippi did not have a synagogue. Evidently, the number of Jewish men in Philippi was fewer than ten, the number of male residents required to build a synagogue in any city. The women with whom Lydia met were probably both Jewesses and God-fearing Gentiles.[7]

One Sabbath morning the apostle Paul and his companions visited them, and Lydia invited Paul to speak. He undoubtedly spoke to them about Jesus as the Messiah, and he ended his speech by inviting the women to be baptized. Most of the woman declined, seeing the invitation as radical and wondering what their husbands would think about their making such a decision without their permission. They were not

7. F. F. Bruce, *Commentary on the Book of the Acts* (Grand Rapids: Eerdmans, 1954), 331.

surprised, however, when Lydia went forward. She was the head of her household and took more liberty with such things. After Lydia came out of the water, her slaves, out of loyalty, followed her in baptism. Afterward Lydia invited Paul and his companions to her house.

Luke tells us that Lydia established the church in her house (Acts 16:40), which probably included many of the women who previously met at the river. The men who attended were probably Jewish and Gentile converts whom Paul referred to her. When Christian congregations met in homes during the first and second centuries, women were prominent leaders.[8] Lydia was among them, and there seemed to be no question that she was capable of leading the church.

Lydia had the poise and the resources to host people from all strands of life; Amina, in contrast, had no resources at all. While Lydia initiated invitations, Amina coveted them. Lydia was a leader with many followers; Amina lost her followers. Lydia and Amina are women with very different backgrounds who found salvation and influenced their respective churches by their presence, highlighting especially the moral ambiguity of women's participation in church services.

The Issue of Participation

The struggle in the early church concerning women was with female participation, not with female leadership. There is no question that Lydia, Prisca, and other women led churches. The problem was that there were not enough women of their caliber to be church leaders. The early church was composed of women more like Amina than Lydia.[9] Female participation was the challenge, especially at Corinth.

The church at Corinth faced the problem of emerging folk religions started by women. Paul prevented this development by allowing both men and women to worship together. As he wrote to the Galatians, in Christ there is no longer male or female (3:28). It is likely that he would have applied this precept to the Corinthians since he wrote to the Galatians before the Corinthians. But Paul's efforts to encourage gender equality in Corinth required measures that seem ironic to twentieth-

8. Karen Jo Torjesen, *When Women Were Priests: Women's Leadership in the Early Church and the Scandal of Their Subordination in the Rise of Christianity* (San Francisco: Harper San Francisco, 1993), 5.

9. Gender was undoubtedly a central organizing principle of the group of women that Lydia led. They probably found more spiritual satisfaction and growth under her than they would have under a man. Amina's group was also organized around gender, but because it focused on indigenous spiritual powers, it was more a folk religion.

century Christians because he advocates gender equality while assuming gender inequality, especially in 1 Corinthians 11:3–8 where Paul advocates traditional Jewish male/female relationships: woman was made from the man and not man from the woman, the husband is to be the head of his wife, and a woman who prays or prophesies with her head uncovered disgraces herself.

In dealing with the Corinthians about this issue, Paul was not initiating propositional truth but mediating a clash between narratives. We generally interpret theological propositions to be normative for all times and places. Narratives, however, absorb propositions as they move through time and space, provoking us to ask how their truth addresses current life situations. Instead of absorbing the propositions about Paul's teaching to the Corinthians as absolute truth, we should ask how we can express gender relationships in a redemptive manner.

Paul's effort to introduce gender equality into the Corinthian church required him to identify and address the critical issues of gender relationships in their narrative. He therefore placed the proposition of gender equality within the context of the Corinthian church, in order to achieve cultural transformation. Paul's central contextual concern was prostitution, a concern that had two parts. The first was addressing the behavior of Christians who participated in the prostitution industry in Corinth. The second part was integrating former prostitutes into the church. Corinth was a Roman port city, famous for its prostitutes, pagan temples, and idols. Prostitutes believed that "having sex with a stranger was in some way an act of service to Aphrodite," the goddess of sex.[10] Likewise, anyone who had sex with a prostitute was also having sex with the goddess.

The Christians in Corinth had no problem condemning temple prostitution. However, they evidently applied Paul's teaching about food sacrificed to idols to prostitution. He taught that Christians could eat food that was sacrificed to idols because "there is no God but one" (1 Cor. 8:4). Through this teaching, the Christians in Corinth evidently concluded that Aphrodite does not exist. Therefore, they could have sex with a prostitute without having sex with Aphrodite. Imagine Paul's dismay when he heard that logic! The early Christians in Corinth just did not grasp the meaning of the Christian message. Paul made an inspired effort to instruct the Corinthians not to be in bondage to the spirituality of

10. Ross Saunders, *Outrageous Women, Outrageous God: Women in the First Two Generations of Christianity* (Alexandria, NSW, Australia: Dwyer, 1966), 123.

Corinth, but they interpreted this freedom much too liberally. They, like the Galatians, were enslaved by the structure of the *kosmos* but in a profoundly different way.

Paul had to redefine the central issue of his teachings by emphasizing that Christians' bodies are members of Christ (1 Cor. 6:15) and temples of the Holy Spirit (1 Cor. 6:19); they should not, therefore, become united with those of prostitutes (1 Cor. 6:16). Thus, Paul resolved the issue of sexual purity, the first part of the problem.

The second part of the issue was the integration of former prostitutes into the church. Paul could have easily appealed to the Jewish tradition of separating men and women in worship. However, he chose not to separate them, despite knowing that many of these women and men possibly engaged in commercial sex with each other. But Paul had to protect the dignity of Christian women who were former prostitutes. His challenge was to blend them into the congregation. He decided to focus on the unique hair styles of the prostitutes of Corinth, their most distinctive feature. He could have asked the women to shave their heads, but this would have equated the former prostitutes with adulteresses, and it would have made them stand out in the congregation. He, therefore, resorted to the Jewish tradition of having women wear veils during worship services.[11]

In solving the problems in the Corinthian church, Paul had to consider their cultural narrative. He began with a current practice and created a process through which the practice was transformed. The pervasive nature of prostitution influenced the manner in which husbands and wives related to each other, making gender equality foreign to that culture as it is in many cultures today. The Corinthian men could not go from viewing women as sex objects to valuing them as equal beings in Christ. They had to engage a process that would result in the full equality of women.[12]

Paul's trajectory of full gender equality creates the interpretive ethic for Paul's other teachings on gender issues. First Corinthians 11:2–16 and Ephesians 5:22–6:9 are good examples. The passage in 1 Corinthians addresses Christ as the head of every man, and the man as the head of his wife (1 Cor. 11:3). It continues by admonishing women to pray with veils and concludes by emphasizing the interdependence of men and women. The passage from Ephesians focuses on wives being subject to their hus-

11. Ibid., 134.

12. This process toward gender equality is similar to the process of removing slavery from Christian ethics. The Bible does not condemn slavery, but it sets a trajectory that leads to the abolition of this institution.

bands and husbands loving their wives. It proceeds by addressing the order of a household, including the relationships of children to their parents and slaves to their masters.

Christians often try to interpret Paul's teachings about women being subject to their husbands, wearing veils, and being silent in churches in a way that supports the idea of mutual submission between husbands and wives and between men and women in general. However, the meaning of the passages should not be stretched to advocate mutual submission. Instead, the passages should be perceived as providing an interim ethic for building a worshiping community in cultures where equality between men and women was not valued. Paul began with the presuppositions of the prevailing cultural narratives and then inspired the people to transform their narratives by grasping the concept of gender equality in Christ.

Paul's difficult teachings on gender move the Christian community from an ethic that focuses on function to one that values the complete human being. Paul concludes that "everything comes from God" (1 Cor. 11:11). Our being is from God, but our functions are cultural; they are the elements of the *kosmos* that have the potential to estrange us from God and from each other. We can transform them, however, in order to bring us into relationship with God as we affirm the full equality of people of different gender.

The subordination of women, which often leads to their exclusion from formal religious practices, creates the conditions for folk religions to breed. Folk religions, while eroding the integrity of orthodox religions, serve as a reminder that the orthodox religious community is engaging in practices that need to be transformed. Conversely, those who are being marginalized need to repent of their helplessness. The elements of culture are fashioned by the people who have the power to fashion it. They place people in a structure but do not govern their morality; each person, having been created in the image of God, is her or his own moral agent. Each person has the responsibility, not to submit to the elements of the *kosmos*, but to transform the elements to reflect the morality of Christ.

This morality is embodied, among other ways, through justice and peace; it beckons people to advocate these virtues in the midst of circumstances where such virtues might be unwelcome. One Hindu tradition advocates that a "wife should always treat the husband as a God, though he be characterless, sensual and devoid of good qualities."[13] The tradition

13. Somen Das, *Christian Ethics and Indian Ethos* (Delhi: Indian Society for Promoting Christian Knowledge, 1989), 25.

carries the subservient role of women to an extreme, denying her any moral agency and raises questions concerning how Christians should respond to it. The moral imperative is that they should work to transform a tradition that denies moral agency to any person as well as any other practice that insults the truth that all people, regardless of gender or any other characteristic, are created in the image of God.

An Excursus and a Prospect

Jack Miles suggests that male circumcision is a fertility ritual of the Hebrew Scriptures, a canon that the Samaritans also accepted. In this interpretation, the value the Hebrew community placed on fertility was neutralized by the ritual of male circumcision. Miles believes that Abraham, in submitting to circumcision, participated in a symbolic act that affirmed, for him and his descendants, that "fertility was not his own to exercise without divine let or hindrance."[14]

While this interpretation is controversial, I want to give it some defense. Circumcision was a rite of consecration throughout the Scripture, beginning with Abraham's fertility (Gen. 17), it was extended to include slaves in the community (Exod. 12:44). It was used metaphorically to consecrate the community to God through the circumcision of the heart (Deut. 10:16; Jer. 4:4), and it became an impediment to affirming the community of Israel as a new creation in Christ (Gal. 6:15). The central tenet of biblical theology in each of these expressions of culture is that God is the only primary symbol of the Hebrew community. Circumcision is the ritual through which the people in the community express the value of consecrating themselves and all aspects of their lives to God.

Fertility is a major value in any culture, and the presence of fertility rites in virtually every culture bears witness to the danger of its becoming reified by making it an absolute expression of God's blessing. God seems to have prevented that possibility, however, by defining circumcision as a ritual that would remind the Hebrew community that all their blessings are divine gifts, which they receive under God's sovereignty. The support for this interpretation of male circumcision stems from the evidence that it was not unique to the Hebrew community. Bodies exhumed in Egypt from 4000 B.C. disclose evidence of circumcision.[15] The

14. *God: A Biography* (New York: Knopf, 1995), 53.
15. Gerald A. Larue, "Religious Traditions and Circumcision" (paper presented at the Second International Symposium on Circumcision, San Francisco, Calif., April 30–May 3, 1991).

Book of Jeremiah attested to the presence of male circumcision among the Moabites, Edomites, and Ammonites (Jer. 9:25).

Since male circumcision was practiced among many ethnic communities during the time of Abraham, the uniqueness of this practice in the Hebrew community must have originated in its function rather than in its form. For the Hebrews it was an act of consecration; men, as representatives of the community, submitted to circumcision to set Hebrews apart from other ethnic communities by affirming God as the agent of causation in every aspect of their lives. God, while initiating circumcision as a sign of the covenant with Abraham and his descendants, put the rite in the context of fertility and progeny. Throughout his discourse with Abraham, God made several references to his descendants as a multitude of nations (Gen. 17:4, 5) and as exceedingly numerous (Gen. 17:2). Abraham, realizing that his wife was ninety years old at the time, fell on his face and laughed, believing that even God could not deliver on the promise. The birth of Isaac, however, bears witness to the validity of the promise that all of Abraham's progeny are produced under God's agency.

The meaning of the circumcision ritual, like that of many other rituals, changes as it moves from one culture to another and throughout the various stages of development in the same culture. The ritual of male circumcision undoubtedly began for hygienic reasons. It could also have served as a rite of passage from childhood to adulthood, symbolizing the death of one stage of life. For the Hebrews, however, it symbolized their ability to create *communitas*[16] by submitting to God, affirming him as their agent of causation, and leveling themselves in submission to him. In the New Testament church, the ritual fractured any sense of *communitas* by insulting the multicultural ethos of the various communities. The apostles, under the inspiration of the Holy Spirit, chose not to export the meaning of circumcision from the Jewish community into the *communitas* of the new creation that became the church.

The apostles, like people in all cultures throughout history, managed cultural change by working with communities, discerning how they could transform the meanings of the symbols, values, and rituals that were indigenous to the community, in order to bear witness to the redemptive work of God in creation. The central goal in this transformation was depicting God as the agent of causation. Likewise, development practitioners throughout the world strive to manage change by discern-

16. A full discussion of *communitas* will be taken up in chapter 11.

ing how the symbols they bring into a community influence the nature of the community in that culture.

As we will see throughout the remainder of this book, all expressions of development work are aimed at influencing the symbols through which the people in the host cultures interpret reality and create community. These symbols, ranging from metal roofs on traditional houses or medical knowledge that distinguishes tumors from fetuses, influence how people view themselves in relation to their symbolic realities, how they modify their cultural narratives, and how they manage change in their communities to reflect God's redemptive work in creation through Christ.

The Book of Revelation ends with a vision of the New Jerusalem that is lighted, not by the sun or the moon, but by the glory of God. The nations will walk in the light; there will be no night, and its gates will never be shut. "The glory and honor of the nations will be brought into it. Nothing impure will ever enter it" (Rev. 21:26–27). The glory of the nations, which will include redeemed traditions and artifacts from all cultures, such as Chinese bridges and classical architecture, will foster an expression of *communitas* that will unite Christians with many cultural narratives as they appreciate and enjoy the redeemed expressions of all human cultures. God seems to have such a high view of the creation and human cultures that he wants to redeem them for eternal glory.

8

Economics:
From Exploitation to Empowerment

The master commended the dishonest manager because he had acted shrewdly. For the people of this world are more shrewd in dealing with their own kind than are the people of the light.

Luke 16:8

Religion brought forth prosperity; and then the daughter destroyed the mother.

Cotton Mather

Economic progress is useful only when it enhances the non-economic values that make up human culture.

Ecumenical Patriarch Bartholomeos
of Constantinople

A young woman sat at the entrance of one of the many third-rate hotels that litter the major cities of the world. She was weeping because she had lost her job as a prostitute and had no idea of how she would support her family. At the tender age of seventeen, this young woman became professionally obsolete because of the belief that AIDS is cured when men engage in sexual intercourse with a virgin. This belief lowers the age of women who enter her profession and causes other women to retire from the profession before they are old enough to drive.

Kate, a Christian missionary, met the young woman after she answered a call to disciple prostitutes. She would visit the red light district of a city, asking God to lead her to women to whom she could minister. Her ministry gave rise to a small group of disciples with which she shared the love of Christ. Kate knew she was ministering to women who were striving to be moral in an immoral society, and she hoped that by teaching them to read, they could find employment in jobs that affirmed their human dignity. She believed she was not only empowering the women to participate in society in a more significant way but also giving them the hope of becoming moral people by making the story of God's redemptive relationship with creation their story.

One of Kate's Bible studies addressed the story of Jesus and the sinful woman who anointed his feet in Luke 7:36–50. Jesus forgave her sins and dismissed her in peace because her actions attested to her faith (Luke 7:50). However, he did not tell her not to sin any more. He undoubtedly foresaw the irony of such a statement, knowing that she might be with a customer shortly afterward because she had no other economic means of support. Her profession was an indictment of her community, not of her character.

The economic welfare of a community is determined by how well the poorest people in the community fare, not by how well the richest people live. The Pharisee in Luke's story, like many people in contemporary cultures, was living quite well. The presence of a prostitute indicates that her way of life was symptomatic of a moral problem within the community. Its structures failed to supply a valuable place for the woman. Kate concluded that her disciples were the twentieth-century counterparts to the sinful woman Jesus met at the Pharisee's house. Their challenge was to transform the structures by overcoming the economic exploitation that victimized them.

Luke 16:1–13: Exposing the Economics of Exploitation

When economists discovered that labor, rather than nature, was the source of a nation's wealth, they discredited the image of limited good, making business profits socially acceptable. Profits were no longer seen as unequivocal indicators of economic exploitation. But exploitation of the poor and powerless continues to be a major way that people gain wealth. In many countries throughout the world, "workers, including children, have become world class competitors by sacrificing their health, lives and futures to subsidize the profits of investors."[1]

The parable of the dishonest manager in Luke 16:1–13 gives insight into the exploitative nature of economic systems that highly esteem profits. The central theme of the parable is that economic systems are slanted against the poor; they lose even when they appear to be winning. Excavating this theme requires us to study it within the context of rural villages during the time of Jesus' ministry on earth, sifting through its irony and humor.

The Structure of the Parable

The structure of the parable is straightforward. The main characters are a rich man, a manager, and debtors. In the first section of the parable, the rich man is threatening to fire the manager, who must either preserve his job or find alternative employment. In the second section, the manager decides upon a scheme that will endear him to his master's debtors when he is without employment. He summons the debtors and reduces the balances of their loans. He decreases a debt of a hundred jugs of olive oil to fifty and a debt of a hundred bushels of wheat to eighty. In the third section, the master commends the manager's shrewd scheme and reinstates him into his employment.

Jesus concludes by saying that the children of this age are shrewder in dealing with their own generation than are the children of light. He continues by advising his audience to make friends for themselves by means of dishonest wealth on the expectation that their friends may welcome them into their eternal homes when the wealth is gone. Finally, Jesus teaches that whoever is faithful with very little is also faithful in much. Conversely, whoever is dishonest in little is dishonest in much. Jesus restates this teaching in the following verses and concludes the parable by reminding the people that they cannot serve both God and wealth.

The Context of the Parable

A full interpretation of the parable requires an understanding of the relationship between the debtors, who are either farmers or landless

---

1. Alexander Goldsmith, "Seeds of Exploitation: Free Trade Zones in the Global Economy," in *The Case against the Global Economy: And for a Turn toward the Local,* ed. Jerry Mander and Edward Goldsmith (San Francisco: Sierra Club, 1996), 269.

peasants, and the manager, a wealthy urbanite. John Dominic Crossan explained that the term peasant "is an interactive term for farmer" and presupposes that somewhere there are oppressors and exploiters,[2] in this case the urbanites, who reduce farmers to peasants by draining their resources through forced labor, high interest rates and taxes, and other terms of trade, making them both poor and powerless.[3] Before the first cities, there were no peasants, only happy farmers.[4] In telling this parable, Jesus spoke prophetically to the people who were perpetuating exploitative relationships between urban and rural cultures by exposing a scheme of exploitation that was as shrewd as it was subtle.

The Meaning of the Parable

This parable is spiced with irony and humor, some derision, and a little mockery, placing it among the most difficult parables to interpret. My interpretation is based on that of William Herzog, whose *The Parables as Subversive Speech* challenges people to step into the drama of life in a rural village economy; it has four interpretive tasks. The first is defining its primary audience, the second is addressing the prohibition of interest, the third is realizing how debts in inflationary economies are valued and measured, and the fourth is learning how people repay debts in impoverished cultures.

Jesus' audience at first glance seems to be his disciples because he addressed it to them. His larger audience and his main target, however, were the Pharisees present at the telling. The Pharisees participated in the economic scheme Jesus addressed in the parable, believing they were not violating the letter of the law regardless of its intent. They were immoral people who strove to be moral in a moral society.

The second interpretative task is explaining why the rich man commended the manager, who apparently worked against his interests. He did so because the manager found a way to overcome one of the most troublesome prohibitions in the Jewish economic structure, the law against charging interest on loans. This interdiction was based on the image of limited good, which assumed that wealth existed in fixed amounts and could not be created. If one person gained, another person lost.

The image of limited good makes reciprocity, rather than exchange, the primary medium of economic transactions. If people believe that all

---

2. *The Birth of Christianity: Discovering What Happened in the Years Immediately after the Execution of Jesus* (San Francisco: Harper San Francisco, 1998), 216.

3. Ibid., 346–47.

4. Ibid., 216.

value exists in limited amounts, they have to build relationships of trust with each other, giving each other the assurance that the economic exchange is just. This trust is built primarily through personal relationships, making them central to the economic welfare of the community and the context in which economic exchanges occur. The ideal expression of reciprocity occurs when people value each other and use money for economic transactions. The economic practice of charging interest insults the nature of community that is central to reciprocity.

The prohibition of interest put the merchants in the predicament of building reciprocity with the people they disdained. The merchants, therefore, insulted the relational ethos of the community by transacting business on the basis of exchange rather than of reciprocity. The merchants had to find a way of getting around the Levitical law and did so by charging considerably higher prices to the peasants to compensate for their loss of interest payments.

The third interpretive task involves an understanding of the method of valuing debts during the first century, where the economy was highly inflationary.[5] The merchants, therefore, had to protect themselves from losing value to an inflated monetary unit. They did this by measuring the value of debt in terms of commodities instead of money because the price of commodities rose during periods of inflation. The merchants buried an effective interest rate by increasing the amount of commodities the debtors had to repay instead of increasing the amount of money. The values of the payment could be converted from commodities to money at the time of payment rather than at the time of purchase, preventing the merchants from losing value if the prices of the commodities increased.

The final interpretive task is understanding how impoverished people made debt payments. Money managers constantly faced the challenge of maintaining their employment by generating new loans and keeping their present accounts active. However, the mechanisms of survival worked against them. The debtors associated them with their old debts and created new debts through new managers. The proliferation of managers prevented the old managers from generating new debts quickly enough to maintain their viability, rendering them obsolete because they were unable to collect on the old debts. The inability of the

---

5. The validity of this statement is supported by the economic principle that inflation occurs during periods of high taxation. The Jewish community, living under Roman occupation, perceived the taxes they paid to Rome as too high, which caused the merchants to raise prices.

old managers to create new accounts caused their rich bosses to seek ways to terminate their employment because new managers generated new accounts, and new accounts generated new money. The rich men lost the face value of the old accounts when they fired the old managers, but they were more interested in cash flow than in ledger balances. By generating new loans, the new managers kept cash flowing into the pockets of the rich.

The Money Manager's Dilemma

Jesus undoubtedly caught the attention of the Pharisees when he started the story about the money manager whose boss was accusing him of mismanaging funds and threatening to fire him. Many Pharisees worked as money managers, and their employment was always endangered. Since Jesus' introduction to the parable hinted at a solution to their predicament, they listened to him.

Jesus' money manager was shrewd; he resolved the quandary that all money managers faced by building the loyalty of existing debtors. He reduced their debts, feigning loyalty to them and giving them the illusion that they did not owe the rich man as much as they previously did. While this sounds generous, the money manager was actually refreshing the old debts and ensnaring the villagers into more debt. The money manager cared little about losing money by reducing debts, since that money was already lost. His central concern was enticing the villagers to borrow more money, which they would do if they believed the old debts were reduced.

Jesus unmasked the scheme and condemned it, noting that the rich man commended the manager for acting shrewdly. He added that the Pharisees should make friends through dishonest wealth, so that they will welcome them into eternal homes. In a sober tone, Jesus concluded with the following lesson:

> Whoever can be trusted with very little can also be trusted with much, and whoever is dishonest with very little will also be dishonest with much. So if you have not been trustworthy in handling worldly wealth, who will trust you with true riches? And if you have not been trustworthy with someone else's property, who will give you property of your own? No servant can serve two masters. Either he will hate the one and love the other, or he will be devoted to the one and despise the other (Luke 16:10–13).

The parable shows the Pharisees that they are participating in a scheme that will eventually make fools of them. God will not be mocked.

From Village Debtors to Urban Prostitutes

Jesus included a statement in the parable that makes it particularly germane to understanding the dynamics of an economic system that drives young women into prostitution. He said that "the people of this world are more shrewd in dealing with their own kind than are the people of light" (v. 8). One expression of this shrewdness is that the people of the light—Christians—think of prostitution as a moral problem. Morality might be a secondary issue, but economics is primary. The global prostitution industry will continue to draft young girls until the economic structures of local communities are transformed.

Since the economic conditions of first-century Palestine were similar to those in many traditional cultures, the parable of the shrewd manager gives us some insights into how to address unjust economic schemes in rural villages. Many villagers, like the people in the parable, live in impoverished subsistence economies. They always need money, particularly for major expenses, such as livestock, health, and funerals, among other things. They do not have credit ratings and collateral to enable them to qualify for bank loans. Therefore, they have to accept loans from money managers at interest rates that often exceed 20 percent per week. At these rates, interest payments escalate, and they can easily represent the debtors' entire income. The money managers mine the villagers for all the money they can get, and the villagers are eventually unable to make the payments. They, like the debtors in the parable, inevitably find themselves in a spiraling cycle of debt, eventually becoming bankrupt. But their societies have no bankruptcy measures.

As the village residents become mired in debt, their villages become economic colonies of money managers, who continue to excavate as many money resources as possible. But they are often more interested in the debtors' greater assets, their daughters. The money managers offer the debtors' daughters employment in the cities as waitresses, but the girls inevitably become fodder for the sex industry. They become not only commodities in the domains of exchange but also sacrifices to market demands in order to produce wealth. Their hope for economic viability lies in their ability to participate in and transform their economies by learning why some villages, like some nations, are rich while others are poor.

From Magic to Morality

Tzvetan Todorov, an advocate of cultural transformation, noted that the social structures of the indigenous peoples of the Western Hemisphere who were exploited during the conquest of America were not incidental to the exploitation of these cultures. He identified agentive causation as a central problem, noting that because many indigenous people "believed in a thousand omens and signs," they lived in "an overdetermined [and] overinterpreted world as well."[6] This prevented them from taking personal responsibility for the their cultural upheavals and working toward significant change.

The Rich and the Poor

Why are some nations rich while others are poor?[7] Among the many answers to this question, there are two from a Western perspective by J. M. Blaut and Max Weber that represent the polarities of the debate.

Blaut argues that the rise of the economic, scientific, and technological development of Europe was the direct result of European exploitation of the people and resources of non-European cultures; "capitalism became concentrated in Europe because colonialism gave Europeans the power both to develop their own society and to prevent development from occurring elsewhere."[8] In contrast, Max Weber proposed that because of John Calvin's theology, northern European cultures transformed their social structures independent of foreign influence, creating the cultural environment in which capitalism could take root.[9] Hence, the people were able to transform the narrative that governed their lives.

In this section, I want to pursue an argument that gives limited support to Weber's thesis but does not ignore the validity of Blaut's thesis. That colonizers have benefited from exploiting the colonized is true. There is ample evidence throughout the world that colonial governments and postcolonial multinational businesses have mercilessly exploited indigenous cultures, which helps explain the poverty of these

6. Tzvetan Todorov, *The Conquest of America: The Question of the Other,* trans. Richard Howard (New York: Harper & Row, 1984), 64.

7. The use of the term "nations" in this debate is antiquated; the current issue no longer concerns nations but ethnic groups and subcultures. The central question is why people of different ethnic backgrounds and subcultures live in poverty amidst wealth.

8. J. M. Blaut, *The Colonizer's Model of the World: Geographical Diffusionism and Eurocentric History* (New York: Guilford, 1993), 206.

9. Max Weber, *The Protestant Ethic and the Spirit of Capitalism* (London: Allen & Unwin, 1930), 2.

cultures to some extent.[10] However, explanations do not always provide an adequate basis for transformation; people can understand the causes of a problem without finding a solution. The values embodied in the social structures of exploited peoples have to be transformed for the people to experience economic growth and empowerment.

Secularization and the Rejection of Mysticism and Magic

Weber perceived that the economic growth of Europe was facilitated, if not inspired, by the secularization of economic values. Calvin's God, according to Weber, was not mystical or magical but intensely practical. Protestants eliminated "magic as a means of salvation," making the world less bewitched, where the freedom of human responsibility could flourish.[11] Calvin taught that the individual believer had "a vocation to serve God in the world—in *every* sphere of human existence—lending a new dignity and meaning to ordinary work. . . . Work was thus seen as an activity by which Christians could deepen their faith."[12]

The Christians who embraced Calvin's theology were no longer enslaved by their agents of causation; they empowered themselves to take the moral responsibility for their economic growth. They created a more secular world, transforming the structures that governed their lives through the creation of a set of values called the "Protestant ethic." These values included industry, frugality, thrift, punctuality, justice, and delayed gratification. By expressing these values, they made their societies conducive to economic prosperity.

Critiques of Weber's Thesis

Weber's thesis has received considerable support and criticism over the years. W. Arthur Lewis supports it by repeating the Calvinist notion that "economic growth depends on attitudes toward work, to wealth, to thrift."[13] Daniel Bell notes that the "Protestant ethic . . . supplies the moral energy and drive of the capitalist entrepreneur."[14] Gunnar Myrdal,

10. See George B. N. Ayittey (*Africa in Chaos* [London: MacMillan, 1998]), who argues that the time to blame African troubles on Europe is over. African governments have to take responsibility for the corruption that has generated such poverty in their societies.

11. Weber, *Protestant Ethic*, 117. See also James M. Byrne, *Religion and the Enlightenment: From Descartes to Kant* (Louisville: Westminster/John Knox, 1996); and R. H. Tawney, *Religion and the Rise of Capitalism* (1922; reprint, London: Penguin, 1990).

12. Alister McGrath, "Calvin and the Christian Calling," *First Things* 94 (June–July 1999): 33, 34.

13. W. Arthur Lewis, *The Theory of Economic Growth* (Homeward, Ill.: Irwin, 1955), 14.

14. Daniel Bell, *The Cultural Contradictions of Capitalism* (New York: Basic Books, 1996), 289.

author *of Asian Drama: An Inquiry into the Poverty of Nations*, also supports it, albeit, negatively. Concerning why people are poor, he notes, "Their unresponsiveness to opportunities for betterment, and their scorn of manual labor, especially working for an employer, may result, directly or indirectly, from long ages of hopeless poverty."[15]

Peter L. Berger, who describes himself as "an unreconstructed Weberian," notes that a value shift was central to the formation of capitalism and suggests that "something *like* Weber's 'Protestant ethic' is probably functional in an early phase of capitalist growth. This ethic, whether religiously inspired or not, values personal discipline, hard work, frugality, and a respect for learning."[16] These authors support Weber by focusing on the relationship between the growth of an economy and values that cultivate positive attitudes toward work.

R. H. Tawney, one of Weber's earliest and most important critics, argues that no relationship can be made between Protestantism—whether Calvinism or other expressions of Protestant faith—and economic growth. Tawney studied the factors of economic growth in England, which were similar to those on the continent, and concluded that "every aspect of English economic life was in process of swift transformation."[17] He claims that Weber ignored the intellectual movement, which was "favorable to the growth of business enterprise and to an individualist attitude towards economic relations, but which had little to do with religion."[18]

Kenneth E. Boulding's criticism of Weber takes a more political approach to the relationship between the Protestant movement and the growth of capitalism. The growth of capitalism, in his view, occurred because of the success of the northern Europeans in dissenting from the authority of the Pope. The legitimization of dissent is necessary for any innovation to become democratized. He postulated that "once the authority of the Pope had been challenged and a high value had been placed in the Protestant countries on successful dissent, the legitimization of dissent in general is a fairly easy step. . . . The development of a religious value system which stressed the immediacy of personal experience as over

15. Quoted in Lawrence E. Harrison, *Underdevelopment Is a State of Mind: The Latin American Case* (Lanham, Md.: Madison, 1985), 20.

16. Peter L. Berger, ed., *The Desecularization of the World: Resurgent Religion and World Politics* (Grand Rapids: Eerdmans, 1999), 16. While Berger notes that the values of the Protestant ethic, or similar values, are functional in an earlier state of economic growth, he also notes that "undisciplined hedonists can do well in the high-tech, knowledge-driven economies of the advanced societies" (ibid., 17).

17. Tawney, *Religion and the Rise of Capitalism*, 141.

18. Ibid., 312.

against the authority of a Pope or even a king ... should provide the groundwork for enormous changes in knowledge and technology."[19]

David S. Landes, a more recent critic of Weber, gives tacit support for Blaut by citing several instances where Weber's values were developed apart from the cultures of his Protestant ethic. Landes quotes the Zen monk Shosan (1579–1655) who "saw greed as a spiritual poison; but work was something else: 'All occupations are Buddhist practice; through work we are able to attain Buddhahood [salvation].'"[20] By citing Shosan and other examples of economic growth in non-European cultures, Landes supports the claim that "one does not have to be a Weberian Protestant to behave like one."[21] He asserts, "Indeed, it is fair to say that most historians today would look upon the Weber thesis as implausible and unacceptable: it had its moment and it is gone."[22]

Admittedly, Weber's thesis that the Protestant movement, through Calvin and his successors, gave birth to the rise of capitalism is difficult to defend. Capitalism has been evident in many cultures throughout history. Even the parable of the shrewd manager assumes the capitalistic nature of economic transactions in first-century Palestine, whether or not the populace realized the implications of their economic transactions.[23] They practiced a form of capitalism that negates Weber's thesis, as it is popularly understood.

The key word in Weber's thesis, however, is "rise." The Protestant movement did not give birth to capitalism. However, it gave rise to capitalism by legitimizing it as an acceptable practice for Christians. It gave them license to overcome the limitations that various agents of causation placed on them and on their counterparts in other cultures throughout the world. The Protestant movement was a secularizing force that democratized capitalism by legitimizing the masses of people to participate in the economic growth in Europe during the seventeenth and eighteenth centuries. Protestant theology, with its emphasis on the value of work, gave the economic growth of Europe the moral foundation it

19. Kenneth E. Boulding, "The Interplay of Technology and Values: The Emerging Superculture," in *Values and the Future,* ed. Kurt Baier and Nicholas Rescher (New York: Free Press, 1969), 546.

20. David S. Landes, *The Wealth and Poverty of Nations: Why Some Are So Rich and Some So Poor* (New York: Norton, 1998), 363.

21. Ibid.

22. Ibid., 177.

23. This statement implies that people understood economic *principles* long before Adam Smith and other modern economists, but they did not understand their *implications.*

needed to transform its economy from reciprocity to exchange and its culture from magic and mysticism to a moral ethos.

Human Productivity and God's Provision

That the values of the Protestant ethic influence cultural narratives to mediate the tension between human productivity and God's provision becomes apparent when a cultural narrative shifts its religious foundation from agentive to empirical causation. One side of this tension is practical atheism, an intellectual assent to the existence of God that does not acknowledge him as having a viable role in creating or sustaining the *kosmos*. Middle-class Americans, for example, depend on their professional values, such as economics or education, not on the providence of God, for survival and success.

The other side of the tension is the belief that God performs miraculous events to enhance the survival of a community, but this belief does not acknowledge that God's redemptive work in creation is realized through empirical means. People who live in cultures governed by agentive causation, either through magic or mysticism or other expressions of religious phenomenology, fail to cultivate the values that foster economic development. They live in fear, rather than in faith, forsaking their human calling to employ their moral responsibility to exercise stewardship over creation. Fear is expressed differently in various cultures throughout the world; the common factor is the fear of the powers that prevent people from controlling their lives and constructing environments that enhance their welfare. It has both passive and active expressions.

The cargo cults of Tanna, Vanuatu, serve as examples of passive fear. The people associated with a cult called the John Frum cult believe that John Frum, a Westerner who once visited them, will return with material wealth and usher in an era of economic prosperity. When Boyd Johnson visited them on behalf of a development agency, he invited them to participate in a community project to improve their living conditions. They refused because they thought that John Frum, or one of his representatives, would bring them all they needed.[24] John Frum was among the many agents of causation who made the people passive and powerless to change their reality. When the goods did not arrive, some of the people converted to Christianity, believing the cargo would come

24. Richard Boyd Johnson, *Worldview and International Development: A Critical Study of the Idea of Progress in the Development of World Vision Tanzania* (Ph.D. diss., Oxford Centre for Missions Studies, 1998), 1.

sooner if they shifted their allegiance. The converts, however, soon became disillusioned when Christianity failed to make them prosperous.[25]

However, like all people who interpret their religious faiths within the contexts of their existing narratives, the converts concluded their lack of instant prosperity was a sign that they were practicing their newly acquired faith erroneously. They attributed their error to their technique, not to their values, so that they decided to imitate the Christian workers by sitting around "tables with bottles of flowers in front of them, dressed in European clothes, waiting for the cargo ship or airplane to materialize."[26] The hope of the people in Tanna is characteristic of those who believe their economic development—or the development of any aspect of their culture—depends on an agent of causation beyond their control. They, like the people Jesus addressed in Luke 19:11–26, believe the appearance of a messianic figure will bring them political autonomy or economic prosperity, a belief that keeps them ignorant of the values they need to create prosperity.

The challenge for development workers who want to manage cultural change in a redemptive manner is empowering people to embrace secularization without assuming secularism. This involves a transformation from experiencing faith as a mystical, liminal experience to perceiving God's redemptive relationship with creation expressed in the normal structures of life. And it demands that agentive and empirical causation be held together, based on the belief that God causes all things but that people have the moral responsibility to manage change.

The story of Nawle, a traditional healer in Ethiopia, is an example of the active fear that prevents people from transforming their culture. While he was cutting grass for his animals one day, he received an inspiration to return to his village and to follow a detailed set of instructions that included healing the sick and casting spells on people. Nawle told the people about his vision, and many of them gathered around him, expecting him to heal their illnesses and to cast spells on their enemies. Nawle's followers brought him many gifts, including their cows, goats, chickens, and money in an effort to build a relationship with him. However, Nawle interpreted these gifts in terms of an exchange and told the people that they might die if they failed to bring them. He frightened them by telling them that he both healed and

25. Peter M. Worsley, "Cargo Cults," in *Magic, Witchcraft, and Religion: An Anthropological Study of the Supernatural*, ed. Arthur C. Lehmann and James E. Myers, 4th ed. (Mountain View, Calif.: Mayfield, 1997), 345.

26. Ibid.

cursed many people with the power the spirits gave him, and he boasted that he caused a man's animals to die when the man refused to give him a gift. The people, like obedient children, did everything Nawle told them to do, believing that they would die if they disobeyed him. Most people sought to find the gifts Nawle demanded from any place they could.

Living in a village where the spiritual governs the physical realm, the people created a direct relationship between their poverty and their fear of Nawle. Unlike the people of the cargo cult, who expressed their powerlessness by waiting for prosperity to come to them, the Ethiopians of Nawle's village transferred their wealth to him. They did not realize he was the source of their problem. The narrative of their culture, which was seasoned with magic, influenced them to believe that he protected them from an evil fate.

Economic Transformation

The Protestant ethic emerged because Calvin and other Protestant theologians grafted the social, political, and economic development of European cultures into the narrative of God's redemptive relationship with creation. The theology that emerged from this integrative effort empowered people to make a relationship between God, their hope for a better life, and hard work. It provided an alternative narrative for people who were weaned from governing their lives through magic, mysticism, or other expressions of religious phenomenology.

Transformation of Philosophical Foundations

The major issue concerning global economic development for Christians who want to manage change across cultures is whether the values of the Protestant ethic can be transported across cultures. These values were developed as an effort to graft the narrative of European cultures into the metanarrative of Christianity during the seventeenth and eighteenth centuries. Such grafting reveals the particularities of the redemptive work of Christ in specific cultures. It raises the question of whether the values of the Protestant ethic are relevant for the people in villages similar to the one in the parable of the shrewd manager. These include the people who reside in Nawle's Ethiopian village, for the members of the cargo cults, and for the people in the Asian village whose daughters are sold into prostitution. The answer to this question is a qualified "yes, but. . . ." William F. Ryan, S.J., researched the cultural portability of modern models of economics and concluded "that Western free-market models, which ignore spiritual and cultural values as 'externalities' . . . do not work in developing countries."[27] The significance of religions and religious values on the process of economic development cannot be underestimated. In analyzing economic development, Ryan asked why the same religion and values have different economic consequences in different historical and cultural settings.[28] I want to propose that the answer to this question is the key to transporting the values of the Protestant ethic across cultures. The same religion and the same values have different economic consequences because people have different understandings of how the agents of causation work in their cultures.

The values of the Protestant ethic express an effort to hold agentive and empirical together; they depict God, the ultimate agent of causation, as holding people morally responsible for the economic decisions they make. Efforts to transport modern economic principles across cultures fail because an agent of causation does not accompany the principles. The Protestant ethic was successful in Europe because the people were weaned from magic. However, unless modern economics is accompanied by a values system that offers an alternative to magic, people like Nawle and his followers will interpret economic development from a magical or mystical perspective rather than a moral one. But morality cannot replace magic unless the agent of causation is explicitly declared.

The ability to hold agentive and empirical causation together is the key to managing cultural change by facilitating economic growth. It is one of the most important issues involved in empowering people to pull themselves out of poverty. While visiting northern Ghana, I observed that villages that had a traditional priest were generally more impoverished than villages that did not. For example, I noticed the children in villages with a traditional priest were generally malnourished; they had poor hygiene and high rates of guinea worm infestation. I shared my observation with my translator, who responded, "Of course the people in this village are poor; they have to use what little money they have to pay for sacrifices."

People who are managing cultural change in such villages must address the influence of the traditional priest. These priests have generally been ignored or disparaged by Christians and are often depicted as the enemies of the gospel. The influence that priests exert calls Christians to

27. William F. Ryan, *Culture, Spirituality, and Economic Development: Opening a Dialogue* (Ottawa: International Development Research Centre, 1995), 13.
28. Ibid., 23.

work toward building a redemptive relationship with them, which does not mean that we approve of what they do, but it calls us to recognize how their power in their communities affects our efforts. We must find a way to use their influence.

During my visit to the Ghanaian villages, I asked my translator if we could visit the traditional priest. He was quite surprised but agreed. When we went to the priest's house, he was a little apprehensive but warmed up after a few minutes of conversation. After we shared our names, he asked what day of the week I was born on. (Names in that culture tell the day of the week on which a person was born.) The crowd who gathered around us laughed hilariously when I told him that I had no idea what day I was born on. Any intelligent person in that culture would have known that detail about their lives. The laughter from the crowd broke any tension that might have existed. I told the priest about my work and asked him about his. He talked about the spirits; I talked about the welfare of the community. He showed me his temple and the fetishes he used in his work; I told him about my concern for the village children who suffered from malnutrition and guinea worm infestation. He agreed with my concern, whether or not he understood it. At the end of the visit, we talked about the need to teach people about the germs that were jeopardizing their health. I emphasized that families needed to spend money on food and medicine to keep their children healthy. He agreed that money spent on food and medicine was well invested. This visit was important because it created the possibility of having the traditional priest endorse the objectives of the development project.

Health educators in a similar culture produced a video that featured a traditional priest who told about the death of his son. He said the child's death could have been prevented had he known what the health educators taught in the video. His endorsement gave the people the hope they needed to take the teachings in the video seriously; it empowered them to change their views of health, economics, and religions, among other things, and gave them the freedom to manage change in at least one aspect of their culture. His concern with magic had to be transformed to address morality.

Transformation through Small Enterprise Development

Capitalism has become globalized. People who have any hope of achieving economic viability in the present global economy can no longer assume that nature is the source of their wealth. They have to shift their economic media from reciprocity to exchange and gain the skills and knowledge that add value to their labor.

Small Enterprise Development (SED) projects are among the most popular methods of enhancing the economic viability of local economies. The good SED projects are successful for several reasons. First, they create employment opportunities, empowering people to build community by participating in an economic system in a significant manner. The apostle Paul was clear that people who take from the community should work honestly in a useful occupation, so that they have something to share with those in need (Eph. 4:28). While Paul directed this teaching to thieves, this passage can also be extended to address people who exploit communities through usury, prostitution, drugs, and various types of exploitation, including religious sacrifice. The creation of jobs is a major enhancement to the economic welfare of a community. The second reason why SED projects are successful is that "they give people opportunities to utilize and develop their faculties; they enable people to overcome their inborn self-centeredness by joining forces with other people in a common task, and they bring forth the goods and services needed by all of us for a decent existence."[29]

The third and main reason for the success of SED is that it fosters the values of the Protestant ethic that facilitate economic growth in a community. These values are apparent in the sixteen operating principles of the Grameen Bank, one of the most successful SED organizations. Some of these principles are discipline, justice, hard work, thrift, and a commitment to sacrifice short-term gains for long-term rewards. The principles also call for the transformation of cultural practices that stifle economic growth, such as practicing child-marriages and exchanging dowries.

Christians establish SED projects on the assumption that the redemptive work of God is embodied in the mundane structures of society. While the stories of Christian spirituality that focus on liminal experiences get the lion's share of attention, those that enhance the mundane structures of life, like local economies, deserve a place in the narrative of God's relationship with creation.

I visited an SED project in Cambodia that involved children raising chickens in the backyard of their school. The children raised the chicks to maturity and sold them to purchase school uniforms and supplies. The money made a valuable contribution to the community by enabling

29. E. F. Shumacher, *Good Work* (New York: Harper & Row, 1979), 118.

children to get an education, preventing them from suffering from the social and economic alienation of child exploitation.

SED projects have the potential to be redemptive; they can transform the distribution of resources in an economy in a just manner, empowering people to live in community with one another. They can generate reciprocity and facilitate exchange. However, SED projects need to be managed with caution to enhance economic welfare because economic growth on its own is not sufficient for reducing poverty. Often "the number of people in poverty can increase even as per-capita income increases."[30] Economic development in a culture can increase the gap between the rich and the poor to the point where it destroys any sense of community by allowing a few to get wealthy at the expense of the many. The values that govern the implementation and management of SED projects have to be interpreted within the context of the narrative of God's redemptive work in creation.

Communities that have successfully engaged in SED projects have the potential to experience the redemptive work of God through the secularization of Christian spirituality. The redemptive challenge in economics is not secularization but secularism. Secularization leads to the "Protestant lift," the idea that people experience economic growth when they are liberated from participating in many traditional cultural practices that detract from their economic well-being. Secularization, rather than secularism, gives economics a place in the redemptive narrative of Christianity.

30. Linwood T. Geiger, "Market Activity and Poverty: An Analysis of the Impact of the Market Economy on Poverty in Developing Countries," *Transformation*, July–September 1995, 19.

9

Science and Religion: Two Different Leading Functions

I don't like tractors, Lord. . . . Tractors are conceited. . . . For a tractor has no soul. . . . I offer you tonight, Lord, the work of all the tractors. . . . I pray that they may not crush [people] with their haughty power . . . but rather that they shall serve [people]; I pray that [people], in the freedom of [their] souls, shall dominate them, and thus praise you by their work, glorify you. . . .

Michel Quoist

In the beginning God created

Genesis 1:1

Moses was a community development advisor who encountered a steep learning curve when he went to a West African village. He expected his Christian beliefs to be different from those of the Islamic villagers, but their beliefs were different in a way he did not expect. The villagers, unlike Moses, perceived every aspect of creation, including technology, to have a spiritual character.

Change across Cultures

Moses received his first lesson on the spiritual ethos of technology when he worked with the villagers to build ventilated improved pit latrines. He thought the particular design he used was an expression of technology that was appropriate for the culture, and he could not imagine anything with fewer spiritual implications than an outhouse. However, he soon learned that the success of integrating any technological artifact into the culture depended on its ability to transform the spiritual ethos of the village. Technology brings its own character into a culture, and people submit to it if they want the technological artifact to work. The villagers, however, unlike people in many cultures, did not surrender to the uncompromising terms of technology, causing the outhouses to lose their effectiveness.

Their efficiency depended on clear specifications. An important feature was that the four walls could not have any windows, and pipes had to be installed from the pit of the latrine, along the exterior south-facing walls, extending above the roof. Solid walls prevented flies from entering the outhouse and odors from exiting. The metal pipes, extending from the pit of the latrine along the exterior walls and above the roof, created an updraft that caused the smells to rise above the rooftops of the village, protecting the villagers from unpleasant odors.

Moses instructed the villagers about the merits of the design and was confident that they understood the value of each feature. He was astonished when the villagers installed windows in the outhouses by cutting holes in the walls, defeating one of the major purposes of the design. He asked the village elders about the windows and learned that they would not use the outhouses without them, because they feared that the dark, moist, smelly structure would attract spirits. They did not care about protecting themselves from flies or odors, but the villagers were not going to make themselves vulnerable to spirits. The belief that the unseen world was far more threatening than the seen world influenced them to exclude spirits at the risk of being bothered by flies and odors.

The villagers rejected the design of the outhouses because Moses failed to interpret their meaning in terms of the values central to the *kosmos* of the village. Along with building outhouses, Moses should have taught the *Christus Victor* theory of the atonement, which would have influenced the people to use them without fear of the spirits. They could have transformed their fears and experienced the redemptive work of Christ in their community.

186

Science and Religion

Exploring the relationship between science and religion is a major issue in managing change across cultures. Most of the innovations introduced into traditional cultures through development projects have scientific and technological natures. These innovations often challenge the validity of traditional religious beliefs and practices and provoke questions concerning the relationship between science and religion. The outhouse design, for example, did not accommodate the indigenous beliefs in spirits.

In another project, village farmers rejected Moses' idea of using insecticides in attempting to control the bugs in their gardens in favor of hiring a sheikh, the spiritual leader of the village, to bury Qurʾan verses along the boundaries of the gardens. The villagers believed the verses had the spiritual power, called *baraka,* to keep insects out of the gardens. They thought everything had a spiritual character, and they assumed, as a self-evident truth, that the spiritual realm controls all aspects of the physical environment, including insects that destroy gardens. The farmers, unlike Moses, did not believe a good wall between religion and science made good neighbors. They reasoned that if Allah had the power to create the world, the Qurʾan, which embodies the power of Allah, must have the power to kill a few bugs.

Religion and science are complementary, even though they have different leading functions. Science's leading function is to unfold the empirical nature of creation by "observing relationships between varying natural events, proposing explanations for these relationships, and testing the validity of these explanations by evaluating their ability to predict future events."[1] Technology, an application of science, includes "all those machines, devices, and other physical apparatuses made and used by humans for instrumental purposes, and the physical products of those machines and devices,"[2] including computers, communication equipment, medical devices, transportation vehicles, and so on. Its leading function is the efficient application of scientific knowledge. People use technology to produce artifacts that enhance the efficiency of their lives. Religion is concerned with inspiring and empowering people to live "within the context of ultimate reality."[3] For orthodox religions, the

1. Bruce Bradshaw, *Bridging the Gap: Evangelism, Development, and Shalom* (Monrovia, Calif.: MARC, 1993), 127.
2. H. Russell Bernard and Pertti J. Pelto, "Technology and Anthropological Theory," in *Technology and Social Change,* 2d ed. (Prospect Heights, Ill: Waveland, 1972), 360.
3. Frederick Ferre, *Hellfire and Lightning Rods: Liberating Science, Technology, and Religion* (Maryknoll, N.Y.: Orbis, 1993), 35.

central concern is discerning truth and morality. Folk religions, in contrast, are concerned with garnering the power to cope with the challenges of daily living.

Science and religion, like pesticides and Qur'an verses, clash when their leading functions are confused. Science and technology have the potential to increase the efficiency of the many activities that comprise the efforts of Christians to extend the narrative of God's redemptive relationship with creation throughout the world. It enhances our ability to treat illnesses, increase food production, and provide clean water and sanitation, among other things. However, it cannot provide the values to address these ills.

Genesis as Narrative of Moral Responsibility

The confusion between the leading functions of science and religion have resulted in numerous debates. The majority of these debates have focused on the nature of the biblical creation narratives, particularly those in Genesis. The central question is whether the creation narratives have scientific validity or credibility.

Despite my conviction that this debate gets more attention than it deserves, I want to address it. Most of the discussion on the scientific integrity of the biblical creation narratives misses the main points of the passages. Some create a conflict between science and religion because they assume that science and religion have the same leading function. Science and religion are not inherently in conflict with each other; they make different contributions to the redemptive narrative of God's relationship with creation.

The Genesis creation stories are not scientific accounts in the sense that they explain how the world was created. Instead, they explicate the values inherent in creation. The central point of the first creation account is that God is the agent of causation. Genesis 1:1–2:4 is clear that God, in the beginning, created heaven and earth. The process through which God created the universe by transforming chaos into order affirms that creation is good; God's redemptive relationship with it gives it purpose and meaning. The story of the fall, the central theme in the second Genesis account (2:4–3:24), bears witness to the moral nature of creation; it affirms that ideas and behavior have moral consequences. As a consequence of their disobedience, Adam and Eve were expelled from the Garden of Eden and made to endure suffering in the struggles of survival.

These passages provide explanations for the human condition as well as values for living. Among these is the belief that human beings are significant because of their unique relationship to God and the world. God gave them dominion over the world but limited their scope of moral authority by preventing them from declaring what is good and what is evil. Adam and Eve ate the forbidden fruit, and God responded to them as morally mature beings by allowing them to bear the consequences of their own behavior.

The significance of the Genesis creation accounts, as well as others in Scripture, is that God has a relationship with creation that is realized primarily through the moral expressions of human beings. The writers of Scripture did not consider whether their inspired teachings could be validated through the methods of modern science. The Scripture is a product of its time, and it was written to address specific issues. The applications of Scripture are timeless, but its historical affirmations are insulted by efforts to extend its intentions beyond their time reference.

Two affirmations of Scripture central to the creation narratives are that God loves creation and that human behavior has moral consequences. Questions concerning the scientific validity of the creation accounts miss these points. The authors of Scripture, particularly those of the creation narratives, were concerned with the moral nature of God's relationship with creation; the Scriptures should not be subject to principles they were never intended to support. Efforts to validate the creation narratives or any biblical teaching through science are reductionist.

Science and technology "treat religious belief as though it were itself a theory"[4] but don't question their own authority. Science oversteps its boundaries when it pretends to answer questions about ultimate reality. The sciences take for granted the existence of the universe and its basic constituents. However, "scientific laws and theories concern only the transformations of everything that now is."[5] Science cannot explain ultimate causes, and it is incapable of making valuations. However, despite these limitations, it is too often interpreted as the "the source of salvation, the agent of secularized redemption,"[6] offering a hope that is morally neutral and value-free.

By treating Scripture "as if it were a book of science ahead of its times, we tend to neglect both the human experiences that lie behind it and the theological affirmations it makes."[7] Our tendency to engage in this ef-

4. Roy A. Clouser, *The Myth of Religious Neutrality: An Essay on the Hidden Role of Religious Belief in Theories* (South Bend, Ind.: University of Notre Dame Press, 1991), 97.

5. Diogenes Allen, *Christian Belief in a Postmodern World: The Full Wealth of Conviction* (Louisville: Westminster/John Knox, 1989), 53.

6. Ian G. Barbour, *Science and Secularity: The Ethics of Technology* (New York: Harper & Row, 1970), 70.

7. Ian G. Barbour, *Religion in an Age of Science* (San Francisco: Harper & Row, 1990), 133.

fort, however, indicates that we do not realize how religion and science have two different leading functions under God's redemptive relationship with creation. It gives us the moral responsibility to interpret all aspects of life, including technology, within the context of the redemptive narrative of Christianity.

The Story of the Spirit in the Well

The West African villagers whom Moses worked with depended on a well for their daily survival. The women gathered there, in the tradition of their ancestors, not only to draw their daily ration of water but also to share the village news and seek encouragement for the daily struggles of life. The villagers believed that a spirit who disapproved of all technological innovations lived in the well and controlled the amount of water in it. Because of this belief, the villagers did not allow development practitioners to cover the well with a concrete slab, install a pump near the well, or drive cars or tractors near it. The spirit also prohibited menstruating women from going near the well.

Moses realized there was no way to prove or disprove the validity of the villager's belief, but he knew that it controlled their lives both physically and morally. For example, it was a physical hazard because not only would the well water be contaminated without a cover but also young children might fall into it and drown. He thought at least the village elders should install a pump to relieve the women of the burdensome task of drawing water. The moral hazard concerned Moses more because he knew that their fear of the spirit gave the villagers the opportunity to relinquish their responsibility of having dominion over creation and building just social and political structures. As long as the spirit controlled their village, the people remained powerless to bring about change in their community.

The power of the spirit to instill fear in the villagers should not be underestimated. The spirit literally held the village hostage, and all the villagers had a story about the well's becoming dry when someone violated the will of the spirit. Moses learned of the belief's enormous power one day when he parked his tractor too close to the well. He moved it, however, when a village elder chastised him, knowing that if he objected he would only get involved in a long conversation about the validity of the villagers' belief in the spirit of the well. Moses forgot about the incident until the village elder asked him for a goat, which was to be sacrificed because the water level of the well had dropped because of his tractor.

Goats were expensive, and Moses preferred not to buy one. He insisted that his tractor had no influence on the water level; it was caused instead by the fluctuations in rainfall and would remain low until the rainy season. But when the villagers shunned him and began to accuse him of witchcraft, he purchased a goat in order to secure the benefits of the development project for the village. He also thought that the sacrifice of the goat would prove to the villagers that the spirit had no power over the water level in the well.

The elders graciously accepted the goat and sacrificed it to the spirit of the well. Everyone benefited from a sacrifice: the spirit thrived on the blood, and the people feasted on the meat. When he noticed that the level of water in the well remained low during the next few weeks, Moses felt vindicated, thinking the low water level affirmed his belief about the influence of the spirit. He decided not to make an issue of it, expecting the villagers to come to the realization that the sacrifice had no influence on the amount of water in the well.

Moses was dismayed, however, to learn that the villagers began drawing water from the well because they believed the spirit had replenished it. They were convinced that the sacrifice had worked and that their belief in the power of the spirit was vindicated. Moses realized that there was another explanation: the level had been low because the people had been drawing water from the well faster than the well was replenishing it. However, the villagers began drawing less water from the well, believing that the water level dropped because of the spirit's anger. Since they used less water, Moses reasoned, the well had an opportunity to replenish itself, causing the water to rise.

Moses thought his explanation was logical, but what he hadn't counted on was that people often assent to an idea that has to do, not with the logical interpretation of evidence, but with reasons grounded in their culture.[8] What Moses encountered was a clash between two kinds of causation that is exasperated by technology. Technology tends to increase the complexity of a culture,[9] not by introducing efficiency, but by rearranging the social structures. In this case it threatened to redefine the roles of the men and women in the village. Technology was the traditional domain of the village men, and the well the domain of the women. If the men had allowed the pump to be moved into the domain

8. J. M. Blaut, *The Colonizer's Model of the World: Geographical Diffusionism and Eurocentric History* (New York: Guilford, 1993), 31.

9. Charles H. Kraft, *Anthropology for Christian Witness* (Maryknoll, N.Y.: Orbis, 1996), 176.

of women, they would have had to transform their absolute categories. They would have had to either surrender their sovereignty over technology or draw water.

While there are several approaches to Moses' dilemma, I want to address the moral implications of the villagers' belief in the spirit of the well. The spirit is an external factor preventing the people from taking responsibility for transforming their culture. The people acquiesced to the power of the spirits, which prevented them from becoming morally mature beings. This statement is not to imply that all people who believe in spirits are morally immature. Instead, it raises the question of whether people who do believe in spirits are taking the moral responsibility to control their lives despite their beliefs in the spirits. Spirits, like technology, cannot relieve people of their moral responsibility. People, unlike spirits and technology, are created in the image of God.

The people who lived in the village needed to exercise their moral responsibility to transform their social structures to enhance the lives of everyone in the village. If we want to frame this issue in terms of spiritual warfare, a notion that is popular in contemporary missions, the people could attempt to cast the spirit from the well, like chasing birds from a tree. The battle with the spirit, though, is not the central issue. The issue is the morality of the people.

The central question is whether the people will accept the moral responsibility to import technology into their village and bear its consequences. The inability of the people to shift their social structures to import technology into the domain of women is an indication of their moral immaturity. Their fear of the spirit was greater than their love for one another. This fear might be genuine, or the people might be using the spirit as a scapegoat. In either situation they are relinquishing their moral responsibility to the spirit by accepting a sense of powerlessness instead of acting with moral integrity, which is the central theme in the redemptive narrative of God's relationship with creation.

Technology and the Transformation of Culture

Rudolf Bultmann, a twentieth-century European theologian, once mused that "one cannot use electric lights and radio and call upon modern medicine in case of illness, and at the same time believe in the world of spirits and miracles." This statement is ironic in light of the widespread belief that science and technology are products of a theistic worldview. Despite the tension between religion and science throughout the history of Western culture, religious convictions set the context for scientific research by affirming that changes within the creation are reliable and predictable. Unlike agents of causation who manipulate changes in the physical world at their capricious will, God's creation has a systematic nature that is reliable and can be studied and documented; without this belief, the labors "of scientists would be without hope."[10] People would expend their efforts to understand the world by battling with spirits and coping with magic.

The tension that technology brings to the ethics of managing cultural change is its ability to transform a culture; technology is a "culturally transformative power that defines the shape of the world we live in and conditions our way of perceiving the world."[11] The narrative of technology organizes a culture around "a belief that the basis of general progress is the sufficiency of scientific innovations; it proposes that if we can ensure the advance of science-based technologies . . . a corresponding degree of improvement in the social, political and cultural conditions of life" will follow.[12]

Legitimizing Indigenous Technical Knowledge

The hegemony of science and technology throughout the world has tremendous impact on the validity of indigenous technical knowledge, which is a growing body of knowledge created within traditional cultures. Indigenous people glean it from developing solutions to the challenges they face as they cope with life; "it is the sum of knowledge . . . [that emerges from] folk wisdom and locally available techniques."[13]

Also known as local knowledge, indigenous technical knowledge emerges from virtually all aspects of a culture. In hunting and gathering cultures, this knowledge includes the various types of plant fluids that are applied to arrow and spear heads to kill animals. People who live in agricultural cultures have developed research to foster animal health. Farmers in Peru, for example, feed artichoke leaves to their cattle to prevent the cattle from getting liver flukes, large flat worms that live in the livers of domestic and wild mammals. The farmers evidently observed

10. Ferre, *Hellfire and Lightning Rods,* 8.

11. Harvey G. Cox, "The Responsibility of the Christian in a World of Technology," in *Economic Growth in World Perspective,* ed. Denys Munby (New York: Association, 1966), 173.

12. Leo Marx, "Does Improved Technology Mean Progress?" in *Technology and the Future,* ed. Albert H. Teich, 7th ed. (New York: St. Martin's, 1997), 9–10.

13. Eric Ram, "Traditional Medicine's Goods," *Together* 34 (April–June 1992): 22.

that cows do not suffer from liver flukes when they eat artichoke leaves.[14]

The credibility of indigenous technical knowledge has suffered from mystical beliefs such as burying Qur'an verses in gardens or appeasing the spirits of a well. Also, the efforts of many development agencies and governments to dismiss it have largely failed because it is ingrained in a people's culture, causing it to be a major factor in the ethical management of cross-cultural change.

A recent edition of the *Indigenous Knowledge and Development Monitor (IKDM)*, an electronic journal dedicated to the dissemination of local knowledge, reported that over 80 percent of the Nigerian population depends on indigenous medical treatment, primarily because modern health care is unavailable and unaffordable. Other research indicates that about 70 percent of the Ghanaian population relies on traditional healers, and only 30 percent benefits from modern medical facilities and service. It predicts that in the immediate future this will not change.[15]

While economics has been a major factor in the continued use of indigenous technical knowledge, it is not the only factor. Most local knowledge has emerged from cultures where agentive causation is supreme, and people in traditional cultures are somewhat satisfied with the tendency of scientific knowledge to deny any agent of causation. We saw this situation with the farmers in chapter 3 who attributed agricultural innovations to witchcraft because the agriculturalists did not name their agent of causation. Similarly, people who live in rural Ghana have categorized sicknesses as "home illnesses" and "hospital illnesses." They believe hospital illnesses do not have agents of causation while home illnesses do. They treat hospital illnesses with medicine and home illnesses with indigenous treatments, including rituals, sacrifice, and prayer.

The various efforts to develop traditional cultures by the conventional methods of importing money, technology, and knowledge have not been entirely sustainable because they tend to ignore local knowledge and practices.[16] The need to take indigenous technical knowledge seriously has led facilitators of cultural change to realize that all knowledge is cultural, and indigenous knowledge embodies the values and

14. See Consuelo Quiroz, "Local Knowledge Systems Contribute to Sustainable Development," in *Indigenous Knowledge and Development Monitor* 4.1 (April 1976); readable online at www.nuffic.nl/ciran/ikdm/4-1/articles/quiroz.html.

15. George B. N. Ayittey, *Africa in Chaos* (London: Macmillan, 1998), 146.

16. Quiroz, "Local Knowledge Systems."

employs the resources of the host culture, making change manageable, affordable, and sustainable. Systems of indigenous technical knowledge have become central factors in cultural change, and development agencies must find a way to work within them.

The Spirituality of Indigenous Technical Knowledge

Missionaries and other managers of cultural change are prone to think negatively of Christians in traditional cultures who use indigenous practices in areas such as health care. However, Christians in many traditional cultures do not have the choice to refuse medical care that is based on local knowledge. The closest modern hospital can be economically expensive and geographically distant. If indigenous technical knowledge is not managed as part of God's redemptive work in creation, it will become among the many traditional practices that go underground.

The central struggle missionaries have with indigenous technical knowledge is its relationship to agents of causation. I once asked a traditional healer in Zambia how he knew what herbs to use when treating people. He told me that a spirit sometimes reveals it through dreams or leads him to specific plants. This was the experience of James Hall, an American journalist who became a traditional healer in Swaziland. While Hall was searching for herbs to treat a person suffering from vomiting, he asked a spirit to guide him to the right plant because he'd heard about "healers who dreamt of places to find medicines: they woke up, went to the place, and there it was."[17] Being a rational American, he was dubious of such experiences. After praying to the spirit, however, Hall noticed a butterfly resting on a bush and interpreted it to be an epiphany of the spirit who guided him. Hall, like the traditional healer in Zambia, treated the person with herbs he believed the spirits revealed to him.

Hall's subsequent use of the herbs engaged a systematic and empirically verifiable method. He developed a hypothesis that a certain herb could cure a particular illness and tested it by treating a person with the illness. He then observed the effects, made some conclusions about the herb's potency, and replicated the process with other patients, modifying the process to accommodate different conditions. The experiences of James Hall and the traditional healer provoke the question of whether knowledge has validity despite its source. Should knowledge be condemned because the people who developed it believe it came from spirits?

17. James Hall, *Sangoma: My Odyssey into the Spirit World of Africa* (New York: Simon & Schuster, 1994), 153.

The answer to this question is no. If God is the source of all knowledge, he evidently works redemptively through all human communities, empowering people to find and use information that enhances their ability to support life in their respective cultures. It is apparently part of God's role in sustaining and reconciling all elements of creation. The validity of the knowledge should not be dismissed simply because people question its source. The production of the knowledge is not value-free or morally neutral; it is a redemptive effort that people from all cultures pursue. Human beings pursue knowledge; it is fundamental to their nature.

Knowledge should be appreciated on its own merits, not on the agreeableness of its sources. Indigenous technical knowledge bears witness to a creation that is radically reliable. The people who discover and use it are among the "people's scientific community."[18] They are among the people throughout the world who have developed a range of knowledge to solve the problems that face them as they cope with the challenges of life in their environments. Their successes and failures contribute to the knowledge of cultural practices and participate in the redemption of the creation.

The Science of Indigenous Technical Knowledge

The discovery of much indigenous technical knowledge is a religious quest in most traditional cultures. It gives the people who engage in the practice a liminal experience that elevates them from the mundane tasks of research, and the knowledge serves as an icon of the spiritual realm.

The ability of local knowledge to put people in a relationship with their agents of causation, or other aspects of their spiritual realm, is an authentic religious experience. For example, the rituals that accompany the search for and the application of herbs used in traditional medical treatments serve the leading function of religion. They put people in touch with their perceptions of ultimate reality. Some of these treatments are effective; the people are cured for a particular ailment.

Indigenous technical knowledge can serve the leading function of religion by empowering people to relate to their agents of causation, but its ability to serve that function does not authenticate its technical application. Local knowledge might be very effective in serving religious purposes. However, its redemptive value in agriculture, medicine, or other

18. Robert Rhoades and Anthony Bebbington, "Farmers Who Experiment: An Untapped Resource for Agricultural Research and Development," in *The Cultural Dimension of Development: Indigenous Knowledge Systems*, ed. D. Michael Warren, L. Jan Slikkerveer, and David Brokensha (London: Intermediate Technology, 1995), 306.

technical pursuits requires scientific validation, which is among the redemptive purposes of science and technology. The authentication of indigenous technical knowledge is one of the leading functions of science.

Science participates in the redemptive narrative of God's relationship with creation by validating indigenous technical knowledge. It recognizes that all knowledge is a product of a culture, and its validity depends on its place within a cultural narrative. The knowledge of gravity, for example, was indigenous to seventeenth-century Europe. Isaac Newton was not the first person to observe that apples fell from trees to the ground, but he created a system that explained the physical behavior. Science legitimated and universalized the laws of gravity. The most successful effort to either validate or invalidate indigenous technical knowledge has been through the transformation of the culture that produced the knowledge. This process seeks to determine what values serve as the foundation of behavior. Because knowledge is a product of values and values are an expression of beliefs, people will either discard or improve practices incompatible with their ethical structures.

The efforts to affirm and improve traditional health care practices by validating indigenous technical knowledge through the process of appreciative inquiry have been significant. Appreciative inquiry examines behavior in order to discern values. A good example of validating local knowledge involves the traditional healers in the Tugen culture, a small ethnic group in Kenya. They developed an effective herbal treatment for visceral leishmaniasis, a tropical parasitic disease.[19] The treatment has enough scientific validity to affirm that it cures the disease reasonably well and inexpensively. It proved effective, not because it agrees with the traditional healers' agents of causation, but because science has confirmed that it is effective. Hence, the treatment is redemptive to the extent that it cures the illness.

Some traditional treatments based on indigenous technical knowledge are being improved by modern medical research. In Tanzania, for example, traditional healers can effectively treat *degede*, a disease that causes high fevers in children. The problem is that traditional healers are unable to distinguish between *degede* and malaria, so that they treat malaria the way they treat *degede*. The inability of traditional healers to distinguish between the two diseases results in preventable deaths. Rather

19. See Kaendi Munguti, "Indigenous Knowledge in the Management of Malaria and Visceral Leishmaniasis among the Tugen of Kenya," *Indigenous Knowledge and Development Monitor* 5.1 (April 1997): readable online at www.nuffic.nl/ciran/ikdm/5-1/articles/mungutiart.htm.

than condemning them, health educators have validated the traditional treatment for one disease and trained traditional healers to diagnose malaria. In this sense, indigenous technical knowledge is being transformed to be redemptive.

Sometimes scientists cannot validate indigenous technical knowledge, and there are at least three reasons for this. First, science has not discovered why the knowledge is effective. Many herbal treatments in African cultures, for example, appear to have some scientific validity, but scientists are still working to discover the reasons for their efficacy. The treatments might have some active agent that science does not understand, or they could have a placebo effect. The redemptive value of these treatments, beyond their use as placebos, is unknown. Second, science has rejected certain kinds of indigenous knowledge as having no validity. Some local knowledge is influenced by the fall and does not fulfill the purposes for which people create it. Traditional treatments to cure AIDS are good examples. Markets are full of elixirs that are sold to cure AIDS. However, the scientific community has not endorsed the effectiveness of any of them. They are not redemptive because they cannot do what they promise; hence, they offer a false hope. The third reason why certain kinds of indigenous technical knowledge are not endorsed by science is that they exist beyond the rational mode of science and cannot be verified. Fertility rites are good examples of transrational knowledge. Somehow many traditional fertility rites are effective, but their effectiveness is attributable to reasons that go beyond the scope of scientific method.

Science and religion have had a tense relationship ever since Nicolaus Copernicus (1473–1543) discovered that the universe is heliocentric rather than geocentric. This tension has created a divorce between science and religion that continues into our postmodern world. People continue to hold religious convictions and scientific observations apart, particularly in the midst of the technological innovations that people currently enjoy.

The challenge for people managing change across cultures is to hold these three products of human culture in complementary relationships. Science, technology, and religion participate in the redemptive narrative of God's relationship with creation by serving different leading functions, each of which has redemptive value in that they enhance the efforts of people to transform the elements of their cultures in manners that support life. The problem that cross-cultural ethicists face when they mediate between science, technology, and religion stems from their inability to interpret science and technology from the redemptive narrative of God's relationship with creation. Science and technology, particularly in Western cultures, have created a narrative of their own, influencing people to believe that they have superseded religion. They depict religion as a set of pre-scientific or pre-technological beliefs that will eventually disappear as they begin to solve more and more problems.

The redemptive response to the relationship between religion, science, and technology, however, is realizing that they have a generative relationship with each other that is based on different leading functions. Religion is focused on a moral response to living in relation to ultimate reality; it is concerned with values, and answers questions concerning why. Science and technology answer questions concerning how. They are not value-free. They participate in the redemptive narrative of God's relationship with creation and with the values that enhance life.

10

Reconciliation: A Commitment to a Better Future

God . . . gave us the ministry of reconciliation.

2 Corinthians 5:18

Forgetting prolongs captivity; remembering is the secret of redemption.

Jewish Proverb

You can't do development in this culture without reconciliation!" This potent statement from a development facilitator exhorted me to include a module on reconciliation in a workshop on managing cultural change. We invited some people from Rwanda who were keen to explore the place of reconciliation in their efforts to manage cultural change after the genocide in their country in 1994.

We started the workshop by identifying expectations. The first person who spoke was from Rwanda. He stood up and said, "Jesus told us to love our enemies and to pray for those who persecute us." I nodded in agreement; then his voice cracked with emotion. He took a deep breath and said, "There is a man who lives in my neighborhood who killed my mother and my three sisters. His daughters wear my sisters' dresses. This man does not show any remorse for killing my family. I want to know how I can love him as Jesus taught."

A facilitator's role is to summarize a participant's statement to a concisely stated objective; that statement spoke for itself. Everyone in the workshop was silent—for what seemed to be an eternity. I recalled how Job's friends comforted him when they sat with him in silence for two weeks. Job rebelled when his friends broke their silence. Their talk changed their roles from comforters to antagonists; in their attempt to interpret the meaning of his tragedy, they devalued his pain. I was relieved when someone broke the silence by suggesting that we pray for our colleague who shared his heart with us.

The workshop participants struggled with these issues, believing that we could shed some light on them, but we could only ask questions about the mystery of God's sovereignty and the role of forgiveness in reconciliation. How does forgiveness relate to loving one's enemies? Is forgiveness, like love, unconditional? How do we hold these two virtues together? What about justice? Should people forgive and forget, believing that justice is unattainable simply because nothing can bring this man's family back to life?

The quest for answers took me on a journey to Rwanda. Upon my arrival, my host took me to a temple of the massacre, a church in Nyamata. The number of entries in the guest book, including ambassadors, government officials, authors, and missionaries, reads like a who's who in international relations and community development. People go there to see what happened, but they leave knowing that they experienced something more profound than they could grasp. Visits to the church transform tourists into pilgrims.

Hundreds of people, including men, women, and children, fled to the church to seek refuge from the genocide, believing the killers, many of whom were members of the congregation, could not touch them there. They did not realize, however, that churches were targeted by the killers in order to desecrate them and to destroy the people's confidence in their protection. Armed with pangas, the killers entered the church and killed everyone in it. More Rwandese died in churches and parishes than anywhere else.[1]

---

1. For a complete account see African Rights, *Rwanda: Death, Despair, and Defiance* (London: African Rights Publications, 1994).

The community leaders chose to leave the bones as a memorial to the massacre; they littered the sanctuary. Skulls, split like melons, had panga blades hanging from them. The stench of death lingered everywhere. The symbols at the front of the church communicated an eerily awesome message. Pictures of Jesus hung on the wall displaying biblical verses such as "God is my shepherd" (Ps. 23:1) and "I am the good shepherd" (John 10:14). An open prayer book lay on the altar surrounded by a trinity of skulls, placed there, perhaps to mock the message, "In him was life, and the life was the light of all people" (John 1:4).

In one sense, the church is a memorial to neighbors who became enemies. The Hutus and the Tutsis lived as neighbors, purchased goods and services from each other, and even married each other. They bore children, called Hutsis, who lived in harmony with their Hutu and Tutsi neighbors. Yet, these neighbors became enemies who were responsible for one of the most ruthless genocides in the history of humankind. In another sense, the church is an indictment of its own moral impotence. Rwanda is often cited as the most Christian nation in the world, with over 90 percent converts. However, the church in Rwanda was seduced by political power and ideologies, ignoring its own message of reconciliation.[2] The "reasons for converting to Christianity were fundamentally social and political. Christian values did not permeate very deeply."[3] The church lost its leading function as a fiduciary agent in the culture; bishops sold their prophetic role in the society for political favors, becoming errand boys to politicians "who have preached murder and filled the rivers with blood."[4] Many of the church leaders were among the last people to denounce the genocide.

Ethnic conflict, like a rash, has infected people all over the world. Like the Hutus and the Tutsis, the Croatians and the Serbians were also neighbors, going to school and working together, even going with the same girls.[5] They too became enemies and sacrificed many lives to kill the "other." The people of Somalia, the most ethnically unified country in Africa, likewise, held themselves hostage as they tried to save them-

2. Laurent Mbanda, *Committed to Conflict: The Destruction of the Church in Rwanda* (London: SPCK, 1997), 51.

3. Gerard Prunier, *The Rwanda Crisis: History of a Genocide* (Kampala, Uganda: Fountain, 1995), 34.

4. African Rights, *Rwanda*, 510.

5. Michael Ignatieff, *The Warrior's Honor: Ethnic War and the Modern Conscience* (New York: Owl, 1997), 35.

selves by self-destruction, adding to the toll of intrastate conflict, whether ethnic, tribal, social, or political and economic.

There is not a part of the world free from destructive conflict; most of its 42 million refugees are victims of violence and conflict.[6] And the cost has been immense. Over 3.5 million people have been killed, 24 million were displaced within their own countries, and 18 million sought refuge in other countries.[7] Yet, the causes have been difficult to understand; some of them border on the trivial. When one journalist asked a Serbian why his people were fighting with the Croatians, he took a pack of cigarettes out of his pocket and said, "These are Serbian cigarettes. Over there . . . they smoke Croatian cigarettes." After a moment of reflection, he added, "The real problem with Croats is that they think they are better than us." Finally, he decided, "We're actually all the same."[8]

The man, like many people, trivialized the reasons for his participation in the war. However, ethnic clashes have more to do with political and economic interests; "time after time, [a] proximate cause of violence is governmental exploitation of communal differences. . . . The 'communal card' is frequently played, for example, when a government . . . finds it convenient to wrap itself in the cloak of ethnic, racial or religious rhetoric."[9] The man who wants to conquer his neighbor is not fighting about ethnic differences; he is being enticed by the persuasive lie that sacrificing his neighbor will empower him to enjoy a larger share of the community's political and economic resources.

Genocide as a Sacrificial Crisis

"Meanwhile, all across Rwanda: murder, murder, murder, murder. . . . Take the best estimate: eight hundred thousand killed in a hundred days."[10] The killings in Rwanda were executed with religious zeal, transforming murder into sacrifice. As a central principle used to interpret reality, sacrifice is an effort to restore order in the *kosmos* when things go terribly wrong. Its victims range from people to chickens. Development

6. Michael Cranna, introduction to *The True Cost of Conflict*, ed. Michael Cranna (London: Earthscan, 1994), xvii.

7. Siobhan O'Reilly, "The Contribution of Area Development Programmes (ADPs) to Peace-Building," in *Working with the Poor: New Insights and Learnings from Development Practitioners*, ed. Bryant L. Myers (Monrovia, Calif.: MARC, 1999), 116.

8. Ignatieff, *Warrior's Honor*, 36.

9. Timothy D. Sisk, *Power Sharing and International Mediation in Ethnic Conflicts* (Washington, D.C.: U.S. Institute of Peace, 1996), 17.

10. Philip Gourevitch, *We Wish to Inform You That Tomorrow We Will Be Killed with Our Families: Stories from Rwanda* (Oxford: Picador, 1999), 133.

practitioners in many cultures throughout the world have witnessed rituals of sacrificing chickens, goats, cows, and bulls to ensure the success of such development efforts as drilling wells, planting gardens, treating illnesses, constructing buildings, and achieving social or political power. In a central African village, the people blamed a crack in the wall of a newly constructed building on the construction worker's failure to make a sacrifice before they erected it. The villagers sacrificed a goat before repairing it, and they believed its stability was due to the efficacy of the sacrifice.

Whether expressed through war, ethnic cleansing, or religious ritual, sacrifices mask the moral nature of reality, preventing people from taking full responsibility for their actions until they experience a sacrificial crisis. The basic assumption of a sacrificial worldview is that external agents of causation, who comprise the elements of the *kosmos*, have capricious natures and require homage to dispense their blessings. The quest for blessing through sacrifice externalizes the moral ethos of a community.

A sacrificial crisis is the realization that a sacrifice has failed to fulfill the purposes for which it was executed. Various forms of violence invariably result in a sacrificial crisis, which happened in Rwanda when people realized that the genocide did not change the fundamental structures of their society. Similarly, the people in the central African village who offered a sacrifice to the spirits prior to repairing a cracked wall in a building will experience a sacrificial crisis until they realize that the adequate mixture of concrete, not the blood of goats, holds the building together.

People will respond to a sacrificial crisis by either transforming their behavior or destroying some aspect of their culture. The collapse of apartheid in South Africa is another example of a sacrificial crisis; the apartheid system collapsed because of its own immorality. The Soviet Union, as well, could no longer sustain itself under Communism, which had lost its leading function of providing order in society and began to deny people their basic human rights. The creation of the Christian church was a response to the sacrificial system of Judaism. The Hebrew prophets were adamant that the temple sacrifices could not facilitate the worship of the people. They offered sacrifices in lieu of mercy, an indication that they were practicing an external expression of their faith without cultivating their moral transformation. The prophets, particularly Hosea, preached that God required mercy, not sacrifice (Hos. 6:6).

The people in the Jewish community at the time of Jesus still didn't fully grasp the meaning of this message. They lived in a culture of limited good and gave more thought to sacrifice than to mercy. Jesus reminded them to consider this teaching, one that they had known for generations: God requires mercy, not sacrifice (Matt. 9:13). The Jewish people, realizing they could not follow every letter of the law, hoped to resolve their sacrificial crises by changing the law. They evidently realized that it was not enhancing their relationship with God and thought it would change, particularly if Jesus was the expected Messiah. Jesus emphatically taught, however, that the law would not change and offered himself as a solution to their sacrificial crisis. He affirmed that he did not come to abolish the law or the prophets; "until heaven and earth disappear, not the smallest letter, not the least stroke of a pen, will by any means disappear from the Law" (Matt. 5:18). The Jews could resolve their sacrificial crisis only by following Jesus; the law was not going to change.

Responses to a Sacrificial Crisis

Sacrificial crises are inherent in virtually every human culture. For instance, people engage in an act of violence only to learn that did not produce the desired result. There are three major responses to a sacrificial crisis. The first is to allow the rituals to reify themselves and to continue practicing them whether or not they are beneficial. The second response is to externalize the problem by blaming a victim, and the third is to solve the problem by taking moral responsibility.

The first response of grafting a practice into the traditions of a culture even when they are obsolete gives people an identity they can neither live with nor live without. Major portions of the New Testament are dedicated to liberating the Jews from their enslavement to a law that had become reified. Paul was emphatic that only Christ could deliver them from their enslavement, but they often continued to obey the law even after they followed Christ.

The second response is to externalize the problem by putting blame onto a victim, or scapegoat. In the Hebrew Scriptures the community cast its sins on a goat or another animal, who then carried them into the wilderness (Lev. 16:10–22). The system assumed that the goats would not return to the community. But they did return, bringing the sins of the people back into the community. They then became living examples of a failed sacrificial system. Casting responsibility of the wrongs in a society onto a scapegoat is a common response to social conflicts, whether ethnic or otherwise. The people who seek to exculpate themselves from moral responsibility cast their sins on the victims and ostracize them from their communities. If the victims stay in the community, those who attempted to sacrifice them have the option either to ignore or to kill them. People from minority ethnic groups or those who are politically powerless, for example, can live in a community as long as they know their place and keep silent.

The sacrificial system requires perfect victims because they must absorb the sin of the community and externalize it (Lev. 22:21). If the sacrificial system fails, those who executed it cannot declare that they tried but failed; they must take responsibility for its effectiveness. And they must ensure that the conditions of the sacrifice are moral and just.

The alternative to the use of a scapegoat, the third response to a sacrificial crisis, is to take the moral responsibility of addressing the conflictive issues and move toward reconciliation. Reconciliation occurs when people realize that "changing oneself is an essential, inescapable first step in changing anything or anyone else."[11] The people on each side of a divisive issue must negotiate with one another and engage in a process of forgiveness, committing themselves to building a better future.

From a Sacrificial to a Moral Worldview

The Gospel accounts of Jesus' feeding of five thousand men and an undisclosed number of women and children illustrate the transition from a sacrificial to a moral worldview. Each of the Gospel writers records the event. It can be found in Matthew 14:14–21, Mark 6:30–44, Luke 9:10–17, and John 6:4–13. I shall refer to the story generally because my interpretation concerns the whole and not the particulars of a specific Gospel account. Most contemporary conservative interpretations of the story focus on the physical expansion of bread and fish,[12] which assumes that a miracle must defy the physical laws of nature. This assumption, however, is not necessarily valid; a miracle can also defy the laws of human nature.

An alternative interpretation of the feeding passages is that Jesus reconciled a crowd of people who were ethnically, religiously, and politically diverse by inspiring them to eat with one another. The twelve baskets of food that were collected at the end of the meal bear witness to the abundance of God's grace as people live in a reconciled community. This interpretation, which focuses on reconciliation, makes the miraculous ex-

11. Michael Henderson, *The Forgiveness Factor: Stories of Hope in a World of Conflict* (Salem, Oreg.: Grosvenor, 1996), 132.

12. See William L. Lane, *The Gospel according to Mark*, New International Commentary on the New Testament (Grand Rapids: Eerdmans, 1974); and Norval Geldenhuys, *Commentary on the Gospel of Luke*, New International Commentary on the New Testament (Grand Rapids: Eerdmans, 1951).

pansion of the bread incidental to the meaning of the event. Its vitality is the belief that miracles have multiple expressions; this miracle was one of inspiring people to overcome the cultural and social barriers that alienated them from each other and prevented them from sharing what little food they might have had. It hangs on the opinion that the boy mentioned by John (6:9) was not the only person in a crowd of more than five thousand people who had any food. Many other people probably had food, but they refused to eat with the others. In a culture where a person's identity was shaped by whom they ate with, the people who had food could not risk becoming what they perceived the other people to be.

We cannot read the accounts of the feeding of the five thousand without realizing that a crowd of that size would have contained a variety of persons, many of whom would be too clean or unclean to associate with one another. The crowd would have contained Pharisees who were too clean to eat with anyone. It would also have contained tax collectors and prostitutes, people who earned their living through sin. There were undoubtedly a few adulterers in the crowd, with some Samaritans sprinkled in. Also, no crowd would have been complete without a few Gentiles lurking on the edge, wondering what this idea of a messiah was all about.

For the early Jews, eating together was a religious experience, and a proper meal for the Jew was a worship service in which the ordinary details of life are sanctified. And "cleanliness was paramount: clean food, clean dishes, clean hands, [and] clean hearts"[13] were essential, but clean company was most important. No self-respecting Jew would eat with unclean people. This act would defy the symbols that governed their lives.

The miracle of the story is inspiring people to overcome the cultural barriers that depict others as unclean and unacceptable. John A. Grassi suggests that "the finding of five loaves hints that there was a willingness on the part of some people to share five of the disk-shaped breads. . . . They were usually kept out of sight and fresh, stored in a pouch or belt wallet."[14] There were numerous reasons why the people in this crowd would not be seen with one another; eating together was simply taboo. Yet, in this feast, which has often been interpreted as a precursor to the Eucharist, people from every social strata came together, creating a mosaic of humanity. The absolute cultural distinctives were

13. Barbara Brown Taylor, "Table Manners," *The Christian Century,* 11 March 1998, 257.
14. *Loaves and Fishes: The Gospel Feeding Narratives* (Collegeville, Minn.: Order of St. Benedict, 1991), 35.

made relative. How could the people in this crowd possibly give up what they protected so tenaciously and eat together?

They ate together because Jesus created a sense of community, liberating them from the cultural barriers that alienated them from one another. He organized them into small groups; they saw one another face to face, and they recognized one another's humanity as they participated in the prayer that Jesus led. As Jesus stepped out on faith and instructed the disciples to feed the multitudes with five loaves and two fish, they were free to reach into their satchels and share their bread with one another. At the end of the day, the surplus was greater than anyone could have imagined.

The important point of the story is that Jesus reconciled the people who would have otherwise alienated one another because of ethnic or religious practices. The bread might have expanded as Jesus challenged the disciples to step out on faith to share the meager offerings of five loaves and two fish because "God multiplies bread that is shared."[15] However, this act of faith also challenged the crowd to consider who they were and who sat beside them. The meal motivated them not only to relate to the "other" but also to recognize that they are like the "other."

Their experience of eating together was a ritual that brought a sense of unity among them. The story has both eucharistic and eschatological implications. It brought the people together and gave them a taste of heaven.[16] Walter Brueggemann, while not giving explicit support to the sharing interpretation, suggests the feeding of the five thousand is a precursor to "the new world coming into being through God. . . . Jesus *took, blessed, broke* and *gave* the bread. These are the four verbs of our sacramental existence. Jesus conducted a Eucharist, a gratitude."[17]

By feeding the five thousand, Jesus reconciled the disparate people of a community to one another, empowering them to affirm one another's humanity, transforming the elements of the *kosmos* that governed their lives, including the religious, ethnic, political, social, and economic structures that separated them. They shifted their image of themselves from "I am because they aren't" to "I am because we are," realizing that Christ transforms people into new creations. The church is composed of these

15. Ibid., 50.

16. C. S. Mann, *The Gospel according to Mark*, Anchor Bible (Garden City, N.Y.: Doubleday, 1986), 300–301.

17. "The Liturgy of Abundance, the Myth of Scarcity," *The Christian Century*, 24–31 March 1999, 346.

new creations, and reconciliation is a central ministry of the global church. It provides the context of civil society.

Civil Society and the Journey to Reconciliation

The workshop participant who asked how he could love and pray for the neighbor who showed no remorse for killing his family displayed the spiritual maturity that bought him beyond the confines of a sacrificial worldview. He wanted to break the cycle of violence that accompanies sacrifices and seeks justice through revenge, prolonging the suffering that has affected everyone. The problem he faced was reconciling himself to his neighbor. He believed that his neighbor's refusal to show any remorse for the killing rendered him unfit for reconciliation.

Reconciliation is a future hope and a present reality; it entails the restoration of individual lives within the context of the larger society. The genocide in Rwanda or ethnic conflict in any culture is a statement that the *kosmos* has crumbled, losing its ability to order human life. It has to be rehabilitated and requires that each aspect of the society be rebuilt in order for it to fulfill its leading function. The economic base has to create employment opportunities and generate the flow of currency; utility systems have to be repaired, providing water, electricity, and transportation; land has to be reclaimed, and houses have to be rebuilt. The restoration process also includes, among other things, social harmony and an integrated spiritual ethos.

The efforts of mission agencies and other nongovernmental organizations to rebuild a society, or significant aspects of it, have introduced the term "civil society" into the vocabularies of missionaries and development practitioners. Civil society, a major outcome of reconciliation, is the web of institutions and relationships neither created nor controlled by the state; it "includes families, religious organizations, businesses, unions, and a vast array of smaller voluntary organizations. . . . Their members 'are personally aware of each other and interact with each other, thereby giving their members a meaningful sense of belonging.' "[18] Civil society provides an arena in which individual freedoms and collective values are complementary.[19] It is the place where our basic humanity expresses it-

18. Ronald J. Sider, *Just Generosity: A New Vision for Overcoming Poverty in America* (Grand Rapids: Baker, 1999), 82, quoting Stephen V. Monsma, "Poverty, Civil Society, and the Public Policy Impasse," in *Toward a Just and Caring Society: Christian Responses to Poverty in America*, ed. David P. Gushee (Grand Rapids: Baker, 1999), chap. 2.

19. Robert Wuthnow, *Christianity and Civil Society: The Contemporary Debate* (Valley Forge, Pa.: Trinity Press International, 1996), 7.

self and where people live out their lives in community with one another, seeking the common good.[20] Civil society, when it is fully functioning, bears the ethos of a redeemed society by assigning "personal moral responsibility to those who [have] no legal or moral authority in their culture."[21] Many Ethiopian villages restored after the famines of the 1980s are prime examples of civil society; the people rebuilt their communities after they received the political freedom to make the choices that suited their best interests.

Civil society transforms the ethos of a sacrificial culture into a moral one, affirming that people have the capacity to invest their personal efforts into the construction of a society that benefits themselves as well as everyone else. Sacrificial cultures, which are based on the image of limited good, imply that people receive benefits at the expense of others and that they exist in an economy of scarcity. The ethos of civil society defies this principle; it affirms that the benefits of morality are self-perpetuating. Like the five thousand or more people who ate when Jesus shared the five loaves and two fish, the individuals benefit when they invest their resources in enhancing the welfare of the group.

The task of building civil society is formidable. It begins by recognizing that the indigenous narrative is coming to a negative conclusion and needs to be transformed; it did not deliver the hope of a better future. The transformation "must come as a consequence of . . . human commitment to collective survival driven by a vision that transcends the behaviors conditioned by existing institutions and cultures."[22]

Toward Building Civil Society

The construction of civil society is a grassroots movement that is central to reconciliation; it is an outgrowth of the realization that the nation states are losing their ability to create social harmony among ethnically diverse people who share the same political boundaries. The growth of strong national states, as a development of modern Western history, depended upon the spread of industry and the rise of national markets.[23] However, the experiences of Somalia, Rwanda, Sudan, and Yugoslavia, among other states, indicate that the failure of nation-states has created a gap for civil society to fill.

20. George B. N. Ayittey, *Africa in Chaos* (London: Macmillan, 1998), 307.
21. John Howard Yoder, *The Politics of Jesus* (Grand Rapids: Eerdmans, 1972), 174.
22. David C. Korten, *Getting to the 21st Century: Voluntary Action and the Global Agenda* (West Hartford, Conn.: Kumarian Press, 1990), 105.
23. Wuthnow, *Christianity and Civil Society*, 2.

Change across Cultures

The challenge for proponents of civil society is determining how to fill this gap. To use a computer analogy, the components of civil society include hardware and software; both are products of the reconciliation process. The hardware includes the infrastructure of the culture. It is composed of the judicial, educational, and economic systems. It includes such things as the delivery of utilities, the building of roads, and supplying medical and health needs. The hardware is the most tangible aspect of a society, and its success depends on the availability of expertise, money, and labor. Its sustainability depends on the effectiveness of its software.

The software of civil society includes a range of issues, particularly the creation of social harmony, trust, and common values, all of which are dependent on a process of forgiveness that gives people opportunities to tell their stories. The opportunity to tell one's story offers a way for people to build the broken connections in their fragmented lives. The people who tell them, however, must have the security that their experiences will be heard and the validity of their experiences will be affirmed. People also need the assurance that some justice will be rendered and that their experiences will inspire changes in the future. This process empowers people to create a new narrative that will unite them with truth and bring them hope; "truth cannot bring people back to life, but truth might be the only justice the dead receive."[24] They receive it for the benefit of the living.

On Forgiveness and Reconciliation

The man in the workshop who asked about loving and praying for his neighbor was among the many people in the aftermath of the genocide in Rwanda who wanted to rebuild their community. His struggle was understanding the nature of forgiveness. The creation of civil society sets the context for forgiveness, a major factor in enhancing the ability of people to live in community. Communities thrive on the ability of people to build relationships through forgiveness. An unwillingness to forgive mocks any efforts to pray for the love and blessings of our neighbors. People must forgive; the central question is how.

The concept of forgiveness is embedded in the narrative of God's relationship with creation. We maintain our relationship with God by asking him to forgive us our sins, as we ourselves forgive everyone indebted to us. Forgiveness, however, is as profound as it is simple, perhaps because of its association with forgetting and loving. Forgiving, forgetting,

24. Robert J. Schreiter, ed., *Faces of Jesus in Africa* (Maryknoll, N.Y.: Orbis, 1991), 119.

and loving seem to be a trinity of Christian virtues, but they have a tenuous relationship. We often hear admonishments to forgive and forget through the power of love. However, such admonishments reduce profound concepts to clichés that embody unsound theology. People cannot forgive and forget, unless they want to deny their pain and bless their adversary with cheap grace that prevents each of them from grasping the profound nature of redemption.

Forgiveness does not mean forgetting; it means remembering well. It is a "decision by a victim to no longer be controlled by the effects of past deeds. . . . It does not eradicate the deed done,"[25] but it beckons the person to "remember well and deeply."[26] Deep remembering takes victims seriously and excavates the meaning of the offense, affirming that no human atrocity is beyond the redemptive power of God's love. It defies the notion that forgiveness excuses behavior as it "strives to heal grief, and reestablish the deepest qualities of humanity."[27] It recognizes that healing involves "an exchange of pain"[28] as it complements perpetrators with the affirmation that they, as beings who are created in the image of God, also suffer. To forgive and forget allows perpetrators to triumph over their own moral demise, preventing them from accepting the pain that they have inflicted on other people and on themselves. "Deep remembering is about taking the victims seriously. This is the only way to rescue the profound importance of forgiveness from its many cheap distortions."[29]

Forgiving and forgetting creates an injustice—and insults the dignity of humankind—by denying people the opportunity to take moral responsibility for their behavior. Reconciliation calls for forgiveness, but it does not excuse injustice. In a quest for justice in Rwanda, Laurent Mbanda expressed his opinion that "it was too soon to call for reconciliation" because reconciliation "was becoming a painful word and insult for genocide survivors. . . . People in the country, especially those who were mourning their loved ones and relatives, wanted to hear and see justice."[30] "Forgiveness is about renouncing unjustified power, not about weakening the pursuit of justice."[31]

25. Robert J. Schreiter, *The Ministry of Reconciliation: Spirituality and Strategies* (Maryknoll, N.Y.: Orbis, 1998), 19.
26. Geiko Muller-Fahrenholz, *The Art of Forgiveness* (Geneva: WCC, 1997), 19.
27. Ibid., 26.
28. Schreiter, *Ministry of Reconciliation*, 26.
29. Muller-Fahrenholz, *Art of Forgiveness*, 17.
30. Mbanda, *Committed to Conflict*, 122.
31. Muller-Fahrenholz, *Art of Forgiveness*, ix.

Forgiveness and Love

Forgiveness is a major factor in the journey toward reconciliation. Loving one's enemies is not synonymous with forgiving them, but it can serve as "a profound and unique guide to human action and morality."[32] Love is unconditional; forgiveness is not. Love sees the worth and value of the other; forgiveness recognizes repentance and embraces it.[33] The man who shows no remorse for killing an entire family of people is worthy of love and prayer, which are efforts to restore a person's human dignity to the point of initiating a relationship of reconciliation. Without showing any sense of remorse, however, the man who killed an entire family of people and allows his children to wear the clothes of his victims is not ready to accept the degree of forgiveness that is a prerequisite for a reconciled relationship.

The workshop participant can love him and pray for him, believing that he is not beyond the redemptive power of God. Forgiveness, however, is not possible apart from a willingness to repent. Love and prayer will prevent the man who lost his family from losing the hope for reconciliation. However, the perpetrator might never repent, causing the workshop participant to express the words of Jesus: "Father, forgive him for he did not know what he did." Forgiving an unrepentant perpetrator prevents the victim from succumbing to the plight of victimization. However, this expression of forgiveness does not foster reconciliation because it requires a sense of mutuality that is expressed in the hope of a better future. Forgiveness inspires the person to love his enemies, which might lead to repentance as the perpetrator accepts moral responsibility for his behavior. The road to reconciliation goes through the house of the neighbor who became an enemy; it is paved with love and forgiveness, but these elements are not its final destination.

The narrative of God's relationship with creation is one of reconciliation. It is the catalyst that unites people from the various strands of humanity, empowering them to express their diversity without fear. Consider the more than five thousand people Jesus brought together; they lived in an economy of scarcity, and they were willing to sacrifice one another's dignity to bolster their own sense of well-being. They could not eat with one another because they knew who they were. However, Jesus transformed their sacrificial worldview by inspiring them to eat together. They could no longer use one another as scapegoats, believing

32. Vincent J. Donovan, *Christianity Rediscovered* (Maryknoll, N.Y.: Orbis, 1978), 168.
33. David W. Augsburger, *The Freedom of Forgiveness* (Chicago: Moody, 1988), 16.

their identities were based on what the other people were not. Jesus, in uniting them, revealed that they were more alike than different. He empowered people to love their neighbors because their neighbors were like them.

The feeding of the five thousand is included in every Gospel, perhaps because it is a metaphor for the church. It demonstrates the hope that people who represent the diverse strands of humanity can be reconciled to one another. The narrative of Christianity is the story of a transformed *kosmos*; it is a story that the world is hungering to experience. This ministry of reconciliation is one major leading function of the church. There has been no time in the history of humankind when this ministry has been more necessary than it is now.

11

Community:
One Narrative with Many Cultural Dimensions

The synagogue ruler said to the people, "There are six days for work. So come and be healed on those days, not on the Sabbath."

Luke 13:14

There is neither Jew nor Greek, slave nor free, male nor female, for you are all one in Christ Jesus.

Galatians 3:28

The people living in a rural East African village frequently complained about the thatched roofs on their mud and stick huts. They leaked, snakes occasionally crawled through them, and the need to harvest thatch contributed to the desertification around the village, making thatch scarce. The Christian development practitioners working in the village suggested that the people replace the thatched roofs with metal ones. The villagers liked the idea but never acted on it. The development practitioners knew that lack of funds and heat were two obstacles to the implementation of the plan, but the development agency offered to subsidize families who couldn't afford them, and the villagers knew they could install ceilings in their houses to keep them cooler.

One day a villager told the development practitioners that the people believed metal roofs would make them victims of witchcraft, which served as "a means of affirming group boundaries and exercising social control."[1] According to village gossip, witches thought metal roofs posed a challenge to their powers and would curse anyone who slept under them. The development facilitators had no idea how the villagers could make a connection between metal roofs and witchcraft. Perhaps they believed that metal was susceptible to witchcraft because it was receptive to lightning. However, they discovered that the source of the story was the traditional priest in the village, and it had more to do with social control than with lightning.

The development facilitators hesitated to confront the village priest because their previous encounter with him about germs and diarrhea had alienated him. The priest, who was a firm believer in agentive causation, had little regard for germs and showed his distrust for the development practitioners by bringing the conversation back to spirits. The development facilitators, wanting to avoid another clash, decided not to pursue the issue. But they were torn between letting the idea die and encouraging the villagers to confront their fears. Before they made any decision, however, they realized that they needed to learn more about the villagers' beliefs in ancestors, witchcraft, and development innovations.

While there were several approaches the development practitioners could have taken to address the problem, they knew the priest's effort to maintain the social harmony of the community was the central issue. The village priest maintained the traditions of the ancestors and defended the cohesion of the village against any intrusions or insults, which the roofs represented by modifying the socioeconomic structure of the village. If the development practitioners want to realize sustainable change for the village, they will have to learn the dynamics of maintaining harmony in the community by understanding the relationship between the ancestors, the villagers, and the priest.

From Reified Ancestors to a Reified Law

The traditional priest's role of fostering social harmony by defending the ancestors is analogous to the role of the synagogue ruler in Luke

1. Paul G. Hiebert, R. Daniel Shaw, and Tite Tienou, *Understanding Folk Religion: A Christian Response to Popular Beliefs and Practices* (Grand Rapids: Baker, 1999), 152.

13:10–17. The leaders of both communities were paralyzed by a law that became reified. Luke records the story of Jesus' healing the woman who was crippled by a spirit for eighteen years. The synagogue ruler, who was entrusted with maintaining the traditions of the community, was indignant because Jesus healed the woman on the Sabbath. He believed that healing should be done only on the six days of work (v. 14). Jesus' decision to heal the woman on the Sabbath threatened a central symbol of the ruler's culture. The central African village priest likewise feared that the metal roofs threatened the integrity of his community by fracturing its harmony.

The original intent of the law was to make the Hebrew community aware of sin (Rom. 3:20), so that the people would see their need for grace. However, the law had become reified and took on a life of its own, enslaving the people it was intended to liberate. The ensuing interactions between Jesus and the synagogue ruler indicate that the reified law caused the people in the community to lose sight of God's grace by disallowing them to celebrate the healing of the woman. Jesus seems to have deliberately chosen to heal her on the Sabbath to expose the powerlessness of the community as a consequence of their reified law.

The traditional African priest, like the synagogue ruler, could not celebrate the welfare of his community until he liberated himself and the community from their fears of ancestors and the threats of witchcraft. Jesus healed the woman to illustrate that the community has stewardship over the law. Similarly, the priest had to mediate a relationship with the ancestors to ensure his liberty to make decisions that fostered the welfare of the community.

Between Community and *Communitas*

The global Christian church, a community called together to embody God's redemptive relationship with creation, is the "primary social structure through which the gospel works to change other structures,"[2] including cultures. Like the traditional priest and the synagogue ruler, church leaders, particularly those engaged in cross-cultural ministries, have to maintain the integrity and solidarity of the community to fulfill the church's role as the agent of cultural transformation. The church is the visible expression of God's redemptive agency; "what our Lord left

2. John Howard Yoder, *The Politics of Jesus* (Grand Rapids: Eerdmans, 1972), 157.

behind him was not a book . . . but a visible community . . . to make explicit who he is and what he has done."[3]

The church, as a community, exists between the concepts of community and *communitas*. Communities are groups of people who organize themselves around similar symbols, such as the ancestors, the Levitical law, or the cross. They are monocultural and multicultural, and they have formal and informal structures that depend on the gifts, talents, and abilities of their members, such as leadership, knowledge specialists, and administrators. The apostle Paul carefully advised the early Christian churches that they needed to respect and affirm the gifts of their members (1 Cor. 12 and 13).

Communitas is a sacred bond that emerges as people gather to worship in communion with one another. They submit to unifying symbols, through the leadership of a ritual specialist, and transcend the structures that normally characterize human communities. *Communitas* is formed as the soul of community through its rituals, making it "less empirical but more substantive than what the term 'community' denotes."[4] Good communities produce *communitas,* empowering people to transcend the structures that normally organize them. It "breaks in through the interstices of structure, in liminality; at the edges of structure, in marginality; and from beneath structure, in inferiority."[5] Through *communitas,* people "break out of the growing tyranny of community, and enter the world . . . where equality, fellowship, and deep feelings of unity are experienced and expressed."[6] Communities, however, do not transform themselves into *communitas*; instead, people experience it within the context of community.

Communitas emerges when the members of a community experience liminality, a state of transition that is necessarily ambiguous since people in liminal states are "neither here nor there; they are betwixt and between the positions assigned by law, custom, convention."[7] This liminal state is facilitated by ritual, equalizing all people in the context of their symbols, especially their agents of causation. It is "often seen as sacred, powerful, holy, and set apart time in which the old structures, rules of order, and identities are suspended."[8]

3. Lesslie Newbigin, *The Household of God: Lectures on the Nature of the Church* (New York: Friendship, 1954), 20.

4. Ibid.

5. Victor Turner, *The Ritual Process: Structure and Anti-Structure* (New York: de Gruyter, 1969), 128.

6. Hiebert, Shaw, and Tienou, *Understanding Folk Religion,* 298.

7. Turner, *Ritual Process,* 95.

8. Hiebert, Shaw, and Tienou, *Understanding Folk Religion,* 297.

The apostle Paul communicated the concept of *communitas* most eloquently by observing that in Christ "there is neither Jew nor Greek, slave nor free, male nor female, for you are all one in Christ Jesus" (Gal. 3:28). Our being in Christ is "a union of separated beings whose primary bond is not of logic but of love,"[9] which empowers people to transcend the normal structures of community, but this transcendence is fleeting. People hold in tension what is already experienced and what is not yet experienced in its fullness. People move between community and *communitas* because they cannot permanently transcend the structures of community and exist in a lifelong state of *communitas*. However, they need the experience of *communitas* to give them a glimpse of eternity.

This tension is constant in the Christian church, and it expresses itself in many ways. I was recently reminded of this when a student claimed that the seminary needed revival before its spirituality withered. Seminaries and other educational institutions are fairly structured communities: semesters begin and end on certain dates, courses have many nonnegotiable assignments, and there is a social structure that governs how students and teachers relate to one another. Structures maintain the integrity of an institution. However, more than one student has questioned the spiritual integrity of seminaries, giving them the nickname "spiritual cemeteries." What would happen if the seminary had a revival? It would last only until the students felt the pressure of preparing for the next examination, reading for the next course, or writing another paper. The students would experience a sense of *communitas,* but its effect would not redefine the structure of the community. All institutions need structures to be what they are.

Communitas is a necessary lift from the mundane to a view of heaven; structure is a necessity of life. Paul G. Hiebert interpreted Peter's desire to live on the Mount of Transfiguration as an effort to live in a permanent state of *communitas*. Had he done so, "he would soon have been fetching water, gathering firewood, cooking meals, and doing laundry—in the process he would have lost the transcendent nature of the moment."[10] The structure of the community makes *communitas* possible and gives people an appreciation for a liminal state of being. *Communitas* is a gift that emerges from healthy communities. The ethical challenge is maintaining the integrity of the community that makes *communitas* possible.

9. Parker Palmer, *To Know As We Are Known: Education as a Spiritual Journey* (San Francisco: Harper San Francisco, 1983), 32.

10. Hiebert, Shaw, and Tienou, *Understanding Folk Religion,* 306.

This challenge was constantly present in the early church, and it is a challenge that continues to this day.

The Nature of Symbols and Rituals

An understanding of community requires some understanding of symbols and rituals.

Discursive and Non-Discursive Symbols

"Symbols are mental categories humans create and label to grasp and order the realities in which they live;"[11] they embody the elements of the *kosmos*. Languages are the most comprehensive symbolic systems of human cultures. They are composed of words and gestures that reveal how people interpret all aspects of reality. In English, for example, people assign meaning to the siblings of their parents, using "aunt" and "uncle" to assign meaning according to gender, regardless of whether the aunts and uncles are paternal or maternal. In Somali culture, however, paternal and maternal aunts and uncles have different symbolic meanings, requiring different words to distinguish them. The metal roofs in the village also had symbolic value in their power to organize people around their socioeconomic meaning, breaking the sense of community in the village.

The meanings of symbols are further defined as discursive and non-discursive.[12] A discursive symbol is one whose meaning is limited to its cultural or functional context. That roofs protect people from rain and that the cross is an execution device are discursive meanings. People organize their cultures around the discursive meaning of symbols because they are expressions of material reality. A non-discursive symbol is one whose meaning transcends its culture, but it can include discursive meanings. The non-discursive meaning of metal roofs in the central African village, for example, is that they are indicators of wealth, but they continue to fulfill their discursive function. Since community is organized around the non-discursive meaning of the symbol, the roofs have the potential of dividing the community as people organize themselves around those who have metal roofs and those who don't.

Virtually all physical artifacts have non-discursive meanings. As I am writing this paragraph, my family is hosting a meal, and we have to decide whether to set the table with silver, stainless steel, or plastic. The function that the utensils serve is not going to change, regardless of their

11. Ibid., 234.
12. For a detailed discussion on these concepts, see ibid., 243.

222

material. However, the materials have non-discursive value; they make statements about the way we perceive our guests and the dinner we will serve. The utensils will influence how the people interpret their relationship to us and to one another, and the meaning of the meal.

The cross of Jesus of Nazareth, likewise, has non-discursive meanings. In one sense, the cross indicates that Jesus did not have the political power to avoid an agonizing and shameful demise. This interpretation caused it to be "a stumbling block to the Jews and foolishness to the Gentiles" (1 Cor. 1:23). However, for the Christian community, the cross is the "the power of God and the wisdom of God" (1 Cor. 1:25). Through the cross, Jesus of Nazareth became the cosmic Christ, the savior of the world; he transformed the people of God into a global community.

The discursive meaning of the cross can be verified by the historical documents of the first century. However, its non-discursive meaning transcends historical verification; it depends on the affirmation of the community that organizes itself around this meaning. The non-discursive meaning of the cross is the central symbol of the narrative of God's redemptive relationship with creation. Narratives, by nature, are more concerned with non-discursive than with discursive meanings of symbols.

Rituals as Symbolic Behavior

Rituals are symbolic actions through which people restore and maintain the non-discursive meanings of their symbols and relate to their agents of causation. They serve three related functions that make them central in building community. First, they legitimize the nature of the symbols of any particular community; second, they establish the order that governs the relationship between the community and symbols; and third, they prescribe change. In serving these functions, rituals create a unified scheme where everything has a place;[13] they integrate disparate symbols into a unified narrative.

Rituals are crucially important for managing change in cultures where people value agentive causation. The traditional priest, like many people who are resistant to development projects, had attributed metal roofs to witchcraft, probably because he did not have a ritual through which he could integrate them into the narrative of his village, which portrayed the ancestors as major agents of causation. By creating a ritual, such as a sacrifice, to integrate the metal roofs into the village, the community can affirm that the ancestors have roofs, or they can transform

13. Mary Douglas, *Purity and Danger: An Analysis of Concepts of Pollution and Taboo* (London: Routledge & K. Paul, 1966), 73.

the way the villagers perceive the causative roles of the ancestors. In either situation, the rituals facilitate the ability of the people to integrate the roofs into their community.

The central issue in understanding rituals is discerning whether they do what they are designed to do. Are they effective? The answer to this question depends on what we expect from rituals. More often than not, they inspire yawns in modern communities, even among people who engage in worship and religious ceremonies. We often hear Christians lament that particular parts of a worship service—or certain traditions of worship—are boring because they are just rituals. People suffer from ritual boredom, losing interest in "the rituals available to them for giving their lives shape and meaning."[14] Ritual boredom is caused by the general lack of understanding of agentive causation. Modern people, who think in terms of empirical causation, watch a priest perform a ritual as though they are watching a magician, expecting a cause-and-effect reaction. When this doesn't happen, they think the ritual was ineffective.

Agentive causation, not magic, is the foundation of ritual change. Priests or other ritual specialists are not performing magic ceremonies when they lead rituals. Instead, they are offering to submit cultural change to the will of the agents of causation. In doing so, they are attempting to hold agentive and empirical causation together, realizing that while the changes are empirical, the agents of causation need to be consulted to affirm the place of the changes in the narrative of the community.

Rituals are successful when they affirm the non-discursive meanings of symbols. The non-discursive meaning of metal roofs, for instance, had economic and spiritual implications that threatened the social cohesion of the community. The traditional priest apparently anticipated that they would reorganize the social structure of the village, separating the rich from the poor families, and he was not sure how the ancestors would accept this. A ritual would have given the metal roofs a legitimate place within the community and beckoned the ancestors' approval of them.

The values of rituals express themselves in many tangible ways. Michael Kirwen illustrates this point by telling a story about several women in a Tanzanian village who could not get pregnant. They consulted a diviner and asked him to discern the reason for their apparent infertility. The diviner sought the guidance of the ancestors and learned

14. Tom F. Driver, *The Magic of Ritual* (New York: Harper Collins, 1991), 7.

that the women could not get pregnant because the people had violated a burial custom.

It had occurred several years earlier when physicians treated a woman from the clan and insisted that she had suffered and died of a stomach tumor. The villagers, however, thought she was pregnant. The customs of the culture dictated that the woman—and what the people thought was an unborn baby—should be buried separately. However, the woman's family evidently believed the physicians, and they chose to bury the woman and her tumor in the same grave. The diviner concluded that he could restore harmony in the village and between the ancestors and the villagers by sacrificing a goat. The story ends with a return of fertility to the clan.[15]

The story recalls an experience a Christian missionary in Cameroon had when he hosted a Bible study for a group of young adults who were first-generation Christians. There was a young married couple in the group who prayed fervently for fertility, but the wife was unable to get pregnant. The couple considered going to a traditional priest who offered to perform a fertility ritual for them. The missionary counseled them to pray for fertility, advising them that their participation in any fertility ritual would be an insult to their faith.

The couple continued to attend the Bible study, praying for fertility during each session. One day they were ecstatic to announce that the wife had become pregnant. The group was relieved, and thanked God for this miraculous blessing. When the missionary met the couple, he attempted to affirm the couple's faith by asking them if they were thankful that they had not gone to the traditional priest. The husband, however, confessed they had participated in the fertility ritual.

These stories challenge people to understand the nature of ritual. My initial responses to both stories was to resist believing that the rituals had any influence on causing pregnancies. I know what causes pregnancy and it does not include a public ritual. Like most Westerners, I believed rituals were supposed to facilitate change in an empirically verifiable, cause-and-effect manner. We tend not to believe rituals can cause pregnancy unless we can make a verifiable relationship between the ritual and the pregnancy. However, we don't see pregnancy as a result of a cause-and-effect mechanism; we believe God blesses us with children, affirming our belief in God as the agent of causation in a cause-and-effect enterprise.

15. Michael C. Kirwen, *The Missionary and the Diviner* (Maryknoll, N.Y.: Orbis, 1987), 82.

We miss the point of ritual if we attempt to understand it as an effort to produce empirically verifiable results by manipulating causes and examining effects. The efficacy of any ritual does not lie in the power to cause empirically verifiable changes. Instead, the power of rituals lies in their ability to create *communitas,* locating the pains of life—such as fertility, illness, and misfortune—within the context of a community's narrative. In empowering people to cope with these pains, rituals absorb the struggles of life, restoring the harmony between the person, the community, and its narrative.

The efficacy of ritual is often realized in its ability to facilitate healing in the absence of cures. People who are not cured from diseases often experience healing by the power of ritual to place the disease in a unified scheme of reality, liberating the person to experience a sense of wholeness. In this context, healing does not mean that the disease is cured but that the people who have the disease place themselves in the redemptive work of God, gaining power to fulfill their leading function of bearing the image of God. I just spent a weekend with a person who has AIDS. His disease was not cured, but he experienced a tremendous sense of healing as he placed himself in the narrative of God's redemptive purpose for creation. AIDS became incidental to his life as he fulfilled his leading function of glorifying God by making the world a more redemptive place in which to live. The rituals in his life are effective.

Rituals are effective when they integrate the transitions of life into the narrative of a community, affirming that they have redemptive values. In the Christian community, births, marriages, and deaths are all ritualized to affirm that they participate in God's redemptive relationship with the community. Ministries that bring substantial transformation to a community also need to be legitimized by ritual to reveal their connection with the agent of causation.

The transitions in life that are not mediated through rituals often reveal a moral dilemma in a community. In many cultures, there are no rituals to integrate children with physical abnormalities into the community; the children are aborted or allowed to die because the people are unable to reconcile the birth of these children with their agents of causation. Children born with physical anomalies are interpreted in many cultures to be the results of a curse or punishment. They provoke their parents or other people in the community to ask "What did we do to deserve this?" The question indicates that the people are unable to interpret the children as blessings from God or other agents of causation.

226

In North American churches, there has been considerable debate on the moral validity of homosexuality. Many churches welcome and affirm people of the same gender who want covenanted relationships. These churches, however, will not fully integrate homosexuals into their communities until they perform rituals to affirm the value of their preference within the narrative of their communities. The churches can be welcoming and affirming, but the communities will continue to perceive homosexual relationships as moral dilemmas until they perform wedding ceremonies or other rituals to legitimize these relationships.

Expressing Cultural Diversity in Universal Community

The ethical tension in creating community in the church is affirming the value of cultural symbols and rituals without compromising the church's leading function of proclaiming the narrative of God's redemptive relationship with creation. Symbols and rituals are among the elements of the *kosmos* because they are necessary to order human life. They are good, fallen, and redeemed. They participate in redemption and enhance the ability of the church to fulfill its leading function. While the church cannot operate without cultural symbols, it does not organize itself around them. By making the symbols of a culture relative, the church becomes a community through which God creates "one new humanity" (Eph. 2:14). "The only absolute in Christianity is the triune God. Anything which involves man, who is finite and limited, must of necessity be limited, and hence relative."[16]

One central challenge in the ministry of the apostles was distinguishing the gospel of Jesus Christ from the symbols of Jewish culture. The apostles, like all cross-cultural ethicists, had to determine how the absolute truth of the gospel could be communicated through culturally relative symbols without compromising its truth. The intent of this effort was to emphasize that the Jewish cultural symbols would not be exported into Gentile cultures but that the narrative of God's redemptive work through Jesus Christ would include Gentiles.

The Judaizers wanted to make the primary symbols of the Jewish culture normative for the universal Christian church. They tried to do this with circumcision by declaring that gentile Christians had to be circumcised and keep the law of Moses in order to be saved (Acts 15:1–5); this issue led to the Council of Jerusalem. The Judaizers could not imagine the

---

16. George R. Hunsberger, *Bearing the Witness of the Spirit: Lesslie Newbigin's Theology of Cultural Plurality* (Grand Rapids: Eerdmans, 1998), 266.

Christian community having any integrity unless its members affirmed this symbol as a central element of their community. Peter, exhibiting an inspired measure of wisdom, made an effort to prevent circumcision from becoming reified. He realized that it was a non-discursive symbol whose meaning was lost to the present generation. In preventing a Jewish symbol from alienating the Christian Gentiles, he reminded those gathered at the council that salvation was achieved by the grace of Jesus Christ, not by an outward sign. It came by cleansing the heart by faith (15:9, 11).

The Jews related to God through their culture, and they did not believe that they could experience any sense of community with the Gentiles unless they embraced the particularities of Jewish culture. They appealed to the apostles to determine how the expressions of their culture could be grafted into the new community of the church. James, the leader of the council, evidently gave this issue serious consideration and concluded the council by proposing that Gentiles abstain from three things: things polluted by idols, sexual immorality, and the meat of strangled animals and blood (Acts 15:20). James's conclusion made an attempt to equalize the balance of power in the relationship between the Jews and the Gentiles, and it reflects the qualities of "grace and truth that came through Jesus Christ" (John 1:17).

The Logic of James's Prohibitions

James's primary concern in offering the three prohibitions was to identify three values that are representative in empowering the church to fulfill its leading function of facilitating redemption. One of the ways it does this is by empowering people to create within their respective cultures communities in which they can worship and express their fidelity to God through Jesus Christ.

James seemed to have defined the prohibitions negatively because the context of the Council of Jerusalem was to discern what the Christians had to protect themselves against in order to define who they were. There is, however, a positive way to interpret the three customs and thereby create a framework to understand the nature of other cross-cultural ethical issues. This framework defines James's prohibitions as comprising transcultural absolute values with culturally specific expressions, and culturally specific values with culturally relative expressions. These values function in the Christian economy of truth and grace.

James's first prohibition, abstaining from things polluted by idols, is an affirmation of monotheism. James recognized that the church was struggling to define its central values in pluralistic cultures, and its integrity required its members to separate themselves from the idols of their respective cultures; their commitment to monotheism was central to their religious identity. The affirmation of monotheism as the central value of the church makes it an absolute transcultural ethical norm that makes truth its central value.

James's second prohibition, abstaining from sexual immorality, is an absolute value with different cultural expressions; it is based on the premise that there are "moral ideals built into the universe that, if lived up to, enable the peoples of the world to experience whatever God intends for them."[17] However, it recognizes that these moral ideals are expressed through the medium of culture. Therefore, I want to depict the prohibition of abstaining from sexual immorality as a transcultural truth with culturally specific expressions; it functions in the moral economy of grace and truth.

The third custom recorded in Acts 15:1–21, abstaining from the meat of strangled animals and from blood, is a culturally relative value with culturally specific applications. This value is the most difficult of the three customs to interpret because it has many applications. The intent of this particular prohibition is to acknowledge the importance of affirming the Jewish taboo against eating meat containing blood. This taboo was based on Genesis 9:4, "you must not eat meat that has its life blood still in it," and it permeates the Levitical law. It is particularly important in light of the fact that the Jews came to the Council of Jerusalem expecting that their symbol of circumcision would be upheld. The council rejected it but affirmed another value that was central to their culture, making the prohibition a culturally specific value with a culturally relative expression; it is an expression of the Christian economy of grace and truth.[18]

Applying the Framework

Transcultural Absolute Values

While the framework of transcultural absolute values and culturally specific values with culturally relative expressions seems clear in the abstract, it becomes complex in practice. The value of monotheism as a

---

17. Charles H. Kraft, *Anthropology for Christian Witness* (Maryknoll, N.Y.: Orbis, 1996), 418.

18. James's effort to acknowledge the importance of affirming this Jewish taboo contradicts Peter's vision that all things are clean (Acts 11:5–10), a vision that was undoubtedly a major factor in holding the council. Paul also had little regard for this taboo. However, James, as the chairperson of the council, evidently concluded to maintain this taboo in consideration of the weaker brethren of Jewish birth. See F. F. Bruce, *Commentary on the Book of the Acts* (Grand Rapids: Eerdmans, 1954), 311.

transcultural absolute, for example, is clear until it addresses such issues as whether or not Christians and Muslims worship the same God. The tension in resolving this is that people from Christian, Muslim, and Jewish faiths agree about who God is, but they do not agree about how God expresses his being. In their agreement the three traditions provide a starting point for affirming the monotheistic transcultural values of the Christian community. However, the narrative of God's redemptive relationship differentiates these religious traditions. The narrative of Islam, for example, includes ninety-nine names of God, but love is not among them, and the narrative of Judaism is still awaiting the Messiah.

The Christian narrative announces the Messiah and challenges Muslims to esteem love as a central expression of God's being. Christians can affirm that the God of Mohammed is the same God as the God of Abraham, Isaac, and Jacob. However, the message of Christ—along with the absence of God's love in the Qurʾan and the Hadith, the central elements of the Islamic narrative—highlight the concept of God's love as central to the discussions of how Christians relate to Muslims. Christians and Muslims are both monotheistic, and the question of whether they worship the same God is not as crucial as the question of whether they affirm love as the central value of God's relationship with creation.

Transcultural Absolute Values with Culturally Specific Expressions

There is no ethical debate that Christians in every culture must be sexually moral. However, there is considerable debate about the definition of sexual morality within particular cultures, causing Christian norms on this issue to have some cultural diversity. The diverse expressions of sexual behavior can range anywhere from educating women to engaging in different expressions of genital contact. When I taught at a college in an Islamic country, any efforts to educate women were interpreted as sexually immoral. The men in the class esteemed their female classmates to be morally inferior, and they believed that no self-respecting man in the culture would marry one of them.

The counterpart to this educating women is the struggle that Christians in Western cultures face in discerning the morality of genital contact between unmarried people. The majority of Christian ethicists in Western cultures agree that the redemptive narrative of the Christian tradition precludes sexual intercourse outside of marriage. However, there is less agreement on defining the boundaries between abstaining from all sexual contact and engaging in sexual intercourse. In his popular book, *Sex for Christians,* Lewis B. Smedes struggles with the ambiguities of sexual contact outside of marriage and concludes with the extremely qualified statement that, "Light petting could be wrong for some couples; very 'heavy petting' could be right for others."[19] My friend Bruce Brander, the author of *Staring into Chaos: The Decline of Western Civilization,* contends that Smedes's statement is another expression of "symbol without substance, the disease of modern society and church alike."[20]

The moral tension in the contrasting statements between Smedes and Brander illustrates the challenge of applying the ethic of an absolute value with culturally specific expressions across cultures. Jomo Kenyatta, the first president of Kenya, laments the stand Christians took toward a sexual practice among the Kikuyus that was roughly the equivalent of petting.[21] In this practice, unmarried men and women sleep in the same bed but do not engage in sexual intercourse. The Christian missionaries condemned the practice because they did not believe that a "young man and a young woman could sleep in one room, let alone in one bed, without copulating."[22] Jomo Kenyatta undoubtedly raised the issue because he believed the missionaries denied that the Kikuyus had the spiritual or moral maturity to participate in making a decision about sexual behavior. Sexual morality is an issue that needs to be determined with grace and truth by the church as a multicultural, interpretive community that is "capable of forming people with virtues sufficient to witness to God's truth in the world."[23] The nature of discerning the morality of transcultural values with culturally specific expressions must respect the moral maturity of the people who are affected by it.[24] These values must express the truth and grace of the gospel; they are central to the church and the medium through which it fulfills its leading function.

19. Grand Rapids: Eerdmans, 1976, 156–57.
20. Personal correspondence with author.
21. The Kikuyus are a major ethnic group in Kenya.
22. Jomo Kenyatta, *Facing Mount Kenya* (Nairobi: Kenway, 1978), 158.
23. Stanley G. Hauerwas, *A Community of Character: Toward a Constructive Christian Social Ethic* (South Bend, Ind.: University of Notre Dame Press, 1981), 3.
24. The Greek word *porneia,* which is translated as "sexual immorality," includes a broad range of sexual behaviors. Christians argue about exactly what it includes in assessing the morality of such practices as genital-to-genital contact, oral-to-genital contact, and hand-to-genital contact between people of the same or different genders inside or outside covenanted relationships. The validity of these arguments provokes a variety of ethical issues, but they are beyond the scope of this book.

CULTURALLY SPECIFIC VALUES
WITH CULTURALLY RELATIVE EXPRESSIONS

Ethical decisions that involve culturally relative values with culturally specific expressions function in the economy of grace, and they are
among the most difficult ethical issues of managing change across cultures. When the apostle Paul addressed the problem that the Corinthians
faced in eating food that was sacrificed to idols (1 Cor. 8:1–13), he had the
choice of employing either the first or the third prohibition. He could
have interpreted the practices of eating food sacrificed to the Greek gods
as an insult to the affirmation that monotheism is one of Christianity's
absolute transcultural truths.

Paul, however, chose not to make the practice of eating food sacrificed
to idols a transcultural absolute ethic; he affirmed that "an idol is nothing at all in the world" and that "there is no God but one" (1 Cor. 8:4).
Paul, perhaps to the chagrin of many Jewish Christians, did not see the
gods of the Greek pantheon as a threat to Christian monotheism. In light
of Colossians 2:8–20, we can infer that Paul considered the idols of
Corinth to be among the elements of the *kosmos*. They distract and estrange people from God, but they do not have a divine nature.

Paul concluded that eating food sacrificed to idols was no threat to
monotheism, giving Christians the liberty to eat whatever they chose.
However, he recognized the complexity of the issue; he had to consider
the weaker brethren. He knew that eating meat sacrificed to idols as well
as other cultural practices might cause them to stumble. In these situations, Paul said he would abstain from eating meat forever (1 Cor. 8:13).
He recognized the need to observe a culturally relative value with a culturally specific application for the sake of nurturing the faith of everyone
in the community. The manner in which he addressed this culturally
sensitive issue depicts it as an item that functions in the Christian economy of grace. The central truth of Paul's teachings on dietary issues is
whether Christians can extend grace to one another.

Cultural Practices That Transcend the Categories

The vitality of this framework depends on being able to fit a particular behavior into an appropriate category, which is one of the reasons
why biblical interpretation is always difficult in ethical inquiry. It is an
issue that can prevent the church from creating a sense of *communitas*
within certain cultures. In Ghanaian culture, for example, a fertility tradition called sacred silence is "the most revered religious ceremony for

the Ga people,"[25] a dominant ethnic group in that country. The ceremony requires all Ghanaians to abstain from singing and drumming for one month. Many Christians in Ghana, at the expense of provoking violence with their traditional neighbors and with many Christians who are sympathetic to the custom, choose not to observe the ritual. They believe that observing the silence would be an act of syncretism, the blending of two religions, which would prevent them from worshiping in a manner that expressed monotheism as a transcultural absolute ethic of Christianity.

In this section, I want to address three issues that are pertinent to managing cultural change and could be interpreted to apply to each of the framework categories. The first issue is the cultural implications of spiritual disciplines, the second issue is bribery, and the third issue is female genital mutilation.

Cultural Implications of Spiritual Disciplines

William Stolzman wrote about contextualizing the Christian faith in the culture of the Lakota people, a native North American ethnic group. He addressed a variety of spiritual behaviors specific to the Lakota culture and advocated the practice of equating the symbols from one culture with those of another. His basic assumption is that symbols are cultural in nature and that the redemptive narrative of the Christian faith can incorporate the spiritual symbols of many cultures.

Stolzman postulated that a person can simultaneously practice "the Lakota religion in a totally orthodox way and also practice the Christian religion in a totally orthodox way."[26] He did not advocate syncretism, but he encouraged Native Americans to preserve their culture—and its religious symbols—by understanding that these symbols are dynamically equivalent expressions of the Western symbols that have gained hegemony in the narrative of popular Christianity.

Stolzman supports his argument to equate these symbols by using a form-versus-function argument. He believes that a Christian function, such as repentance, can be expressed through a cultural form, such as verbal confession, or it can be done by spending time in a sweat bath. Verbal confession, he argues, is a European expression of faith. However, the narrative of Lakota traditions is more experiential, making the prac-

25. "Toppling Tradition? Christian Teachings Conflict with Tribal Customs, National Laws," *Christianity Today,* 6 September 1999, 31.
26. William Stolzman, *The Pipe and Christ: A Christian-Sioux Dialogue* (Chamberlain, S.D.: Tipi, 1986), 218.

tice of confession through verbal expression less meaningful for them than a visit to a sweat bath. According to Stolzman, confession is a transcultural absolute value with culturally specific expressions. Christians in all cultures must confess their sins. However, the form of confession, whether verbal expression or a sweat bath, is a culturally specific value. The form of the discipline is incidental to its function.

Whether or not we agree with Stolzman, the issue provokes a clash between Christianity and culture that is going to be a focal point of ethical discussion for a long time. *Christianity Today* noted that "the clash between Christian faith and ethnic tradition remains as worrisome as ever."[27] It became critical during the conference of the World Christian Gathering of Indigenous Peoples in Rapid City, South Dakota, in September 1998, during which many participants questioned the spiritual validity of many cultural artifacts. One participant, when discussing the validity of using cultural artifacts in worship, emphasized that the only mandate for indigenous people is to become like Christ. He took a dim view of someone who challenged the practice of offering food to deceased relatives. It is a ceremony that honors the dead and symbolizes the new life to which they move on after death.

When a European-American chided the Native American about the practice, asking, "When are the deceased going to eat that food?" the Native American answered, "About the same time your relatives get up and smell those flowers."[28] If this Native American was faced with the issues of whether Ghanaians should observe the ceremony of sacred silence in their culture, he would have undoubtedly advised them to transform this cultural tradition to honor God. He would have reminded them that Christmas and Easter, the central holy days of Western Christianity, have their roots in pagan practices. While these practices and disciplines have spiritual value, they embody culturally specific values with culturally relative expressions.

The Ethics of Bribery

All Christians who engage in some form of cross-cultural mission will eventually be asked to pay a gratuity for a service rendered, such as receiving packages through a customs office, expediting a visa, or registering a motor vehicle. The more serious gratuities involve payments to send medical supplies and food to people who are dying. The lore of

27. "Toppling Tradition?" 30.
28. Ken Steinken, "Native Christians Reclaim Worship," *Christianity Today,* 26 October 1998, 13.

missions organizations are full of stories about payments for services; my favorite one is about a government official who insisted that a development organization from Germany give him a Mercedes-Benz before he could allow them to deliver medical supplies to a hospital.

The Christian community has created a wide range of views about these payments. Some Christians call them bribes and refuse ever to pay them, believing that "bribery . . . is universally condemned in both testaments" and that "a wicked man accepts a bribe in secret to pervert the course of justice."[29] The Christian who pays bribes "places pragmatism over obedience" and becomes "a victim of extortion."[30] It "is not an option for a Christian, let alone a missionary."[31]

Other Christians take a softer view of the cultural customs that appear to be bribes in the legislated cultures of Western societies. They believe they are not offering bribes but are paying tips, giving gifts, and rendering fees for services in the relational cultures of traditional societies. They see that gifts or bribes serve as incentives for officials to do their jobs well. Even though it may violate Western cultural ideals, it does not violate Scripture.[32] Christians on this side of the issue recognize that many cultures throughout the world are organized around the ritual behavior of giving gifts. The gift bonds relationships, honoring those who serve. The Book of Proverbs reminds us that "a gift opens doors; it gives access to the great" (Prov. 18:16) and that "a gift in secret averts anger" (Prov. 21:14).

These two sides of the debate are often unresolved, despite the many biblical passages that the proponents from each side use to support their position. Those who argue against bribes believe the Bible prohibits them because they violate justice, a transcultural absolute value of Christianity. The opponents of bribery argue that people who pay bribes support Isaiah's observation that "rulers are rebels, companions of thieves; they all love bribes and chase after gifts. They do not defend the cause of the fatherless; the widow's case does not come before them" (Isa. 1:23). The Bible prohibits bribes because it will only make a bad situation worse.

29. Steven Falkiner, "Bribery: Where Are the Lines?" *Evangelical Missions Quarterly* (January 1999): 23, 25.

30. Ibid., 24–25.

31. Ibid., 29.

32. Gregory Nichols, "A Case for Bribery: Giving versus Taking," *Evangelical Missions Quarterly* (January 1999): 31.

Christians who support the payment of incentives agree that payments cannot be made if they support injustice; they should not pay bribes for illegal or immoral services. However, the practices of giving gifts and incentives support culturally specific values with culturally relative expressions. In this sense, giving tips, gifts, and incentives to public servants in many countries is somewhat analogous to giving tips to people in other cultures who provide personal services, such as servers in restaurants, hair stylists, and cab drivers. The payment is not an effort to endorse corruption; it is a recognition that public servants, like other people who provide personal services, supplement their incomes by receiving fees for rendering personal services.

The argument between these two positions can be resolved by analyzing the leading functions of the institutions that are employing the people who are receiving the payments. A payment for services, whether money or material, is a bribe if it impedes an institution from fulfilling its leading function. Otherwise, it can be an incentive that encourages people to work toward contributing to the leading function of their work place; it has the potential to build reciprocity in cultures where people value relationships over impersonal exchanges. Neither Christians nor anyone else should make payments to influence people to pervert justice or to perform a service that is not among the leading functions of their organization. Therefore, Christians should not pay police officers to ignore traffic violations, and they should not pay fines for fabricated violations. However, the payment of incentives, tips, and gifts to customs officials might be appropriate if they encourage officials to expedite the services of their institution.

Payments of this nature can be culturally relative expressions of culturally specific values. They function in the economy of grace; they should be commensurate with the nature of the services, preventing extortion or other forms of injustice. As expressions of grace, they should be negotiated to recognize gratitude rather than obligation.

Female Genital Mutilation

Female genital mutilation (FGM) has received considerable attention in the global media in recent years. It is defined by the World Health Organization as constituting all procedures that involve partial or total removal of the external female genitalia or other injury to the female genital organs, whether for cultural or any nontherapeutic reasons. People in about forty countries of the world practice it, primarily Muslims in Africa. It is often attributed to Islam, but there is no support for it in its early traditions or in the Qur'an. Most likely, it was practiced in these cultures prior to the advent of Islam, and it was imposed on Islamic teachings. Young girls usually undergo the operation at the onset of puberty.

The practice of FGM has received a wide range of ethical inquiry. The initial publicity it received in recent years was almost unanimous in condemning it. However, a few anthropologists and theologians have sought to justify the practice, if not support it. The reasons for supporting the practice range from preparing women for adulthood to protecting their sexual integrity. They also include many fallacies; people in some cultures claim that female genitals will grow to a woman's knees if they are not cut, and other people say that a man will die if his penis touches female genitals that aren't mutilated. People in most cultures where FGM is practiced, however, resign themselves to the fact that women cannot get married unless their genitals are mutilated, regardless of what they or anyone else thinks of the practice. It survives simply because the marriage prospects are dismal for women who are not mutilated.

The condemnation of FGM usually focuses on such issues as pain, hygiene, and sexual satisfaction. Each of these reasons justify condemning the practice. However, since these reasons fall short of capturing the ethical severity of the issue, I want to suggest that the eradication of FGM is a transcultural absolute value. The eradication of the practice has moral implications that are cultural and sexual in nature. However, the eradication of the practice is a transcultural absolute value, primarily because it denies that women have any moral agency, which suggests they are not created in the image of God.

The moral implications of FGM stem from managing *fitna* in a culture. *Fitna* is the destructive power that results when people cannot manage their sexuality; it usually results when men are uncontrollably attracted to women. However, people attempt to control it by stifling female sexual expression.[33] I once asked a college professor who lived in an African-Islamic culture what he thought about female circumcision. Since this professor was educated in Europe, I expected him to give me an enlightened answer such as, "I think it is horrible, and I wish it

---

33. The lack of logic in burdening women to solve a male problem has not gone unnoticed by Islamic theologians. In his attempt to grasp the logic of the seclusion and veiling of women and the basis of sexual segregation, the Muslim feminist Qasim Amin (1863–1908) suggested that women can control their sexual impulses better than men can control theirs. He concluded that sexual segregation is a device to protect men, not women (see Fatima Mernissi, *Beyond the Veil: Male-Female Dynamics in Modern Muslim Society* [Bloomington: Indiana University Press, 1987], 31).

would end." However, much to my dismay, he said, "It must be done. Otherwise, women could not control their sexuality, and our society will be in moral chaos." He believed the society would become a victim of uncontrolled *fitna* if its residents stopped practicing FGM.

The need to regulate sexual expression is a result of the fall. Most cultures have found adequate ways of regulating it through marriage, clothing styles, and gender relationships. None of these regulatory efforts, however, deny that approximately half of the human population is incapable of becoming morally mature beings. FGM not only insults the moral integrity of women, it also prevents men from realizing the fullness of God's being. The narrative of God's redemptive relationship with creation begins with the affirmation that people bear the image of God by expressing their moral maturity.

John Howard Yoder depicted community as *"an alternative construction of the world."*[34] It is composed of people who have voluntarily united to express their affirmation for similar non-discursive meanings of symbols. These symbols can include roofs, sabbaths, the cross, and a host of other issues; they are cultural in nature, but their ability to unite people into community bears witness to their transcultural nature. They empower people to bear witness to the same story; they "express a new reality by which they have been grasped."[35]

In reflecting on the story of the Magi coming to Jerusalem from the East to pay homage to "the one who has been born king of the Jews" (Matt. 2:2), I wonder who the Magi were and when they came. However, their presence in Matthew's Gospel clearly indicates God's intention to empower people to form community by making relative their cultural differences without abolishing these differences. The Magi are a foretaste of the universal nature of the church, an alternative community through which God welcomes all to participate in the narrative of God's redemptive relationship with creation.

34. John Howard Yoder, "The Believers Church and the Arms Race," in *For the Nations: Essays Public and Evangelical* (Grand Rapids: Eerdmans, 1997), 153.
35. Paul Tillich, *Theology of Culture* (New York: Oxford University Press, 1964), 41.

12

Toward Constructing the Narrative: From Teaching to Learning

If anyone else thinks he has reasons to put confidence in the flesh, I have more: circumcised on the eighth day, of the people of Israel, of the tribe of Benjamin, a Hebrew of Hebrews; in regard to the law, a Pharisee; as for zeal, persecuting the church; as for legalistic righteousness, faultless. But whatever was to my profit I now consider loss for the sake of Christ.

Philippians 3:4–7

When health educators asked the women in a Somali village how many children they had, the women included the numbers of both living and deceased children. Their answers confirmed the health educators' impression that infant mortality rate in that region was particularly high. The educators responded by implementing a child survival program but were perplexed when it made no noticeable impact on reducing infant deaths in the village. The project raised the question that always emerges in the missions and development communities, "Why is so much that is said, written, and spent on development having so little effect on the problems it seeks to address?"[1] There are many answers to

1. Michael Edwards, "Rethinking Social Development: The Search for 'Relevance,'" in *Rethinking Social Development: Theory, Research, and Practice,* ed. David Booth (London: Longman, 1994), 279.

this question, the best of which focus on the need to empower people to transform the structures that govern their lives so that they can change their story.

While the health educators understood the high infant mortality rate as a problem and a tragedy, the mothers perceived it as a blessing because they believed deceased children went to heaven to become the advocates for their parents' salvation. The people had integrated a folk tenet into their Islamic faith to absorb a serious problem in their community. These efforts to theologize their pain challenged Christians who worked with the Somali villagers to discern how an infant survival program expressed Good News to the community. How can the project empower them to tell a different story?

The Need for Participation

"We cannot change the world successfully unless we understand the way it works."[2] To manage cultural change, development facilitators and missionaries must first understand the narratives of the communities they serve because they reveal the nature of the structures that govern life and explain the way the world works. The irony of learning narratives, however, is that people are often unaware of them and of the structures they represent; they are among the elements of the *kosmos*. They have tremendous influences on efforts to cope with the struggles of daily life. People need to empower themselves to transform their narratives and thereby their social structures.

Participatory Rural Appraisal

Development facilitators have devised a variety of tools in recent years to foster community participation. The most popular is a collection of exercises, Participatory Rural Appraisal (PRA), which is "a family of approaches and methods to enable rural people to share, enhance, and analyze their knowledge of life and conditions . . . to plan and act . . . to monitor and evaluate."[3] PRAs comprise a collection of exercises that include maps, time lines, seasonal calendars, and charts that empower people to discern how they use time, money, and natural resources, and matrices that illustrate the various domestic and foreign influences on the village. These influences can include churches, mosques, temples, devel-

2. Ibid., 280.
3. Robert Chambers, *Whose Reality Counts? Putting the First Last* (London: Intermediate Technology, 1997), 104.

opment agencies, and political organizations. Good PRAs also pay attention to the folklore, stories, and proverbs of a culture.

The significance of PRAs is that they change the nature of managing cultural change in their efforts to make knowledge creation less professional and to return the activity to the people it directly affects.[4] They transform teachers and trainers into learners. PRAs that are done well comprise a variety of exercises that facilitate the ability of indigenous people to communicate in a nonverbal way. They minimize interviews and invite people to draw maps and make diagrams, and they reject surveys because they are flawed and unreliable.[5] The health educators in the Somali village, for example, were unable to interpret statistical information that was apparently valid. A good PRA would have exposed the meaning that the people assigned to the high infant mortality rate in the village by focusing on the non-discursive meaning of the statistics.

Figure 12.1 illustrates the contributions PRAs make to development research. The diagram was created by a group of people who lived in a Hindu village in India. By arranging an assortment of plastic disks to illustrate the power of each of the village's gods, the development workers were able to understand the hierarchy of both their gods and values.

Figure 12.1 Hierarchy of Gods in a Hindu Village
(Circles Indicate Degree of Power and Geographical Location within Village)

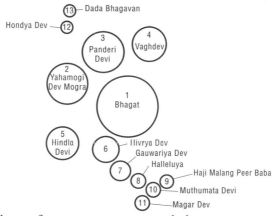

The larger disks in figure 12.1 represented the more powerful gods, who were also closest to the geographical center of the village. The PRA

4. David Hulme, "Social Development Research and the Third Sector: NGOs as Users and Subjects of Society Inquiry," in *Rethinking Social Development,* ed. David Booth.

5. Chambers, *Whose Reality Counts?* 5.

researchers listened as the people explained the power and function of each god. The people's explanation of the eighth god on the chart perplexed the researchers because the god's name, "Halleluya," sounded familiar but not in that context. The villagers told the researchers that "Halleluya" was the Christian god and recounted the story about an evangelist who had visited the village several years earlier, preaching about "Halleluya." The people said some residents of the village became Christians, and the community included their god among the others. When the researchers asked the villagers why they ranked this god as number eight, they said the evangelist would not pray for their animals. They concluded that the Christian god, therefore, did not have the power to meet one central value of the village.

Survival Strategies

The ultimate purpose of a PRA is to empower the people in a community to learn their survival strategy. Survival strategies embody the central values of a community and are the medium through which cultural change is managed. Survival strategies include, among other things, systems for health care, economics and employment, provisions of food, clothing and shelter, justice, social harmony, education, community guidance and planning, and salvation. Figure 12.2 represents the survival strategy of the Pokot community of Kenya and illustrates activities that the development practitioners who work in that community believed were central to its survival.

Figure 12.2 Pokot Survival Strategy[6]

Justice
courts of elders

Social Harmony
oathing, burning arms,
sacrificing animals

Healing
traditional healers and
surgeons, herbalists,
exorcists

Tororoot

Provision
livestock as basis
of economy

Guidance
fortune-tellers, seers,
diviners

Salvation
ancestors, the living
dead

6. This diagram was drawn by participants in the transformative development workshop in World Vision–Kenya.

The activities included in figure 12.2 are organized around *Tororoot,* the high god of Pokot culture, who influences a cadre of specialists that serve the community's welfare. For instance, healers and fortune-tellers provide guidance by interpreting the meaning of stars, animal tracks, and cow droppings, among other natural phenomena. The ancestors advocate salvation for the people who are living. Social harmony is achieved by sacrificing animals, scarring arms, and oathing. Justice is mediated by the court of elders, who consult the living dead.

All communities have survival strategies. When a workshop with people from Ethiopia asked me about the survival strategy of my suburban American community, they were surprised when I said that economic viability is the central value of my neighborhood. I explained that people often do not go to church on Sundays because they don't believe it helps sustain their way of life. I mentioned that many people feel the church is a negative influence on the community because it takes resources, such as money, from their community but does not reciprocate with equal services. When the Ethiopians asked me why United States currency bears the inscription "In God We Trust," I realized that survival strategies also reveal how traditions in cultures have changed.

The purpose of managing cultural change through development work is to enhance the survival strategy of a village. The capabilities and vulnerabilities of a community are directly related to its social, economic, and political structures. The initial step in enhancing the sustenance of a community, therefore, is to conduct a PRA that focuses on its narrative. The success of this effort requires people who are managing change in the community to listen to the stories people tell about themselves, to read novels about the culture, and to understand folklore and religious beliefs. Both the Christian evangelist and the health educators could have been effective had they understood the narratives of each community and thereby gained insight into the way influential people interpreted the meaning of their innovations.

The need for understanding the narrative of a community is essential for people who are engaging in grassroots development as well as for those who are conducting international diplomacy. It was essential to the success of the United Nations' effort to intervene in Somalia in the early 1990s. The effort failed, to a large extent, because UN peacekeepers did not read Somali poetry. Consequently, they knew little about the values that fostered the survival of that culture. Consider the values inherent in the following lines of poetry, written in the late 1890s:

> Grievous times are now upon us, times of death and woe . . .
> Close kinsmen align themselves in rival factions . . .
> Supporting the unbelievers, who offer them grain for food . . .
> Foreign solders are the ones they choose . . .
> In preference to the Prophet, on whom be peace . . .
> When they enlist in the strangers' army . . .
> May god smite them with torments . . .
> They come to see unbelievers as a source of goodness . . .
> Bringing provisions, animals and shares of wealth . . .
> I shall take nothing from them . . .
> even if swords and rifles are taken up against me and bullets shot . . . [7]

The international community was shocked when the Somali militia destroyed a United States helicopter and celebrated the death of the pilot by dragging his body through the streets of Mogadishu. The act, however, was embodied in the narrative of the community. Richard Corfield, a British military officer, suffered the same fate eighty years earlier. The story of Corfield's death is embedded in the narrative of Somali culture in the following poem:

> You have died, Corfield . . .
> When you see the companions of the faithful
> and the jewels of Heaven . . .
> say "Yesterday in the holy war a bullet
> from one of their rifles struck me. . . ."
> Report how savagely their swords tore you,
> Show the past generations [where] the daggers plunged
> Say, "My eyes stiffened as I watched with horror. . . .
> "The mercy I implored was not granted.
> "The risk I took, the mistake I made, cost my life.
> "The schemes the [evil spirits] planted in me brought my ruin. . . .
> "Beasts of prey have eaten my flesh and torn it apart. . . .
> "The crows plucked out my veins and tendon. . . .
> "The [Somali fighters] are like the advancing
> thunderbolts of a storm, rumbling and roaring."[8]

The UN efforts in the early 1990s "should have given top priority . . . [to]

7. Mohamed Abdille Hassan, "Perhaps the Trumpet Has Sounded," in *An Anthology of Somali Poetry,* trans. B. W. Andrzejewski with Sheila Andrzejewski (Bloomington: Indiana University Press, 1993), 42–46.

8. Said S. Samatar, *Oral Poetry and Somali Nationalism: The Case of Sayyid Mahammad 'Abdille Hasan* (Cambridge: Cambridge University Press, 1982), 175.

Somali music, national songs and poetry,"[9] the ingredients of their cultural narrative.

The Church's Role in Survival Strategies

Since development projects cannot be value-free or morally neutral, communities are becoming more intentional about basing their development efforts on a set of values. The role of the church is to offer the redemptive values of Christ to the community with the ultimate hope that the narrative of the community will eventually be transformed into the narrative of God's redemptive relationship with creation. This effort to transform the community's narrative will make Christ the center of the survival strategy.

This effort, however, cannot be accomplished without a strong community. One of my friends conducted research on the survival strategy of a village in Russia. His concern was that the village had become dysfunctional when it was dominated by communism. With the fall of the Soviet Union, however, the village lost its strategy for survival; life became chaotic and the leaders of organized crime took over. People had to pay them for the services the government could not provide. The Christians in the community were divided about their moral response. Some of them, who believed in graded absolutes, believed they could pay homage to the leaders because it was necessary for their survival. Other Christians, who had more absolute approaches to ethical dilemmas, believed they should not support organized crime in any way. They believed God would provide a means for them to survive without sinning.

After a long discussion we concluded that the narrative of the village was undergoing a severe transition from communism to capitalism, through chaos. The major issue was not whether the Christians should pay for services to organized crime but whether they could garner any value in paying for them while they transformed the narrative of the community. The Christians could decide not to pay the fees to organized crime and suffer by living without services necessary for their survival. They might even become like many Sudanese Christians, who suffer because they are barred from participating in their national economies. They had a moral obligation not to pay for the services even if they could afford them.

9. Mariam Arif Gassem, *Hostages: The People Who Kidnapped Themselves* (Nairobi: Central Graphics Services, 1994), 127.

245

The Christians in the Russian village could also decide to pay organized crime for their services. They might find justification for this by believing that their political situation was somewhat analogous to that of the Christians living under Islamic rule during and after the Islamic conquests. *Dhimma,* the Arabic term for *dime,* was a tax the Muslims imposed on Christians under their rule as payment for their protection. While the Christians lived as second-class citizens with no political or economic power, by paying the *dhimma* they received the services necessary for their sustenance. The central issue in both situations is whether the Christians in the community took responsibility to establish a survival strategy that resembled the values of the narrative of God's redemptive relationship with creation. Are the Christians doing the good God requires in Micah 6:8, "to act justly and to love mercy"?

A similar issue emerged when the Pharisees asked Jesus if they should pay taxes to Caesar. He replied, "Give to Caesar what is Caesar's, and to God what is God's" (Matt. 22:21). In giving this answer, Jesus was not endorsing the morality of the Roman government. Instead, he was reminding the Pharisees that they lived according to a different narrative. Their decision to pay or withhold taxes did not change who they were; the political structures in which they lived were incidental to their ability to live as God's people. The bigger concern was whether they could organize themselves into a community to express their virtues and values and to be who God wanted them to be. The Roman government did not have that power over them. Similarly, the calling of Christians is to organize themselves in a community that produces a survival strategy to enhance justice for the poor, the widow, and the orphan. "The primary social structure through which the gospel works to change other structures is that of the Christian community,"[10] the church.

The fiduciary responsibility of the church dictates that Christians in the Russian village should work toward the transformation of the current system. Either decision bears witness to a *kosmos* that is groaning and pleading for redemption; these groans are made by the millions of people who are dying from disease and wars and suffering from economic and political exploitation. The pleas for redemption are heard by the billions of people who are struggling for justice as they strive to cope with the daily challenges of life. They need a story of hope that will empower them to believe that God has not abandoned the world he made.

10. Ronald J. Sider, *One-Sided Christianity: Uniting the Church to Heal a Lost and Broken World* (Grand Rapids: Zondervan, 1993), 37.

The narrative of God's redemptive relationship with creation brings to mind the elderly woman who was walking to the market carrying a pot of butter in one hand and holding a goat with a leash in the other. She had hoped to sell the goat and the butter to buy food for her family; she was caring for many of her grandchildren because their parents had died from AIDS. As she approached the market, a man, pretending to be blind, asked her to lead him to the market. She told him that her arms were full. The man offered to hold the goat leash if she held his arm. The woman agreed and handed him the leash.

Before long, she noticed that the man was no longer holding the goat. He acted astonished and said he must have dropped the leash. When she went to look for the goat, she left the man holding her pot of butter. The man continued walking to the market and joined his friend, who had taken the goat. They sold both the goat and the butter for a tidy profit, while the woman mourned her loss. To the Somalis the story is humorous; to Western readers it is a tragedy. The woman, willing to assist a victim, became a victim. She deserves our compassion; "protecting or rescuing innocent victims has become the cultural imperative everywhere the biblical influence has been felt."[11]

There is no time when the world has been in greater need of the gospel of Jesus Christ; yet, there has also been no time in the history of Christianity when the gospel has been more trivialized. The *kosmos* is hungering for redemption, not through propositional truth, but by means of a narrative into which we live.

11. Gil Bailie, *Violence Unveiled: Humanity at the Crossroads* (New York: Crossroad, 1995), 20.

Selected Bibliography

Adeney, Bernard T. *Strange Virtues: Ethics in a Multi-cultural World.* Downers Grove, Ill.: InterVarsity, 1995.

African Rights. *Rwanda: Death, Despair, and Defiance.* London: African Rights Publications, 1994.

Allen, Diogenes. *Christian Belief in a Postmodern World: The Full Wealth of Conviction.* Louisville: Westminster/John Knox, 1989.

Anderson, Mary B. *Do No Harm: How Aid Can Support Peace—Or War.* Boulder, Colo.: Rienner, 1999.

Anderson, Mary B., and Peter J. Woodrow. *Rising from the Ashes: Development Strategies in Times of Disaster.* Boulder, Colo.: Rienner, 1988.

Augsburger, David W. *Helping People Forgive.* Louisville: Westminster/John Knox, 1996.

Aukerman, Dale. *Reckoning with Apocalypse: Terminal Politics and Christian Hope.* New York: Crossroad, 1993.

Ayittey, George B. N. *Africa in Chaos.* London: Macmillan, 1998.

Bailie, Gil. *Violence Unveiled: Humanity at the Crossroads.* New York: Crossroad, 1995.

Banfield, Edward C. *The Moral Basis of a Backward Society.* New York: Free Press, 1958.

Barber, Benjamin R. *Jihad vs. McWorld: How Globalism and Tribalism Are Reshaping the World.* New York: Ballantine, 1996.

Barbour, Ian G. *Religion in an Age of Science.* San Francisco: Harper & Row, 1990.

———. *Science and Secularity: The Ethics of Technology.* New York: Harper & Row, 1970.

Batchelor, Peter. *People in Rural Development.* London: Paternoster, 1981.

Beckmann, David, and Arthur Simon. *Grace at the Table: Ending Hunger in God's World.* Downers Grove, Ill.: InterVarsity, 1999.

Selected Bibliography

Bediako, Kwame. *Christianity in Africa: The Renewal of a Non-Western Religion.* Maryknoll, N.Y.: Orbis, 1995.

Bell, Daniel. *The Cultural Contradictions of Capitalism.* New York: Basic Books, 1996.

Benedict, Ruth. *Patterns of Culture.* Boston: Riverside, 1934.

Bennet, Jon. *The Hunger Machine: The Politics of Food.* Yorkshire, England: Polity, 1987.

Berger, Peter L. *Facing Up to Modernity: Excursions in Society, Politics, and Religion.* New York: Basic Books, 1977.

———. *The Rumor of Angels: Modern Society and the Rediscovery of the Supernatural.* Garden City, N.Y.: Doubleday, 1969.

———. *The Sacred Canopy: Elements of a Sociological Theory of Religion.* New York: Doubleday, 1969.

———, ed. *The Desecularization of the World: Resurgent Religion and World Politics.* Grand Rapids: Eerdmans, 1999.

Berger, Peter L., and Thomas Luckmann. *The Social Construction of Reality: A Treatise on the Sociology of Knowledge.* New York: Anchor, 1966.

Berkhof, Hendrikus. *Christ and the Powers.* Trans. John H. Yoder. Scottdale, Pa.: Herald, 1962.

Berry, Thomas M. *The Dream of the Earth.* San Francisco: Sierra Club, 1988.

Blaut, J. M. *The Colonizer's Model of the World: Geographical Diffusionism and Eurocentric History.* New York: Guilford, 1993.

Blomberg, Craig L. *Neither Poverty nor Riches: A Biblical Theology of Material Possessions.* Grand Rapids: Eerdmans, 1999.

Booth, David, ed. *Rethinking Social Development: Theory, Research, and Practice.* London: Longman, 1994.

Bosch, David J. *Transforming Mission: Paradigm Shifts in Theology of Mission.* Maryknoll, N.Y.: Orbis, 1991.

Bradshaw, Bruce. *Bridging the Gap: Evangelism, Development, and Shalom.* Monrovia, Calif.: MARC, 1993.

Brown, Robert McAfee. *Unexpected News: Reading the Bible with Third World Eyes.* Louisville: Westminster/John Knox, 1984.

Bujo, Benezet. *The Ethical Dimension of Community: The African Model and the Dialogue between North and South.* Nairobi: Paulines Publications Africa, 1998.

Burnett, David. *Clash of Worlds.* Eastbourne, U.K.: MARC/Monarch, 1990.

Byrne, James M. *Religion and the Enlightenment: From Descartes to Kant.* Louisville: Westminster/John Knox, 1996.

Chambers, Robert. *Rural Development: Putting the Last First.* Essex, England: Longman, 1983.

———. *Whose Reality Counts? Putting the First Last.* London: Intermediate Technology, 1997.

Christian, Jayakumar. *God of the Empty-Handed: Poverty, Power, and the Kingdom of God.* Monrovia, Calif.: MARC, 1999.

Clouser, Roy A. *The Myth of Religious Neutrality: An Essay on the Hidden Role of Religious Belief in Theories.* South Bend, Ind.: University of Notre Dame Press, 1991.

Cobb, John B., Jr. *The Earthist Challenge to Economism: A Theological Critique of the World Ban.* New York: St. Martins, 1999.

Cox, Harvey. *Fire from Heaven: The Rise of Pentecostal Spirituality and the Reshaping of Religion in the Twenty-First Century.* New York: Addison-Wesley, 1995.

————. *The Secular City: Secularization and Urbanization in Theological Perspective.* New York: Macmillan, 1965.

Craig, Jenni M. *Servants among the Poor.* Wellington, N.Z.: Servants to Asia's Poor, 1998.

Crane, Julia G., and Michael V. Angrosino. *Field Projects in Anthropology.* Prospect Heights, Ill.: Waveland, 1992.

Cross, Nigel, and Rhiannon Barker, eds. *At the Desert's Edge: Oral Histories from the Sahel.* London: Panos, 1992.

Crossan, John Dominic. *The Birth of Christianity: Discovering What Happened in the Years Immediately after the Execution of Jesus.* San Francisco: Harper San Francisco, 1998.

Cummings, Mary Lou. *Surviving without Romance: African Women Tell Their Stories.* Scottdale, Pa.: Herald, 1991.

Dale, Reidar. *Evaluation Frameworks for Development Programmes and Projects.* Thousand Oaks, Calif.: Sage, 1998.

Daly, Herman E., and John B. Cobb Jr. *For the Common Good: Redirecting the Economy toward Community, the Environment, and a Sustainable Future.* Boston: Beacon, 1989.

Davis, John Jefferson. *Evangelical Ethics: Issues Facing the Church Today.* 2d ed. Phillipsburg, N.J.: Presbyterian and Reformed, 1993.

Donovan, Vincent J. *Christianity Rediscovered.* Maryknoll, N.Y.: Orbis, 1978.

Douglas, Mary. *Purity and Danger: An Analysis of Concepts of Pollution and Taboo.* London: Routledge & K. Paul, 1966.

Driver, John. *Images of the Church in Mission.* Scottdale, Pa.: Herald, 1997.

Driver, Tom F. *The Magic of Ritual.* New York: Harper Collins, 1991.

Dyrness, William A. *Invitation to Cross-Cultural Theology: Case Studies in Vernacular Theologies.* Grand Rapids: Zondervan, 1992.

————. *Learning about Theology from the Third World.* Grand Rapids: Zondervan, 1990.

Edgerton, Robert B. *Sick Societies: Challenging the Myth of Primitive Harmony.* New York: Free Press, 1992.

Ellul, Jacques. *The New Demons.* New York: Seabury, 1975.

———. *The Subversion of Christianity.* Trans. Geoffrey W. Bromiley. Grand Rapids: Eerdmans, 1986.

Eze, Emmanuel Chukwudi, ed. *Postcolonial African Philosophy: A Critical Reader.* Oxford: Blackwell, 1997.

Fackre, Gabriel. *The Christian Story: A Narrative Interpretation of Basic Christian Doctrine.* Grand Rapids: Eerdmans, 1996.

Ferre, Frederick. *Hellfire and Lightning Rods: Liberating Science, Technology, and Religion.* Maryknoll, N.Y.: Orbis, 1993.

Finger, Thomas N. *Self, Earth, and Society: Alienation and Trinitarian Transformation.* Downers Grove, Ill.: InterVarsity, 1997.

Fisher, Julie. *Non-Governments: NGOs and the Political Development of the Third World.* West Hartford, Conn.: Kumarian Press, 1998.

Fletcher, Joseph. *Situation Ethics: The New Morality.* Philadelphia: Westminster, 1966.

Fortman, Bas de Gaay, and Berma Klein Goldweijk. *God and the Goods: Global Economy in a Civilizational Perspective.* Geneva: WCC, 1999.

Foucault, Michel. "Two Lectures." In *Power/Knowledge: Selected Interviews and Other Writings, 1972–1977,* ed. Colin Gordon. New York: Pantheon, 1980.

Geertz, Clifford. *The Interpretation of Cultures: Selected Essays.* New York: Basic Books, 1973.

Geisler, Norman L. *Christian Ethics: Options and Issues.* Grand Rapids: Baker, 1989.

Gelfand, Michael. *Medicine and Custom in Africa.* London: Livingstone, 1964.

Giorgis, Dawit Wolde. *Red Tears: War, Famine, and Revolution in Ethiopia.* Trenton, N.J.: Red Sea, 1989.

Girard, Rene. *Things Hidden Since the Foundation of the World.* Trans. Stephen Bann and Michael Metteer. Stanford, Calif.: Stanford University Press, 1987.

Gittins, Anthony J. *Bread for the Journey: The Mission of Transformation and the Transformation of Mission.* Maryknoll, N.Y.: Orbis, 1993.

Goldberg, Michael. *Theology and Narrative: A Critical Introduction.* Nashville: Abingdon, 1982.

Gonzales, Justo L. *For the Healing of the Nations.* Maryknoll, N.Y.: Orbis, 1999.

Goulet, Denis. *Development Ethics: A Guide to Theory and Practice.* South Bend, Ind.: University of Notre Dame Press, 1995.

———. *The Uncertain Promise: Value Conflicts in Technology Transfer.* New York: Horizons, 1989.

Granberg-Michaelson, Wesley. *Ecology and Life: Accepting Our Environmental Responsibility.* Waco: Word, 1988.

Grassi, Joseph A. *Loaves and Fishes: The Gospel Feeding Narratives.* Collegeville, Minn.: Order of St. Benedict, 1991.

Green, Edward C. *Indigenous Theories of Contagious Disease.* Walnut Creek, Calif.: AltaMira, 1999.

Grenz, Stanley J. *The Moral Quest: Foundations of Christian Ethics.* Downers Grove, Ill.: InterVarsity, 1997.

———. *A Primer on Postmodernism.* Grand Rapids: Eerdmans, 1996.

Groothuis, Douglas. *Truth Decay: Defending Christianity against the Challenges of Postmodernism.* Downers Grove, Ill.: InterVarsity, 2000.

Guder, Darrell L., ed. *Missional Church: A Vision for the Sending of the Church in North America.* Grand Rapids: Eerdmans, 1998.

Halteman, James. *The Clashing World of Economics and Faith.* Scottdale, Pa.: Herald, 1995.

Hancock, Robert Lincoln, ed. *The Ministry of Development in Evangelical Perspective.* Pasadena: William Carey Library, 1979.

Hargrove, Eugene C., ed. *Religion and Environmental Crisis.* Athens: University of Georgia Press, 1986.

Harris, Marvin. *Cows, Pigs, Wars and Witches: The Riddles of Culture.* New York: Vantage, 1974.

———. *Theories of Culture in Postmodern Times.* Walnut Creek, Calif.: AltaMira, 1999

Harris, Myles F. *Breakfast in Hell: A Doctor's Eyewitness Account of the Politics of Hunger in Ethiopia.* New York: Poseidon, 1987.

Harrison, Lawrence E. *Underdevelopment Is a State of Mind: The Latin American Case.* Lanham, Md.: Madison, 1985.

Hart, John. *Ethics and Technology: Innovation and Transformation in Community Contexts.* Cleveland: Pilgrim, 1997.

Hartman, Robert H., ed. *Poverty and Economic Justice: A Philosophical Approach.* Ramsey, N.J.: Paulist, 1984.

Hatch, Elvin. *Culture and Morality: The Relativity of Values in Anthropology.* New York: Columbia University Press, 1983.

Hauerwas, Stanley C. *A Community of Character: Toward a Constructive Christian Social Ethic.* South Bend, Ind.: University of Notre Dame Press, 1981.

Hauerwas, Stanley, Richard Bondi, and David Burrell. *Truthfulness and Tragedy: Further Investigations into Christian Ethics.* South Bend, Ind.: University of Notre Dame Press, 1977.

Hauerwas, Stanley, and L. Gregory Jones, eds. *Why Narrative? Readings in Narrative Theology.* Grand Rapids: Eerdmans, 1989.

Hay, Donald A. *Economics Today: A Christian Critique.* London: Apollos, 1989.

Haynes, Jeff. *Religion and Politics in Africa.* Nairobi: East Africa Educational Publishers, 1996.

Selected Bibliography

Hays, Richard B. *The Moral Vision of the New Testament: A Contemporary Introduction to New Testament Ethics.* New York: Harper Collins, 1996.

Hege, Nathan B. *Beyond Our Prayers: Anabaptist Church Growth in Ethiopia, 1948–1998.* Scottdale, Pa.: Herald, 1998.

Herzog, William R., II. *Parables as Subversive Speech: Jesus as Pedagogue of the Oppressed.* Louisville: Westminster/John Knox, 1994.

Hiebert, Paul G. *Anthropological Reflections on Missiological Issues.* Grand Rapids: Baker, 1994.

———. *Cultural Anthropology.* 2d ed. Grand Rapids: Baker, 1983.

Hiebert, Paul G., and Frances F. Hiebert. *Case Studies in Missions.* Grand Rapids: Baker, 1987.

Hiebert, Paul G., and Eloise Hiebert Meneses. *Incarnational Ministry: Planting Churches in Band, Tribal, Peasant, and Urban Societies.* Grand Rapids: Baker, 1995.

Hiebert, Paul G., R. Daniel Shaw, and Tite Tienou. *Understanding Folk Religion: A Christian Response to Popular Beliefs and Practices.* Grand Rapids: Baker, 1999.

Hoedemaker, Bert. *Secularization and Mission: A Theological Essay.* Harrisburg, Pa.: Trinity Press International, 1998.

Hopkins, Willie E. *Ethical Dimensions of Diversity.* Thousand Oaks, Calif.: Sage, 1997.

Hughes, Dewi. *God of the Poor: A Biblical Vision of God's Present Rule.* Carlisle, Cumbria, U.K.: OM, 1998.

Hunsberger, George R. *Bearing the Witness of the Spirit: Lesslie Newbigin's Theology of Cultural Plurality.* Grand Rapids: Eerdmans, 1998.

Huntington, Samuel P. *The Clash of Civilizations and the Remaking of World Order.* New York: Simon & Schuster, 1996.

Ignatieff, Michael. *The Warrior's Honor: Ethnic War and the Modern Conscience.* New York: Owl, 1997.

Irvin, Dale T. *Christian Histories, Christian Traditioning: Rendering Accounts.* Maryknoll, N.Y.: Orbis, 1998.

Jackson, Edward T., and Yusuf Kassam. *Knowledge Shared: Participatory Evaluation in Development Cooperation.* West Hartford, Conn.: Kumarian Press, 1998.

Johnston, Douglas, and Cynthia Sampson, eds. *Religion, The Missing Dimension of Statecraft.* New York: Oxford University Press, 1994.

Jones, L. Gregory. "Alasdair MacIntyre on Narrative, Community and the Moral Life." *Modern Theology* 4.1 (1987): 53–69.

———. *Embodying Forgiveness: A Theological Analysis.* Grand Rapids: Eerdmans, 1995.

Kaufman, Gordon D. *Nonresistance and Responsibility, and Other Mennonite Essays.* Newton, Kans.: Faith and Life, 1979.

Kirwen, Michael C. *The Missionary and the Diviner*. Maryknoll, N.Y.: Orbis, 1987.

Klassen, Walter. *Armageddon and the Peaceable Kingdom*. Scottdale, Pa.: Herald, 1999.

Knappert, Jan, compiler. *Myths and Legends of the Swahili*. Nairobi: East African Educational Publishers, 1979.

Korten, David C. *Getting to the 21st Century: Voluntary Action and the Global Agenda*. West Hartford, Conn.: Kumarian Press, 1990.

Kraft, Charles H. "Animism or Authority?" In *Spiritual Power and Missions: Raising the Issues*, ed. Edward Rommen. Evangelical Missiological Society Series, no. 3. Pasadena: William Carey Library, 1995.

———. *Anthropology for Christian Witness*. Maryknoll, N.Y.: Orbis, 1996.

———. *Christianity and Culture: A Study in Dynamic Biblical Theologizing in Cross-Cultural Perspective*. Maryknoll, N.Y.: Orbis, 1979.

Kraus, C. Norman. *An Intrusive Gospel? Christian Mission in the Modern World*. Downers Grove, Ill.: InterVaristy, 1998.

Kraybill, Donald B. *The Upside-Down Kingdom*. Rev. ed. Scottdale, Pa.: Herald, 1990.

Kreeft, Peter. *Back to Virtue: Traditional Moral Wisdom for Modern Moral Confusion*. San Francisco: Ignatius, 1991.

Ladd, George Eldon. *The Gospel of the Kingdom: Scriptural Studies in the Kingdom of God*. Grand Rapids. Eerdmans, 1959.

Landes, David S. *The Wealth and Poverty of Nations: Why Some Are So Rich and Some So Poor*. New York: Norton, 1998.

Lansing, J. Stephen. *Priests and Programmers: Technologies of Power in the Engineered Landscape of Bali*. Princeton, N.J.: Princeton University Press, 1991.

Lean, Mary. *Bread, Bricks, Belief: Communities in Charge of the Future*. West Hartford, Conn.: Kumarian Press, 1995.

Lederach, John Paul. *Building Peace: Sustainable Reconciliation in Divided Societies*. Washington, D.C.: U.S. Institute of Peace, 1997.

Lee, Phillip J. *Against the Protestant Gnostics*. New York: Oxford University Press, 1987.

Lehmann, Arthur C., and James E. Myers, ed. *Magic, Witchcraft, and Religion: An Anthropological Study of the Supernatural*. 4th ed. Mountain View, Calif.: Mayfield, 1997.

Lewis, W. Arthur. *The Theory of Economic Growth*. Homeward, Ill.: Irwin, 1955.

Lingenfelter, Sherwood. *Agents of Transformation: A Guide for Effective Cross-Cultural Ministry*. Grand Rapids: Baker, 1996.

Lohfink, Gerhard. *Jesus and Community: The Social Dimension of Christian Faith*. Trans. John P. Galvin. Philadelphia: Fortress, 1984.

MacIntyre, Alasdair. *After Virtue: A Study in Moral Theory*. 2d ed. South Bend, Ind.: University of Notre Dame Press, 1984.

Selected Bibliography

Mander, Jerry, and Edward Goldsmith, eds. *The Case against the Global Economy: And for a Turn toward the Local*. San Francisco: Sierra Club, 1996.

Mbanda, Laurent. *Committed to Conflict: The Destruction of the Church in Rwanda*. London: SPCK, 1997.

Mbiti, John S. *Introduction to African Religion*. 2d ed. Nairobi: East African Educational Publishers, 1991.

McClendon, James W., Jr. *Systematic Theology: Ethics*. Nashville: Abingdon, 1986.

McDonald, Hugh Dermot. *The Atonement of the Death of Christ: In Faith, Revelation, and History*. Grand Rapids: Baker, 1985.

Mernissi, Fatima. *Beyond the Veil: Male-Female Dynamics in Modern Muslim Society*. Bloomington: Indiana University Press, 1987.

Midgley, Mary. *Science as Salvation: A Modern Myth and Its Meaning*. London and New York: Routledge, 1992.

Moltmann, Jürgen. *God in Creation*. Minneapolis: Fortress, 1993.

Mott, Stephen Charles. *Biblical Ethics and Social Change*. New York: Oxford University Press, 1982.

Mouw, Richard J. *Politics and the Biblical Drama*. Grand Rapids: Eerdmans, 1976.

Muller-Fahrenholz, Geiko. *The Art of Forgiveness*. Geneva: WCC, 1997.

Murphy, Nancey. *Anglo-American Postmodernity: Philosophical Perspectives on Science, Religion, and Ethics*. Boulder, Colo.: Westview, 1997.

———. *Beyond Liberalism & Fundamentalism: How Modern and Postmodern Philosophy Set the Theological Agenda*. Valley Forge, Pa.: Trinity Press International, 1996.

Murphy, Nancey, and George F. R. Ellis. *On the Moral Nature of the Universe: Theology, Cosmology, and Ethics*. Minneapolis: Fortress, 1996.

Myers, Bryant L. *Walking with the Poor: Principles and Practices of Transformational Development*. Monrovia, Calif.: MARC, 1999.

———, ed. *Working with the Poor: New Insights and Learnings from Development Practitioners*. Monrovia, Calif.: MARC, 1999.

Newbigin, Lesslie. *The Gospel in a Pluralist Society*. Grand Rapids: Eerdmans, 1989.

———. *Honest Religion for Secular Man*. Philadelphia: Westminster, 1966.

———. *The Open Secret*. Grand Rapids: Eerdmans, 1981.

———. *Truth and Authority in Modernity*. Valley Forge, Pa.: Trinity Press International, 1996.

Nicholls, Bruce J., and Beulah R. Wood, eds. *Sharing the Good News with the Poor: A Reader for Concerned Christians*. Grand Rapids: Baker, 1996.

Niebuhr, H. Richard. *Christ and Culture*. New York: Harper & Row, 1951.

Niebuhr, Reinhold. "The Christian Witness to the Social and National Order." In *The Essential Reinhold Niebuhr: Selected Essays and Addresses*, ed.

Robert McAfee Brown. New Haven, Conn.: Yale University Press, 1986.

Noble, David F. *The Religion of Technology.* New York: Knopf, 1997.

———. *A World without Women: The Clerical Culture of Western Science.* New York: Knopf, 1992.

Otis, George, Jr. *The Twilight Labyrinth: Why Does Spiritual Darkness Linger Where It Does?* Grand Rapids: Chosen, 1997.

Palmer, Parker J. *To Know As We Are Known: A Spirituality of Education.* San Francisco: Harper & Row, 1983.

Passmore, John. *Man's Responsibility for Nature: Ecological Problems and Western Traditions.* New York: Scribner, 1974.

Pittman, Don A., Ruben L. F. Habito, and Terry C. Muck, eds. *Ministry & Theology in Global Perspective: Contemporary Challenges for the Church.* Grand Rapids: Eerdmans, 1996.

Polner, Murray, and Naomi Goodman. *The Challenge of Shalom: The Jewish Tradition of Peace and Justice.* Philadelphia: New Society, 1994.

Pope-Levison, Priscilla, and John R. Levison, eds. *Return to Babel: Global Perspectives on the Bible.* Louisville: Westminster John Knox, 1999.

Postman, Neil. *Technopoly: The Surrender of Culture to Technology.* New York: Vintage, 1992.

Prunier, Gerard. *The Rwanda Crisis: History of a Genocide.* Kampala, Uganda: Fountain, 1995.

Ram, Eric, ed. *Transforming Health: Christian Approaches to Healing and Wholeness.* Monrovia, Calif.: MARC, 1995.

Rasmussen, Larry L. *Earth Community, Earth Ethics.* Geneva: WCC, 1996.

Robinson, James M., ed. *The Nag Hammadi Library.* San Francisco: Harper Collins, 1990. Readable online at http://www.webcom.com/gnosis/naghamm/nhl.html.

Rosaldo, Michelle Zimbalist, and Louise Lamphere, eds. *Woman, Culture, and Society.* Stanford, Calif.: Stanford University Press, 1974.

Ryan, William F. *Culture, Spirituality, and Development: Opening a Dialogue.* Ottawa: International Development Research Centre, 1995.

Sampson, Philip, Vinay Samuel, and Chris Sugden, eds. *Faith and Modernity.* Oxford: Regnum, 1994.

Sannah, Lamin. *Religion and the Variety of Culture: A Study in Origin and Practice.* Valley Forge, Pa.: Trinity Press International, 1996.

Saunders, Ross. *Outrageous Women, Outrageous God: Women in the First Two Generations of Christianity.* Alexandria, N.S.W., Australia: Dwyer, 1966.

Schreiter, Robert J. *The Ministry of Reconciliation: Spirituality and Strategies.* Maryknoll, N.Y.: Orbis, 1998.

———. *Reconciliation: Mission and Ministry in a Changing Social Order.* Maryknoll, N.Y.: Orbis, 1992.

Schreiter, Robert J., ed. *Faces of Jesus in Africa.* Maryknoll, N.Y.: Orbis, 1991.

Selected Bibliography

Sen, Amartya. *Poverty and Famines: An Essay on Entitlement and Deprivation.* New York: Oxford University Press, 1981.

Shumacher, E. F. *Good Work.* New York: Harper & Row, 1979.

———. *Small Is Beautiful: Economics As If People Mattered.* New York: Harper & Row, 1973.

Sider, Ronald J. *Just Generosity: A New Vision for Overcoming Poverty in America.* Grand Rapids: Baker, 1999.

———. *One-Sided Christianity: Uniting the Church to Heal a Lost and Broken World.* Grand Rapids: Zondervan, 1993.

———. *Rich Christians in an Age of Hunger: Moving from Affluence to Generosity.* Twentieth anniversary ed. Dallas: Word, 1997.

———, ed. *Evangelicals and Development: Toward a Theology of Social Change.* Philadelphia: Westminster, 1981.

———, ed. *For They Shall Be Fed: Scripture Readings and Prayers for a Just World.* Waco: Word, 1997.

Sine, Tom. *Mustard Seed versus McWorld: Reinventing Life and Faith for the Future.* Grand Rapids: Baker, 1999.

Sisk, Timothy D. *Power Sharing and International Mediation in Ethnic Conflicts.* Washington, D.C.: U.S. Institute of Peace, 1996.

Slim, Hugo, and Paul Thompson. *Listening for a Change.* Philadelphia: New Society, 1995.

Stassen, Glen H., D. M. Yeager, and John Howard Yoder. "A New Vision." In *Authentic Transformation: A New Vision of Christ and Culture.* Nashville: Abingdon, 1996.

Stolzman, William. *The Pipe and Christ: A Christian-Sioux Dialogue.* Chamberlain, S.D.: Tipi, 1986.

Stout, Jeffrey. *Ethics after Babel: The Languages of Morals and Their Discontents.* Boston: Beacon, 1988.

Swartley, Willard M., ed. *The Love of Enemy and Nonretaliation in the New Testament.* Louisville: Westminster/John Knox, 1992.

———. *Slavery, Sabbath, War, and Women: Case Studies in Biblical Interpretation.* Scottdale, Pa.: Herald, 1983.

Tawney, R. H. *Religion and the Rise of Capitalism.* 1922. Reprint, London: Penguin, 1990.

Thiselton, Anthony C. *Interpreting God and the Postmodern Self: On Meaning, Manipulation, and Promise.* Grand Rapids: Eerdmans, 1995.

Thomson, William Irvin. *Imaginary Landscape: Making Worlds of Myth and Science.* New York: St. Martin's Press, 1989.

Tillich, Paul. *Theology of Culture.* New York: Oxford University Press, 1964.

Tippett, Alan R. *Solomon Islands Christianity: A Study in Growth and Obstruction.* New York: Friendship, 1967.

Torjesen, Karen Jo. *When Women Were Priests: Women's Leadership in the Early Church and the Scandal of Their Subordination in the Rise of Christianity* San Francisco: Harper San Francisco, 1993.

Tschuy, Theo. *Ethnic Conflict and Religion: Challenge to the Churches.* Geneva: WCC, 1997.

Tucker, Mary E., and John A. Grim, eds. *Worldviews and Ecology: Religion, Philosophy, and the Environment.* Maryknoll, N.Y.: Orbis, 1994.

Turner, Victor. *The Ritual Process: Structure and Anti-Structure.* New York: de Gruyter, 1969.

Tutu, Desmond. *No Future without Forgiveness.* Parktown, R.S.A.: Random House South Africa, 1999.

Vallely, Paul. *Bad Samaritans: First World Ethics and Third World Debt.* Maryknoll, N.Y.: Orbis, 1990.

Van Leeuwen, Mary Stewart. *Gender and Grace: Love, Work, and Parenting in a Changing World.* Downers Grove, Ill.: InterVarsity, 1990.

Volf, Miroslav. *Exclusion and Embrace: A Theological Exploration of Identity, Otherness, and Reconciliation.* Nashville: Abingdon, 1996.

Wakatama, Pius. *Independence for the Third World Church: An African's Perspective on Missionary Work.* Downers Grove, Ill.: InterVarsity, 1976.

Walsh, Brian J., and J. Richard Middleton. *The Transforming Vision: Shaping a Christian World View* Downers Grove, Ill.: InterVarsity, 1984

Warren, D. Michael, L. Jan Slikkerveer, and David Brokensha, eds. *The Cultural Dimension of Development: Indigenous Knowledge Systems.* London: Intermediate Technology, 1995.

Weaver, J. Denny. *Keeping Salvation Ethical: Mennonite and Amish Theology in the Late Nineteenth Century.* Scottdale, Pa.: Herald, 1997.

Weber, Max. *The Protestant Ethic and the Spirit of Capitalism.* London: Allen & Unwin, 1930.

Wehr, Paul, Heidi Burgess, and Guy Burgess, eds. *Justice without Violence.* Boulder, Colo.: Rienner, 1994.

Wells, David F. *God in the Wasteland: The Reality of Truth in a World of Fading Dreams.* Grand Rapids. Eerdmans, 1994.

Wilson, Jonathan R. *Living Faithfully in a Fragmented World: Lessons for the Church from MacIntyre's After Virtue.* Harrisburg, Pa.: Trinity Press International, 1997.

Wink, Walter. *Engaging the Powers: Discernment and Resistance in a World of Domination.* Minneapolis: Fortress, 1992.

———. "The Hymn of the Cosmic Christ." In *The Conversation Continues: Studies in Paul and John,* ed. Robert T. Fortna and Beverly R. Gaventa. Nashville: Abingdon, 1990.

Wolfe, Regina Wentzel, and Christine E. Gudorf, eds. *Ethics and World Religions: Cross-Cultural Case Studies.* Maryknoll, N.Y.: Orbis, 1999.

Selected Bibliography

Wright, Christopher J. H. *An Eye for an Eye: The Place of Old Testament Ethics Today.* Downers Grove, Ill.: InterVarsity, 1983.

———. *God's People in God's Land: Family, Land, and Property in the Old Testament.* Grand Rapids: Eerdmans, 1990.

Wright, G. Ernest. *God Who Acts: Biblical Theology as Recital.* Chicago: Regnery, 1952.

Wuthnow, Robert. *Christianity and Civil Society: The Contemporary Debate.* Valley Forge, Pa.: Trinity Press International, 1996.

———. *Rediscovering the Sacred: Perspectives on Religion in Contemporary Society.* Grand Rapids: Eerdmans, 1992.

Yoder, John Howard. *The Christian Witness to the State.* Newton, Kans.: Faith and Life, 1964.

———. *For the Nations: Essays Public and Evangelical.* Grand Rapids: Eerdmans, 1997.

———. *The Politics of Jesus.* Grand Rapids: Eerdmans, 1972.

———. *The Priestly Kingdom: Social Ethics as Gospel.* South Bend, Ind.: University of Notre Dame Press, 1984.

Index